THE
LOVING
ABDUCTOR

When protecting your child
is against the law.

JAN FORD

To Ann
Thank you
for listening.
Enjoy.
Jan x

Printed in the United Kingdom
First Printing, 2022
ISBN: Print (Soft Cover): 978-1-915472-18-2
        eBook: 978-1-915472-19-9

Book design by Viv Ainslie at Purple Parrot.
Published by Purple Parrot Publishing.
www.purpleparrotpublishing.co.uk

Dedication

For every Plagued Mother,
my precious sons,
Tom, Owen & Morgan
& everyone who needs
a pirate in their life.

Acknowledgements

Enormous thanks to Viv, my editor and friend who steadied my hand on this incredible journey whilst we laughed, cried and worked our socks off. Thank you for believing I had a story to tell in the first place and for your subsequent patience, humour and authenticity.

Humble thanks to all the wonderful characters in the book. Whether as a friend, or a kind-hearted stranger, your support reassured me there are good people in the world. You gave me hope.

Captain Jim, I'll never forget you. I'm forever indebted to you for helping me to defend the priceless treasure we'd stowed safely aboard. Blessed to have a true pirate on my side, I wish you'd lived to see yourself portrayed in this book, as the hero you were and always will be. I'd like to think you and the butter lady might drop by sometime and we'll toast to undying friendships and seeking justice by whatever means.

My boys. There'll never be enough words. We've had sayings aplenty over the years which we've identified as being unique to us and employed each one with humour to either alleviate or exaggerate our feelings at the time. Many of these are derived from watching too much Disney, so I daren't quote them here for fear of copyright infringement. Let's just mention *"infinity"* '(the position ranking after first) star on the right', *"ah aww, ah aww..."* and leave it there! Above all, I want to pay tribute to all that you are; three incredible individuals, who, rather than letting your suffering get the better of you, grip it in both hands, strangle it into submission, and refuse to be defined by it. Your responses to the 'If France hadn't happened' conversation, focussing solely on the positives:

- we wouldn't have Morgan
- we wouldn't know what it's like to have nothing apart from each other
- we wouldn't appreciate the things we used to take for granted
- we wouldn't realise just how strong we are as a family

I'm blessed to be your mother. Thank you.

It goes without saying that I wish to acknowledge every protective mother for your endless bravery and courage. May the love for your children be your greatest weapon of strength, arming you with a strategic arsenal of power and endurance, superior to that of the enemy, making your victory inevitable.

A donation from every sale of this book will be made to the Hague Convention Mothers charity.

Contents

Prologue
Somewhere near Bordeaux – 1982

Isabelle

She senses his presence before she sees him. Intuitively she turns her head in his direction, eyes now transfixed, body frozen as the fear rises. The warm terracotta of the sunlit terrace forms a bleak contrast to the cold, dark rage that emanates from the familiar form of the man who continues to close the distance between them. Somehow, she is not surprised to see the barrel of his handgun, sun glinting off its tip, aimed directly at her head. The gap between them continues to close, stifling the oxygen from her small frame as it does so. The inevitable day of reckoning has finally arrived. How desperately stupid to have believed that she could outwit this man. Freedom had been a temporary state of affairs, a brief interlude in which she dared to hope. The reality that confronted her now was the final, debilitating proof that she had deluded no one other than herself. All forms of escape had proved futile, and now she will pay the ultimate price. How many times had she played out endless possible scenarios in her head in a desperate bid to keep one step ahead, to maintain the upper hand in an attempt to give herself the best chance of survival? Isabelle could not have prepared for this eventuality despite everything that she has endured to date. It is in a league of its own. The perpetrator's mind extends far beyond the limits of her imagination. Most people are not capable of such thoughts. However, once imagined, they are no longer non-existent but lay waiting in the darkest, most remote corners of the psyche, ready to be called to action by their creator. It is with a dawning sense of dread that Isabelle knows why the predator has returned. He is going to take them.

When he had swooped the first time, he had successfully extracted one of their three children. She had only turned her back momentarily but had let her guard down in the process. That brief lapse of vigilance on her part was all it took. The consequence of it had changed her life forever. Time had passed, and stupidly she had lulled herself into a false sense of security, convincing herself that he would be satisfied with just one of her brood. Isabelle condemned herself for not realising that given the predator's innate need to inflict pain and suffering on others, in a bid to dominate and control them, his appetite for cruelty craved satiating. Now he was back for more and, Isabelle knew that he would take whatever action he deemed necessary and by whatever means, to get what he wanted. The stirrings of a string of depraved screams rise to meet the bitter bile in her throat, only to be silenced by the raw technicolour reality of what is happening. He wants her two remaining children. Gun twitching in his hand with tight lipped determination, he spits his order, demanding an immediate response.

'Tell me where they are.'

Out of nowhere, Isabelle is conscious of a sound akin to the rapid breathless panting of an animal — almost indistinguishable at first but increasing in resonance as it takes ownership of its voice. It continues to soar in strength, rising to become the depraved screams of manic, uncontrollable laughter. As the sound catches her attention, she pauses momentarily, tilting her head to detect its source. Seconds pass. Realisation dawns. She is both its centre and creator. The predator has noticed it too, and his grip on the gun falters as her terrified screams rise once more into the air with an unabated howling, scattering their hidden consequences into the ever-gathering dusk.

Chapter 1
Malta – Summer 1998

It was the early hours of the morning when Mum and I finally arrived with two over-tired boys in the hotel's lobby on the north coast of Malta. As we stood in the marbled foyer, amidst an assortment of massive palms, I felt that maybe I would relax for the first time in a long time. It was a struggle trying to juggle full-time teaching with the needs of a six and four-year-old who were still coming to terms with the idea of seeing their father alternate weekends following our divorce. This holiday would do us all good and allow us the opportunity to spend some much-needed quality time together. I was thrilled that my mum had jumped at the idea of coming too. We'd always had adventures together, and she was the one permanent fixture in our lives. Ever since her husband, my father, died about fifteen years ago, she chose to devote the majority of her free time to us. I always felt blessed by her presence.

Eventually, the night porter appeared at the deserted reception desk and handed us the keys to our apartment. We made our way wearily along a meandering pathway, following the directions the porter gave us and found ourselves outside the door to a low-level building with blooms of bougainvillaea adorning its ochre walls. I noticed that even the cicadas were quiet at this time of night. Like us, perhaps they also needed time to rest and found peace in the silence. However, in the stillness, I became aware of the sound of the distant sigh of the sea, and I smiled. Opening the front door, I guided the boys inside, and Mum and I exchanged tired yet excited looks, which, although unspoken, hinted at the prospect of what delights a new day might bring.

The following day we awoke to our new surroundings and were hit by a wall of heat as we left the front door of our air-conditioned apartment. Following breakfast, we discovered the swimming pool area, and to the delight of the boys, access to the sea via a ladder on the side of the ancient sea wall. The water was crystal clear, and although not sandy, the sea bed was teaming with a variety of aquatic life which looked intriguing to both Tom and Owen. It was not long before both boys had donned their animal character swimming rings and were gleefully bobbing around in the water. They took it in turns to jump off the lower rungs of the old ladder on the sea wall and into my waiting arms. Gran was also on hand, and between us, we were able to steer our precious cargoes back to dry land as and when necessary.

We geared our sightseeing of the island to activities that would keep the boys entertained. On one occasion we took a boat trip around Valetta with its honey-gold bastion walls. While Mum and I marvelled at the architecture, Tom and Owen, armed with wooden souvenir swords, became gallant Knights of St John, enacting their version of defending the mighty seaport.

Ninu's Cave, 'The Cave' to the boys, proved to be the most memorable part of our day trip to the neighbouring, tiny island of Gozo. It was an experience that we talked about long after our visit. Having viewed the unremarkable exterior of a Maltese townhouse, we could not have imagined what lay beneath its interior floors. Invited inside by the proprietor, we followed him into a cold tile entrance hall from which he escorted us down a narrow, dimly lit staircase to venture beneath the property. At the bottom of the long descent, we were astonished to find ourselves in a cave, surrounded by an assortment of oddly shaped stalactites and stalagmites. Visually it was so remarkable and unusual that it gave the impression of being borrowed directly from a Doctor Who film set. Young imaginations ran wild once more. Tom and Owen quickly abandoned their previous roles of Maltese knights in favour of the excitement of becoming *'extra-terrestrial investigators'*. Their Maltese swords proved versatile in their implementation as highly technical equipment capable of detecting any forms of alien life.

Apart from these select sightseeing trips, we spent most of our holiday within the extensive hotel grounds. We didn't need to look any further than the hotel swimming pool for the boys to keep themselves entertained. Languishing on the sunbeds, Mum and I took it in turns to supervise the splashing boys as they bobbed up and down. Intermittently, we would join them to coax them into trying to swim without inflatable rings or armbands. Tom mastered the arm movement for a front crawl technique that looked extremely impressive when viewed from the water's surface. However, his credibility rating soon dropped in the revelation that he was keeping one foot planted on the bottom of the pool, using it to propel himself forward in a series of energetic hopping motions. Owen seemed at his happiest, leaping into the pool amidst an array of show-off shrieks of delight, forming crazily dramatic body shapes in mid-air before landing in the water.

There was always live entertainment geared to enthralling the hotel guests in the evening. On one particular occasion, we were listening to a live band. The music was very upbeat, one song in particular, became a favourite, 'The Lemon Tree' by Fool's Garden, and Tom and Owen were busy creating their musical interpretation of it, seated at our table and haphazardly wriggling their shoulders to the rhythm. It was clear that the music appealed to the other guests who were tapping their feet or their fingers in time to the music. In true British fashion, everyone remained seated, a restrained air about them as if they could not allow themselves to relax fully. Tentative tapping was the peak of self-expression for the Brits it seemed, and so, when I spotted a middle-aged couple from across the terrace push back their chairs in a sudden flourish, they caught my full attention. The balding gentleman, sporting a loudly coloured Hawaiian shirt that was button-poppingly taut around the tummy, stepped with remarkable light-footed ease onto the dance floor. He tilted his head in anticipation towards his partner and proceeded to take a small, dignified bow. She responded by putting on a show of majestic delight, shimmying onto the floor, her doll-size dress swirling out from her minuscule waist as she met the hand that he proffered to her. It was not long before they had captured the attention of everyone who was now as equally enthralled as I was to observe their obvious enjoyment of dancing together. They were well practised and had got the execution of their dance off to an art, a basic waltz but with little touches thrown in, making it exclusive to them. As I watched in awe, I reflected upon how special it must be to have a relationship whereby each person knows the other's moves and can predict them. I envied their evident togetherness. There was something to be said for this style of dance that involved two people, as opposed to the isolating dances of the 'dancing around the handbags' style, that I had enjoyed while growing up! The band finished playing, and the couple completed their performance – the gentleman twirling the lady around and around before ending in a dramatic finale in which she threw herself back into his waiting arms with trusting well-heeled confidence. Everyone clapped and cheered loudly. Tom and Owen, excited by the excitement in the air, clapped and shouted too, jumping up and down on the spot and launching themselves intermittently into exaggerated body gestures that would have rivalled any Travolta enthusiasts! It felt as if the air had become charged with infectious positive energy. Everyone was smiling and laughing, and surrounding conversations seemed to have taken on renewed leases of life. It felt good, and so I welcomed the appearance of the loud shirted gentleman advancing in our direction. Coming to a stop at our table, he gestured towards the ashtray that was placed on it, waving the remains of a strongly scented cigar, pinched firmly between index finger and thumb.

He spoke in fractured English, 'Excuse me.'

He shook the cigar butt in a dramatic gesture once more, and smiling, I pushed the ashtray towards him, showing that I understood his request.

I replied, 'No problem.'

His suntanned face broke into an enormous grin, his teeth leaning like an irregular row of bent trees suffering from prolonged exposure to an unrelenting wind.

'Ah! Very good! No problem! Ah yes! No problem!'

I gathered from this response that his English was

quite limited and, feeling a sudden burst of confidence, decided to dig into the recesses of my mind for something appropriate that I had learned from studying O-level French. I was just about to start when Mum intervened. Of course! She had lived in France with my father many years ago. As I watched her embark on an animated conversation with the newcomer, so Tom and Owen stared in open-mouth bewilderment, as if their Gran had suddenly turned into some alien speaking creature. They continued their wide-eyed stare when the gentleman's partner walked purposefully yet gracefully towards us.

She introduced herself, 'I am Josie, and this is my partner, Jean-Claude.'

Jean Claude looked relieved to have someone for linguistic backup purposes, and he rattled something off to her in their native tongue.

She smiled and said, 'He says that your mother speaks excellent French.'

I saw my mum visibly swell with pride and reply, 'Mais vous êtes très gentil.'

The pair of newcomers shone broad smiles back at us. I warmed to them as they helped us continue to converse in a mixture of *'Franglais'* and bestowed endless offers of sweets, ice-creams and drinks on the boys who lapped up the attention and promise of treats.

As the evening progressed, we learned that Josie and Jean-Claude, whom we now referred to as JC, lived near Paris in France. They had been partners for many years but had made the conscious decision not to marry. JC had been previously married, but the bitter divorce had put him off any notion of a repeat performance. Josie spoke fluent English due to having lived in America for several years. JC relied upon her to translate for him as we conversed. The couple made me feel relaxed to be around, so I found myself daring to recall some of the French I had learned at school. I began to put the theory into practice. The more I tried, the more Josie gently prompted and encouraged me.

The time passed quickly, and it was soon even later than the boy's lenient holiday bedtime. We said our *'goodnights'* and mutually agreed that we would be sure to see one another again. It was, therefore, a pleasure to resume our newly found friendship the following day and the day after that. In fact, for the remainder of the holiday, we saw both Josie and JC every day. When the time came for us to leave, Josie embraced me like an old friend, kissing me twice on each cheek in quick succession and giving me her contact details.

'Jan. You must come to Paris. Come to Paris with the boys and visit us! You can take the ferry from Cornwall. Come to our home, and I will show you all the sights of Paris, and you can sample proper French food.'

She turned to my Mum and added, 'You too, Mary. You must come as well.'

I told her that I would look forward to it and keep in touch.

I then turned to JC, who said, 'Jan (but with his accent, it sounded more like Jen) – *A bientôt mon pote.*'

I had spent long enough with them to know that this was a term of endearment. It was not a phrase consigned to textbook French but an informal expression used between friends. Translated, it meant 'see you soon, buddy.' For that reason, it felt all the more extraordinary that JC had felt our friendship was such that he could refer to me in that way. I hoped that this would not merely be a holiday friendship but that we really would keep in touch. I vowed that I would make every effort to see Josie and JC again and was thrilled at the prospect of taking Tom and Owen to Paris in the not-too-distant future.

Chapter 2

Cornwall – 1998

The autumn months marched in, blown by the relentless, south-westerly winds which gathered momentum as they crossed the Atlantic. They hailed the time for my need to retreat to the comfort found within the walls of our home. Natural daylight hours were receding, which meant I reluctantly had to put the lights on and close the curtains earlier each evening. Although it was comforting to light the fire in the evenings, I would have preferred a period of hibernation. Sleeping the coming winter months away was preferable to enduring the long hours of darkness. I longed for the natural warmth of perpetual summer and the splendour of outdoor colour associated with it. It was now mid-October, and our diet reflected the change in the season. I started to cook more casseroles and roasts than the lighter meals we had enjoyed only a month before.

My working days seemed more of a challenge due to getting up before dawn to get the boys ready to go to the childminder. I said my habitual goodbyes to them on a cold granite doorstep at a quarter past seven in the morning, drove the seventeen miles to work, only to return to collect them in impending darkness. I hated leaving Tom and Owen for so long. I did not like the thought of them being taken and collected from school by someone other than me. I think this was because I felt a sense of duty to them. Since my divorce, their father, Nick, only saw them at alternate weekends. It was, therefore, my responsibility to care for them daily. I wanted to keep them feeling secure. They'd been through enough upheaval, and I knew I would feel guilty if I was in some way adding to it. However, there was no alternative. To stay at Mithian Farm, I had to keep earning to pay the mortgage and cover the living expenses. It was a beautiful place for the boys to grow up, so I was determined to keep it that way for as long as possible.

With my evening household chores complete and school books marked ready for tomorrow, I felt thankful to finally sit down to relax. The boys were fed, bathed, and put to bed and were finally asleep. The latter was a feat in itself. The simple act of saying goodnight had become something of a drawn-out ritual. We had several repeat performances of 'night night, sleep tight. Mind the bugs don't bite'. If one person started the phrase, it couldn't be left hanging in the air but had to be completed by someone else! Between them, Tom and Owen had added a good six rounds, thereby successfully delaying their bedtime. It proved to be a useful ploy in their tactical tool bag of sleep avoidance techniques.

Although I appreciated having what I classed as the luxury of 'me' time, a period, however small, that I could devote to myself, I found that I was struggling with the emptiness of it. The notion of having space to myself that I could fill in whatever way I chose was supposed to be appealing. I had seen articles and watched snapshots of chat shows where celebrity mothers talked about the importance of 'me' time. It appeared to add sugar-coated, frosted tops to the perfect icing of their already glamorous lives. Their only trials and tribulations depended upon their decision of where and how to get their nails done, source exclusive salons for hair extensions, or indulge in luxury spa treatments. These choices were pivotal to their sense of wellbeing. My reality was a stark contrast to theirs. I had found that it was in the quiet times when I was entirely on my own with no diversions, no need to meet deadlines or the demands of others, that a dark void bellowed up from my very soul. The bleakness of the emptiness brought with it the thoughts of the child I had lost, the child I had never had, the one that would have made our family complete.

I remembered how thrilled I had been to discover that I was pregnant just after moving into Mithian Farm. The timing was not ideal because Nick and I worked all hours to get the basics done. The property needed re-wiring, and the floorboards had to be taken up and treated for woodworm. I recalled the stench of the woodworm treatment and how it gave me the urge to retch. Nonetheless, I was elated at the prospect of having a third child and nothing could diminish the joy I was feeling. Despite my pregnancy coinciding with a restoration project, I chose not to see it as an inconvenient hindrance but rather a challenge to be conquered. It made it even more important that everything should be just right.

The pregnancy had been so different from my experiences with the boys. For this reason, I convinced myself that my baby was a girl. Morning sickness was a bit a misnomer as I found I was nauseous for most of the day. Reminding myself that the feeling would eventually pass, I willed myself to focus on the outcome instead. The joy of a little sister for Tom and Owen would make it all worthwhile. But it was not to be.

At twelve weeks, almost to the day, she went; taking my dreams and a part of my heart with her. I was devastated. Neither Nick nor I could deal with the situation in which we found ourselves. We threw blows of blame and punches of guilt at one another in the emotional boxing ring. Scars ran deep and proved too deep for us to heal. Resentments reigned. It felt mutually intolerable to continue living together, and aware of the detrimental effect on the boys, there was only one option left. Three months later, we split up, and divorce proceedings got underway.

It dawned on me how time passed so quickly. It was now almost two years ago, and yet the ferocity of the loss still held me in its un-relinquished grasp. In the silence of the living room, an emotional outpouring sent rivulets of tears engraving their invisible patterns of grief down my cheeks. I told myself that this was a good thing. Externalising the internal pain was a necessary part of the healing process. Only when I was on my own could I allow this emotion to surface. After all, I had to be strong for my boys; I had to wear a mask to hide my fragility. Well-meaning friends had assured me of the adage that 'Time was a great healer.' No one seemed able to clarify the length of time that a person would have to wait for the healing. Consequently, I found no solace in the concept. The phrase was overused and overrated, spewed from the unwitting mouths of those who had never experienced loss themselves. It did not cut it for me. My healing had to come from the inside out. Simply capping the emotional wound with an Elastoplast of well-intentioned words was merely a temporary fix.

As I began to contemplate what might constitute a more permanent option, the ringtone of the landline penetrated my self-consumed thoughts.

Who would be ringing at this time of night? My mother had been over earlier and stayed for tea. A sudden thought rushed through my mind. Had she got home safely? Supposing this was a call from the hospital to say there had been an accident involving my mum? When the phone rings at an unusual time, I admit that I automatically react with morbid thoughts. They originated when the phone rang late one winter's night some fourteen years ago. It was a call from my mother. She had an almost forced tone of brightness to her voice when she asked if I was alright. We exchanged pleasantries, but I could hear that something was not right. Although my mum was always one to put the needs of others before herself, there was something about how she was asking how I was this time.

I was increasingly uncomfortable, so I'd stopped her mid-conversation.

'Mum. I know there is something wrong. You're covering it up as if you're checking how I am before telling me whatever it is. Please tell me. What's happened?'

In doing so, the emotional floodgate opened to the shocking news that my father had suffered another stroke, this time on the stairs on his way to bed. Whether he had known that it was the end or whether he was trying to tell her that he thought he might fall on the stairs, we will never know.

His last words to his devoted wife of over thirty-five years were, 'Mary – I'm going.'

He did just that. He went, and I never got to say 'goodbye'. He went, and I lost my Dad. All those years ago and yet, the ring of a phone late at night instils that same sense of fear and dread.

Tentatively, I lifted the receiver.

'Jan? It's Josie,' said the voice.

A sense of relief flooded over me.

It was lovely to receive her call. She thanked me for the postcards that I had sent her of Cornwall. I was proud of my county and wanted to share my passion for the place with my French friends across the channel. In the course of the conversation, it became apparent that Josie's main reason for calling was to invite us to visit them in France during the half-term holiday. She pointed out that the boys would love it as they held a Halloween Party every year. I knew the boys would be bouncing off the walls in excitement at the thought of going on holiday yet again! Eagerly, I provisionally accepted her invitation, pending my ability to make the necessary travel arrangements. It would mean taking the nearest ferry from Plymouth over to Roscoff in Brittany and travelling the remaining distance by car to the town of Maurepas, on the outskirts of Paris. Thankfully, I enjoyed driving, so it would be an exciting challenge rather than a daunting prospect. In a couple of weeks, I would escape any further thoughts of the darkness of approaching winter and, more importantly, I could leave grief, who had become my reliable fireside companion, behind. Instead, my boys and I would embark on an adventure and build memories together that I hoped we would be able to look back upon and cherish.

Having booked the ferry, I contacted Josie to confirm that we would visit them at their home in Paris at half term.

The simple act of accepting that invitation was all it took. How could I possibly have known that in doing so, I was effectively throwing the pebble into the rock pool, creating a ripple effect that would have consequences far beyond the furthest boundaries of my imagination.

Chapter 3

The journey proved more of an ordeal than I had anticipated, given that gale force winds delayed our ferry's departure from Plymouth by eight hours. We finally left port when the captain announced that he was taking advantage of a 'window in the weather,' and we embarked on the gruesome six-hour crossing.

Leaving the majority of other green-faced passengers, poised with their seasickness bags, as they groaned in the cramped bowels of the ship, I took the boys up on deck. Amidst the torrents of spray from the wind-whipped water, we clung to the cold, wet passenger rails, steadying ourselves as the ship rolled and skewed beneath our feet. I channelled my energies to create a sense of excitement and adventure, hoping this tactic would divert attention from the hostile heaving thrust of the storm-stricken vessel.

'We're the Cornish pirates!' I hollered into the wind. 'The wilder, the better for us!'

I had a duty to be a positive role model to show them that this experience was not to be feared but embraced wholeheartedly. Tom and Owen were looking to me to take the lead, and with this in mind, I shouted to them excitedly.

'I love it when it's like this on a ship! Come on, you pirates! I've got some games we can play! Let's go and investigate the other side of this deck. I wonder what we might find.'

With a firm grip of Owen on one hand and Thomas on the other, we set off, eager to explore, thoughts of nausea vanishing overboard as we did so. For the duration of the voyage, we occupied ourselves with a range of spur-of-the-moment games. We played a salty I-Spy, then pretended to be fearsome pirates scanning the darkness for lights of approaching enemy vessels. As we lent over the rails of the foredeck, we strained to be the first person to spot which of the oncoming waves would create the most significant bow wave. We whooped with excitement as the nose of the ferry lifted its grumbling bulk onto each peak of the ongoing swell, shuddering and groaning before being slammed down hard into the inevitable salty black trough.

It was four hours before land came into view on the horizon. The sea was now calming as the storm had blown itself out, and other passengers made their way onto the decks to express their huge relief that the end of their ordeal was in sight. As we drew ever closer to the French port of Roscoff with its pink granitic outcrops, I took a moment to speak to Tom and Owen, who were now eagerly awaiting the next leg of our journey.

'Listen to me, you two. There is something important I want to tell you.'

They turned their gaze from the rapidly approaching French coastline to look at me, unsure of what might be coming next.

'I want to tell you that I am proud of you both. That sea was incredibly rough out there, and it was a tough crossing. I didn't want to tell you at the time because there was nothing I could do to stop the storm. But listen, if you can weather a rough sea like that, you can manage anything! I don't think either of you will ever need to worry about being seasick!'

Two bedraggled boys, hair plastered haphazardly around their sea-soaked faces, grinned confidently back at me, proving that the lesson learned over the seemingly endless hours had been worth every exhausting minute of it.

Within an hour, we disembarked from the ferry and began the last stretch of the journey. Not being accustomed to driving on the opposite side of the road proved challenging, but it became increasingly enjoyable as my confidence levels rose with every kilometre covered. Opportunities for observing foreign driving techniques were aplenty. To describe the French as having a 'unique' driving style was kind! Speed restriction signs served as prompts to exceed whatever was the displayed speed. It was equally evident that the French had never encountered the concept of 'safe stopping distances,' clearly having omitted to make any reference to it in their version of the Highway Code. Vehicles appeared suddenly, out of nowhere, looming into vision in my rear-view mirror at colossal closing speeds, making the ramming of my car a genuine possibility unless I took immediate avoiding action. With yet another quick-witted swerve on my part, it crossed my mind that road users were targeting me for having an English number plate. Not to be outdone and refusing to be a victim, I decided to play them at their own game and adopt the same 'driving with a purpose' attitude. With renewed vigour, I squeezed hard on the accelerator pedal, quickly closing the distance between ourselves and the vehicle now lying directly in my path. As the driver pulled dutifully over to the right, thus letting me pass, we surged on up the adrenalin-fuelled A11 AutoRoute. Before long we were following the large blue overhead signs denoting Paris as the destination. As each mile notched up, so our sense of excitement surged. We were closing the distance between us and our friends.

Chapter 4

Maurepas, Paris – October 1998

A long tree-lined avenue wound ahead of us, and with relief, I saw that the image before me matched the final detailed directions that Josie had sent. Our destination was only a few yards away, and I could already make out the shape of two cars parked on the driveway. Although dark, their silhouettes resembled the cubed squat shape of a four by four and the sleek line of a Mercedes saloon alongside. The house was inviting, a beacon of warm light, hailing us through the darkness.

'Guess what, boys?' I said with a hint of humour in my voice, 'You can stop the "Are we there yet?" because we're HERE!'

The boys were excited that we had finally arrived. Parking my car on the street behind a rather stylish Porsche, I was all too aware that my own trusted steed appeared out of place. The Porsche was gleaming white under the street light, and I inwardly cursed myself for not having washed the Cornish mud off my maturely mucky Volvo.

Tom and Owen raced up the path to the front step in a bid to see who could be first to ring the doorbell. I could hear the sound of music emanating from behind the front door, and it was not long before I saw the outline of a figure approaching through the pane of the bottle glass-style window. The door opened, and Josie stood there in high-heeled black thigh boots, covering half of her small five-foot frame, teamed with a leather mini-skirt. She flung out her arms to greet us with eyes twinkling a greeting from behind her leopard print spectacles.

'Jan! You made it! And To-ma and O-ven!'

Her greeting reminded me how the French accent affected the pronunciation of our names. 'Jan' was always pronounced 'Jen.' Similarly, 'Thomas' lost the 's,' and the 'w' in Owen was replaced with the familiar 'v,' making my second son sound like a bulky kitchen essential.

'Oh, it is so lovely to see you all again!' she continued, hugging each one of us in quick succession.

A shout came from behind her, spoken in speedy French, but I recognised the voice immediately. It was none other than JC, larger than life, just as fun-filled as I had remembered him. He strode into the white marbled hallway to greet us. He was wearing the same tooth-leaning grin that I remembered so well, coupled with his familiar air of boyish, mischievous confidence.

'Ah – Jan!' he beamed

I wondered if he would say what I thought he might say. I was hoping that he might because I had already rehearsed my reply.

'Ça va mon pote ?' he asked, teasingly, right on cue

'Ça va mon pote,' I replied, my grin matching the scale of his own, pleased he had chosen to class me as his mate.

'You remembered Jan. You have been practising, perhaps?'

I turned to face Josie, needing help with further communication.

'Can you tell JC that I have been doing a bit of practice? Please point out that I have so much to learn. It's a long time since my school day French! I'll dare to try some of it out, but I think I shall have to rely on you to translate most of the time!'

'*Pas de problème* or in English, not a problem,' smiled Josie turning to quickly relay what I had said to the expectant JC before adding, 'Now come in. We have awaited your arrival to have dinner. And boys – I have some Halloween treats for you, but I think they will have to be for after you have eaten. Is that right, Mummy?'

'Yes – you are right,' I replied, 'Halloween treats have to be after tea, boys.'

Looks of dejection from the boys quickly evaporated as JC gestured to follow him to see where they would be staying. Moments later, I heard squeals of delight echoing down the stairway as they discovered the surprise toys that Josie had carefully selected for them. I was relieved. If they were happy, then I was delighted. It also meant that I would not have to contend with two overtired boys. After the journey we had just had, all I wanted was a bit of time to relax and savour the notion of being reunited with my friends.

Josie appeared to have read my mind as she said, 'Jan – you must be feeling tired after your long journey. Now you are here, and so you can relax. I have a special dinner planned for tonight. It is called a *'Raclette'*. I thought it would be a good idea because I did not know how hungry you would feel after your drive, and I am not sure what type of food the boys like.'

I smiled in appreciation of her thoughtfulness, and she continued to explain.

'A raclette is so much fun! We put a large pot of potatoes in a pan of boiled water on a hotplate, and underneath it, we have a grill. Each person has a little grill pan that slots under the grill. You can choose what you would like to cook in the grill pan, although it is normally cheese, which, once melted, is poured over the tops of the potatoes that you have put on your plate. We eat it with a selection of meats, pickles, and salad. You can help yourself. I think you will like it, and I am sure the boys will enjoy it too.'

'That sounds amazing!' I replied, relieved that this would not be a 'formal' dining experience.

The French were renowned for taking their mealtimes very seriously, and neither of my boys would have a clue what to do if they faced a place setting with numerous pieces of cutlery. In our household, mastering the correct use of an essential knife and fork was challenging enough.

Josie showed me to my room, the only bedroom on the ground floor. It had an en-suite bathroom in one corner. The style of the bedroom's decorative features was just as I had imagined they would be. They were a striking contrast to anything I had seen in the UK and gave me a sense of immersion in a different culture. There was a bronze sculpture of two naked lovers that wound their way seductively up the base of the bedside table lamp. Ornate ceiling-to-floor curtains draped their velvety opulence in front of a pair of similar-sized white, louvered shutters.

From what I had glimpsed, my initial impression was that the house sported predominantly earthy oak furnishings. However, my room was a direct contrast. Its white furnishings portrayed a highly sanitised, sleek, show-home feel. It was certainly very different from my home in Cornwall, where fingerprints were intrinsic to the decoration. This room was almost frighteningly pristine. Continuing to scan my room in awe of its degree of cleanliness, I noticed a fresh, pure white, towelling cotton robe hanging on the back of my door. It matched the perfectly folded set of bath and hand towels that lay on the double bed with a carefully arranged selection of complimentary toiletries. I was astounded. Josie had gone to great lengths to make me feel welcome. I made a mental note that I would have to do the same, should they ever visit us in Cornwall, although it would be challenging.

There was a tap on my door, and Josie poked her head around the opening.

'Jan, I have someone I would like you to meet! *Mon petit frère* or in English, my little brother; Claude. He has a quiet nature and does not speak English at all. I told you about him on holiday. Do you remember? I told you that he went through a bitter divorce, making him sad for a long time. Come and meet him. He is rather shy, but despite this, he is looking forward to meeting you and your boys.'

I recalled that Josie had said something about her favourite brother when she was on holiday. If my memory served me correctly, I was sure that she regarded Claude as being particularly special to her out of all her brothers and sisters. Was he the brother who had children and had brought up one of them single-handed? I could not be sure. I remembered her telling me about his divorce, which led me to recount my situation as a divorcee, living in a farmhouse on the north Cornish coast. Josie had fully understood, commenting that it took time to readjust to such emotional changes. I had been grateful for her ability to empathise with me.

Jolting myself back to the present, I realised that I was not relishing the prospect of putting myself in the unenviable position of spending time with a stranger who did not speak English. I winced visibly at the sounds of absolute foreign hilarity emanating from across the other side of the house. The party was in full flow with flamboyant French voices echoing off the walls, interspersed now and then with raucous unrestrained laughter. I was about to be thrown full force out of my comfort zone. How could I possibly converse with these people? Being naturally quietly spoken was going to cause even more of a hindrance.

Josie watched me expectantly from the doorway, and I flashed her a quick, nervous smile. Taking a deep breath, I proceeded to follow her out across the hallway, passing a large terracotta planter from which foliage extended so high that it was in line with the first-floor landing. I paused in admiration, noticing how a long string of unruly orange paper pumpkin faces peeped out to grimace at me, adorning the lower leaves of the plant. Suddenly there was a thunder of feet above me on the landing, followed by two small figures descending the carpeted stairs at an alarming rate. Thomas launched himself off the lower step, intent on putting as much distance as possible between himself and his brother.

'I've got it, and you haven't!' shrieked Tom in mockingly triumphant tones as he skidded past me, legs working furiously to gather momentum while his stocking feet failed to find traction on the marble floor.

As he scrabbled and slid determinedly only to disappear through the adjacent doorway, an equally persistent Owen brought up the rear of the chase. The scowl on his brow shouted far louder than any words could have achieved. An immediate form of intervention was necessary. Forgetting my fears, I shot after the two boys, my only focus, to de-escalate the conflict before they came to blows.

Once through the doorway, I saw that Owen had succeeded in cornering his older brother, who stood with his arm held aloft, ensuring that the object in his hand remained firmly out of the reach of his younger brother. Owen's attempts to jump and grab the item sent crazed beams of light in the shape of pumpkin faces, dancing across the walls. I realised that the prized possession was none other than a Halloween torch. No wonder Owen wanted to play with it! It was the first time I had seen anything like this, and I was intrigued. Tom could be a rascal. He knew how to wind his younger brother up like a top, teasing him and sending him spinning in a spiral of frustration. He was relishing the impact he was having.

'I want it!' yelled Owen. 'Mum, Thomas won't let me play with it.'

Tom grinned, making no move to lower his arm, his fingers still gripping the much sought-after toy. I gave a wry smile. Owen could be very astute. By addressing his brother by his full name, he had highlighted the fact that there was a misdeed afoot. 'Tom' became 'Thomas' when admonishments were necessary within our household.

'OK. OK, boys! That's enough! Thomas, you need to share with your brother.'

Becoming increasingly stern, I added, 'You have had your turn. Now give Owen a chance to play with it. Give me the torch.'

I extended my hand in anticipation. Thomas reluctantly relinquished his grasp on the item and placed it in my outstretched palm. Looking at the torch's face, I noticed a dial that, if turned, would alter the subject matter, thus allowing a witch's cat to replace the flashing pumpkins. Using this discovery as a diversion tactic to diffuse the situation, I excitedly waggled the torch.

'Oh, look! I think we can change the picture!' I exclaimed, squatting to floor level, and both boys drew close, eager to find out more. With our heads now touching, I began to turn the dial on the torch. 'Let's see if we can get the witch's black cat and then...'

My sentence was interrupted by the sudden appearance of an arm wrapped in a white-sleeved, crisply pressed shirt. It extended towards my crouching position on the floor. A man's hand held another torch, a replica of the first. I looked up inquisitively. The face that looked back belonged to a man about my age, clean-shaven, with an olive complexion and a shock of neatly styled black hair. His strong bone structure and slightly hooked nose gave me the impression that this person would not be out of place on the grassy plains of North America had it not been for the fact that he wore a white shirt and contrasting black leather trousers. Our eyes met briefly, just long enough for me to notice that he had smile lines at the corners of his brown eyes. The edges of his mouth spread into a shy smile, and with a brief nod of his head, he indicated that I should take the torch from him. I did so, and he pointed to Tom and Owen in turn, his gesture indicating that they now had a torch each. I thanked him profusely and was even more relieved to express my gratitude to him in French.

'Merci monsieur. Merci beaucoup.'

My words were almost a whisper as a sudden feeling of shyness flooded over me. Trying to shake off my embarrassment, not sure it was purely the result of speaking a foreign language, I pulled myself together, back into mother mode.

'Look, boys! How kind is that? Now you've both got a torch. How lucky is that? No more squabbling! Here – let's get this one going Owen.'

I handed the torch flashing 'witch's cat' to him and returned the other to Tom.

'Now, before you carry on playing, I'd like you both to go and say a massive thank you to Josie and to JC for getting these for you.'

All previous warfare forgotten; two big smiles set off in the direction of the kitchen to say their respective thank yous. Scanning the living room, I sought the man who had rescued me from what had been a potentially awkward situation in front of strangers. He had retreated to a seat on one of the two large black leather sofas that faced the roaring log fire.

Josie emerged from the adjoining kitchen, where she had been busy with her final preparations for dinner.

'Ah, Jan. I am glad the boys like their torches. It's just a little gift. I love that they said 'thank you, Josie. They are good boys, very well-mannered. Now let me introduce you to our friends!'

Nervously, I followed her to where JC was sitting alongside an older couple on one of the large leather sofas. They were all talking animatedly, obviously passionate about whatever they were discussing. JC's arms flew upwards in a series of wildly uncoordinated gestures as he became more and more exasperated in making his viewpoint clear to his audience. The grey-haired, heavy-set gentleman next to him seemed completely unperturbed as his deep voice doggedly rumbled his resolute response. A lady of a similar age and with various bangles and pendants jangling from about her person nodded and threw in the odd 'Bien sur,' indicating she agreed whenever the two men paused for breath. I glanced once more in the direction of the 'Indian in leather trousers' in the slim hope of finding a friendly face amidst this exuberant collection of strangers. He was sitting quietly, reserving judgement as if he had made the conscious decision to listen and observe rather than partake in any of the drama. Although solemn and unspeaking, there was a hint of amusement in his eyes as he watched them. The room fell suddenly silent, conversation ending abruptly as the settee occupants realised that a newcomer was present. All eyes were on me, making me shift my weight from one foot to another in awkward anticipation. Josie smiled widely and exclaimed

'Jan – you already know JC. He is always the one that has lots to say. You do not forget him!' Then she continued. 'These are our neighbours, Celine and Christian. They have lived next door to us for many years.'

I smiled shyly at the couple and advanced to shake their extended hands. Silently I gave thanks that no one had leapt up to offer their cheek for a kiss. Celine and Christian expressed in well-rehearsed English that they were pleased to meet me. Introductions over, Josie then turned around to face the submissive Indian in leather trousers. As if she was saving the best bit until the last, her face melted into an adoring smile, which told me what to expect.

'And this is my brother Claude. *Mon petit frère.*'

She gazed at him dotingly while he smiled up at her in return. It amused me that even though Josie referred to him as her 'little brother,' it was apparent that he had taken her share of the gene for tallness. Concertinaed on the sofa, he looked at least six feet tall. He proceeded to unfold his lengthy frame as he rose to shake my hand formally. So this was the brother that Josie had spoken of so highly, the guy whose divorce was particularly traumatic. Based on his appearance, I found it incomprehensible that any woman in their right mind would contemplate divorcing this man. He was far too handsome. Perhaps, he was too quiet. Maybe he lacked a zest for life. Could he be one of those good-looking men who lack a backbone? I wondered if he might be egotistical and arrogant but dismissed the thought because he appeared far too quiet to have any of those traits. There was no doubt that he had caught my attention, and I was intrigued by him. Further contemplations ceased when Josie called for everyone to take their seats at the ornately large dining table.

It was just how I imagined it. Dining in France took on a different connotation to dinner of the type we had at home. 'Dining' smacked of a far more formal affair, and I hoped that I could master the correct etiquette, even though Josie had assured me that it was a relaxed occasion. Nonetheless, the side plates, baskets of bread, and selection of wine glasses – seemingly two per person made me nervous. Josie sat at the head of the table with Tom and Owen on either side. They were looking eagerly at the spread in front of them, and Josie gave them a piece of baguette which they ate with newfound relish. At home, supermarket value bread was obviously in a different league and a non-contender compared to this!

As I approached the table, unsure whether I should assume my natural place adjacent to either Tom or Owen, Claude seemed to sense my uncertainty. He touched me gently on my back and gestured to a seat, which he proceeded to pull out for me. I was not used to this. I smiled and thanked him, convinced that a pink flush of sudden self-consciousness appeared on my cheeks. Gently pushing my chair in behind me as I took my place next to Owen, he proceeded to fold himself into the vacant seat on my other side. As he did so, I was acutely aware of his proximity and the distinct scent of a slightly floral yet musky aftershave.

It was not long until I realised that I felt genuinely relaxed and began enjoying myself. Whether it was the heavy-bodied Bordeaux in the glass that Claude kept replenishing for me or the convivial atmosphere, I was not sure, but it felt good. It was lovely to be among a group of genuine people, and I felt touched to be a part of it. The raclette was a great success, just as Josie had predicted. Tom and Owen enjoyed making faces out of the morsels of sliced cornichons, onions, and tomatoes, melting them along with the cheese in the little triangular grill pans. I wondered if they would have eaten any of them if faced with the same foods at home. I had the distinct feeling they would not. Josie certainly knew how to play the perfect hostess in every way, and I was very grateful to her. Dessert was followed by an ample selection of different types of cheese. I had no idea that there were so many different regional varieties. There was a moment of awkwardness as both Claude and I reached for the breadbasket simultaneously, our hands touching. I drew mine away as if seared by an unknown source of heat. He smiled with those amused eyes of his, picked up the basket, and offered it to me. Tentatively I took a piece of bread and thanked him, aware that I could not maintain eye contact for any time, in case my eyes gave too much away. I did not want him to think that I was some silly English girl that could typically fall for the handsome French man. That was far too Mills and Boon for my liking. There was certainly something going on that I was not in control of though, and I cursed myself for even letting momentary romantic thoughts flit into my head. I'd only just met him, and we were yet to have a conversation! However, I sensed that non-verbal communication was already underway.

Having wiped the ice cream off the now sleepy faces of my little boys, I excused us from the table, explaining to Josie that I would get the little ones to bed before re-joining the adults. As I stood up to leave, I heard a name spoken by Claude to the rest of the group. I faltered because it came as such a surprise to witness him speaking. The person's name to whom he was referring seemed familiar, yet I failed to place it. Puzzled, I glanced up only to find all eyes focussed on me and everyone nodding in agreement with what Claude had just said. I looked expectantly at Josie, hoping that she would enlighten me.

Through her large rounded glasses at the head of the table, she said, 'Claude has just told everybody that he thinks you look like Lady D. I think he is right. We all do.'

'Lady D?' I echoed, perplexed.

'Yes. Lady D. Lady Diana. She was beautiful.'

I could feel a flush of embarrassment flood over me, rising from my feet and rapidly making its way towards my face.

'You have the same gestures as her too. It is the way that you dip your head like you are embarrassed or slightly shy, but your blue eyes glance out,' she added.

Now that she had pointed this out, I could see a physical similarity in how I held my head when I felt reserved or unsure. This comparison was overwhelmingly embarrassing. After all, Lady Diana was a veritable icon, loved the world over.

All I could muster was a quiet, 'Oh! I'm not so sure, but thank you.'

I retreated from the room, thankful that I had the excuse of needing to get my sons into bed. As we climbed the stairs, a weary boy in each hand, I could not get those words out of my mind. Had Claude just paid me the utmost compliment? Still mulling it over, I tucked the sleepy boys into their respective beds, each with their teddies, and found that Josie had already installed a night light. I had brought one with me, complete with an adaptor, but it was surplus to requirement. Josie had thought of everything. Smiling, I turned and made my way back downstairs to join everyone.

Perhaps it had taken me longer than I thought to settle the boys because when I arrived downstairs, the sitting room was empty. A rattle of crockery came from the direction of the kitchen, replacing the sound of the previous conversations. Josie was busy loading the dishwasher, and JC was up to his elbows in bubbles, washing up a range of large pans in the sink. I looked for a tea towel to make myself useful. There was no sign of Claude, and I found myself secretly hoping that perhaps he had needed to use the toilet and would be returning soon.

Catching my giveaway expression, Josie enlightened me, 'You are wondering where everyone has gone? Celine and Christian ask me to say goodnight. They are going away tomorrow and so need their night's sleep. Claude has to work in the morning, so he has gone too, but I have invited him back to join us tomorrow evening. He enjoyed it tonight. It is nice to see my little brother looking happy.'

She looked lost in thought for a moment before adding, 'At the time that he was so sad, he came back here to live with us. I wanted to look after him. I did not want him to be on his own. The room that you are sleeping in used to be his bedroom. He installed the small en-suite. He can turn his hand to most things although he works in computers now. He has his apartment in Paris, but sometimes he comes over here and stays in his bedroom rather than driving home. I keep it for him. It will always be the bedroom for my *petit frère*.'

I smiled, thinking how lovely it must be to have a close brother and sister bond. Josie cared very strongly for her brother, and I imagined she would be fiercely protective of him.

Drying up duties now complete, I hung the damp tea

towel back on its hook and said, 'It's been a charming evening. Thank you both so much. Josie! You manage to think of every detail, and it's so kind. We've had an amazing welcome! I'm going to wish you goodnight now, though, and head off to bed. I need my sleep!'

I embraced both friends in turn.

Josie replied, '*De rien*, (you're welcome). I hope that you sleep well tonight, Jen. Tomorrow we will go to the city of Paris and take a boat trip and see the Tour D'Eiffel.'

'That sounds great!' I said, my enthusiastic response not centred purely on sightseeing but about the prospect of seeing Claude again.

Chapter 5

I awoke to a glassy November light filtering through the closed shutters of my room and stretched lazily. The house was silent, which indicated that the boys were still sleeping off yesterday's adventure. The hours spent travelling, combined with the excitement of a late night, had caught up with them, and they needed their rest so they were not too tired for the day ahead. It was a luxury not to have to get up at stupid o'clock to get the boys ready in order for me to be at work on time. Instead, I could allow myself to languish in my luxurious, tranquil surroundings. I looked about the room to re-familiarise myself with its décor. Immediately opposite me was a large mirror inset into the dressing table. I caught a view of myself in it and stifled a giggle. I wondered how the person who returned my gaze with her blurry eyes and tousled blonde hair could remotely resemble anyone as elegant as a member of royalty!

Another thought occurred to me as I realised that the length of this mirror opposite me could capture every movement of the occupant of the bed. Deciding that it was a safer option not to linger on this line of thought for too long, I cast my eyes further around the room and spotted a small cartoon picture of a black and white cat. From a distance, it appeared to be Sylvester. I wondered who had drawn it. Adjacent to this, the sheen of a silver photo frame highlighted a red Lamborghini captured within its polished surround. It was all rather flashy with no real depth, and I wondered why it was so appealing to Josie. Then I remembered. It was not her room but Claude's. I was looking at his choice of interior decorations. As I pictured what he had worn last night, it suddenly all made sense.

The pristine whiteness of the room was like an extension of the crisply white shirt that he had worn. My eyes scanned their surroundings once more, looking for clues to give me an insight into the person to whom this room belonged. The scarcity of the ornaments told me that he only displayed those items that were meaningful to him. I deduced that maybe he had an affinity with cats, liked fast cars, possibly red ones in particular, and then my gaze landed squarely back on a bronze lampstand with the seductively entwined nudes. I averted my gaze and leapt rapidly from the bed, conscious of the implication. Swooping the towelling robe off its hook on the back of the bedroom door, the enormity of its size swamping me, I wrapped it rapidly like a rolled newspaper around my body. Pulling its belt tight in an overly exaggerated fashion, I left the room to check on my boys.

Owen was still sound asleep, but Tom lay quietly, torch in hand, quietly swinging his arm above his head as he watched the pattern dance on the ceiling. Its beam had faded to a less than vibrant yellow, resulting in a set of somewhat jaundiced pumpkins waving across the bedroom walls.

'Hey, Tombo,' I whispered, 'Did you sleep well?'

Tom nodded a yes. He was not one for making a lot

of noise first thing in the morning, and he was still very much preoccupied with his torch, which remained the preferred focus of all his attention.

'Shall we go and find some breakfast and leave Owen to wake up; I think he needs his sleep at the moment?' I asked.

The mention of breakfast had Tom throwing back his covers and eagerly taking my hand to pad down the stairs.

Josie was already in the kitchen. She looked up and smiled, 'Bonjour Jen, bonjour Tom-a.'

She proceeded to offer Tom what she described as a real French breakfast. The genuine item involved chocolate, and so Tom took little persuading. In a matter of moments, he was enjoying a bowl of Benco chocolate powder mixed into milk, hungrily dunking his croissant into the blended contents of the cereal bowl. Fresh coffee hissed in the percolator, and I helped myself to a cup, briefly noting that the French mugs seemed much smaller than those at home. I hoped I would be in line for a re-fil. I had already encountered new experiences on this holiday, and I felt a swell of excitement as I felt sure that today was just the start of creating some long-lasting memories.

Chapter 6

I was relieved that JC was in charge of driving, not because it enabled me to take in the scenery but because of the rush hour traffic. These French drivers took no hostages! It was each to his own in a competition to be the first to fill an inch of road space. Like ants to grains of sugar, a swarm of hot-headed commuters would accelerate towards any available bit of tarmac. Pipped at the post, fury and frustration were vented by a wild waving of arms, and a torrent of verbal abuse that fought to be heard above the angry beeping of car horns. Undeterred by the commotion and congestion that surrounded us, JC inched the jeep forward as we edged to encircle the *Arc de Triomphe*. My clammy hands tightened their grip on the leather seat in the rear of our vehicle as JC had just insisted that we should circle the magnificent piece of historic architecture once more. The experience was horrifying enough the first time and now he was about to repeat the process! Under starters' orders, we jockeyed for position, only to lurch in a series of forward and backward motions as we rode the gridlocked carousel in a series of unexpected starts and stops. I cringed as my body threw itself forward once more, hearing an ensuing string of expletives gush from JC as he waved his left arm out of the open window in a gesture that required no translation. Mightily amused by his antics, Tom and Owen were soon chanting encouragement to him, only to be reprimanded by myself when they took it upon themselves to copy his hand signals in all their glory, to the disgusted occupants of an adjacent vehicle.

Despite the terror of navigating the congested Parisian roads, the holiday was surpassing all my expectations. As promised, our attentive tour guides took us on an evening cruise on the River Seine. We marvelled at the architecture around us as we glided under one bridge after another before going ashore at the foot of the illuminated Eiffel Tower.

Much to the delight of Tom and Owen, we also visited the Parisian version of McDonald's. Josie informed us that this particular fast-food outlet had been the first to open in Paris and that Claude had managed the franchise. As I scanned the French menu, I was surprised to see alcoholic lager on the list of beverages on offer instead of the more familiar mundane options of coke or milkshakes in the UK.

Claude would appear every evening after he finished work to dine with us throughout our vacation. As the days passed, I noticed he was becoming increasingly outgoing, relaxing in our company. One evening he amused the boys greatly by offering them an impersonation of the cartoon series about Sylvester the cat cartoon character that I had seen on my bedroom wall. The boys were shrieking with laughter as he launched into an impersonation of Sylvester's foe, Tweety Pie's famous words, "I tawt I taw a puddy tat."

It warmed my heart to see Tom and Owen so obviously enjoying themselves. Seeing their happy faces helped me relax, and I began to lose my inhibitions when speaking in French. On the fourth day of our visit, Josie had ruled that I should converse in French all the time from this point onwards. It was challenging, but she assured me that this would be the best way to learn, so I took her advice. I started to pick up the everyday phrases and hear the intonation used. I still struggled at times, becoming all too easily frustrated in my endeavours to find the words that continued to escape me. I would lapse into English on these occasions, only for Josie to patiently correct and encourage me to keep trying. JC was particularly pleased with my ongoing efforts, and whenever I faltered, he would remind me with a warning wag of his finger and the words, "When in France, you speak French. No English."

By the time it came to our last night, not only had I re-visited all the foundations of school day French, but I was also fluent in a range of swear words. I attributed this to spending so much time in the company of the unruly JC. Tom and Owen were also picking up a splattering of words, and Owen, in particular, proved to have excellent mimicking skills. On one occasion, when the last remnant of his ice lolly fell off its stick to land on the floor, he loudly exclaimed his disgust with a singular, "*Putain!*"

JC threw back his head in delight and guffawed while Josie looked on in abject horror at the fact that her partner had taught Owen how to use one of the oldest swear words in France.

As the last evening of our visit drew to a close and the boys were already asleep in bed, I found myself not wanting our holiday to end. I was not relishing the thought of the drive home to our empty house and, in particular, the lack of amicable adult company. Resignedly, I fetched the roadmap from my room to look at the route needed the following morning. I needed to retrace my steps back to the ferry port at Roscoff. Josie was in the kitchen, where she added the final touches to the food hamper that she had made up for us. She delighted in telling me that it was a gift from France to take home to remind us of our friendship, and it comprised an array of products that we had sampled during our stay with them. A kind gesture, indeed. I was impressed to see Claude using a cloth to remove crumbs from the dining table. He was not opposed to helping out and tidying up.

Opening out the map, I sat on the sofa with it sprawled across my lap, a pattern of haphazard coloured lines of varying thicknesses splaying across the waxy paper in front of me. I endeavoured to locate my current location, knowing it was somewhere southwest of Paris. The uncooperative map kept bending, making it difficult to follow, and it was rapidly proving to be a frustrating exercise. Claude, who had finished wiping the table, approached me and nodded in understanding of what I was trying to do. He sat down next to me on the sofa, taking the straying end of the map that straggled off the edge of my lap. I told him that I was trying to find my current location to look at the route I needed to follow to go home. I was armed with paper and pencil to make a note of the road numbers and place names that I would need to look out for on route. He bowed his head and, without hesitation, pointed to our current location, which happened to be cited right in the middle of my right leg. I felt myself blush.

'Nous sommes ici,' he smiled. He did not remove his hand.

I thanked him for pointing out where we were. Still, his hand remained on my leg. He smiled, looked at me, and said, 'C'est sur – nous sommes ici.'

I was powerfully aware that what he said was entirely

accurate. There was no doubt where we were at that moment. I could have leapt up and thanked him for his help. I could have folded the map away and returned to it later, but that would have closed the door of possibility. In retrospect, that is precisely what I should have done. Instead, I took a risk and left the door ajar on the chance that it might open onto something beautiful.

So with this in mind, I played with fire and asked him to show me the route to the ferry port. He wrapped his left arm around me with natural ease, pulling the map across my lap and towards him with his right hand. His left cheek against mine, he spoke quietly and intently as his index finger gently traced the directions, pausing now and then to check for my reaction. I knew that he was looking to interpret something far more profound than my cartographic skills, and as my body relaxed into his, he found all the direction he needed.

Cosseted in his arms, we spent several hours talking about the places where we had lived to date. Claude told me that while married, he had owned a boulangerie in Bordeaux and had made rustic bread in an oven he had designed specifically for that purpose. I learnt that he'd had a Labrador called 'Snoopy' and made a mental note to tick this attribute off my checklist. So far, he certainly seemed to be meeting all the criteria!

I endeavoured to describe where I lived in Cornwall or en Cournouille. He nodded in appreciation as I told him about the farmhouse within walking distance of the wild splendour of the Cornish coast. I did not want the evening to end and realised that I would happily continue conversing with him because I knew that once the conversation closed, so did the door of opportunity. We overcame potential hitches in discussions via a drawing pad, taking turns to guess the images that each other sketched. It was rather like playing the word game 'Pictionary,' and I thanked myself that our successful means of communication to date had not had to rely upon any mathematical aptitude on my part. Had that been the case, I would have failed abysmally. Mathematics had never been my strong point. I was more of a creative art type.

We discovered that we shared similar tastes in music. Claude introduced me to the sounds of some of his favourite French singers, one of whom was Patricia Kaas, a lady with a bluesy jazz edge to her voice. I was impressed. He handed me the inside cover of the CD, revealing all the lyrics for each song on the album. I particularly liked one entitled '*Mon Mec a Moi*.' I pointed to it and told him that it was my favourite, only for him to confirm that it was also his preferred song. He put the track on to play again and returned to sit alongside me, wrapping his arm around me. We sat in companionable silence, listening to the song. I followed the words on the inside sleeve of the CD with my fingers. The first couple of lines were easy to understand. They sang of a man playing with a girl's heart, messing with her life, and lying to her, yet despite this deception, she chooses to believe everything that he tells her because she loves him. Stifling a yawn, I realised that fatigue had finally caught up with me. While my heart told me to linger, my head instructed me that I had to be sensible as there was a long drive ahead of me in less than five hours.

Claude seemed to sense my thought pattern, and in French he told me, 'It's necessary for you to go to bed now. You need to sleep.'

I nodded in agreement. Claude picked up the doodle pad, tore out a clean sheet of paper, jotted something down and passed it to me. It was his contact details. Why had I not thought of that myself? I quickly wrote down both my mobile and landline numbers before passing my piece of paper to him.

'You can call me,' he said.

'Ok. Thank you. I can try.'

My reply was cagey, given that it would be challenging to hold a conversation in French with no visual prompt available and no 'doodle' option to help us. With many miles between us, the distance alone made it impractical. However, despite my misgivings, my heart told me otherwise.

Chapter 7

Cornwall – January 1999

'Come on then Jan. Bean spill! I want to know what is going on! I need details,' implored Moira, one of my closest friends, as she lent with her chin cupped in her hands, facing me in a state of complete unadulterated intrigue at her large pine kitchen table.

It was a wintery Friday night, and already more than three months had passed since I had come back from France. I relished the time that I could spend with my dearest friend, especially at the start of a weekend, a time that other couples were preoccupied with planning their quality time together. Weekends often proved difficult for me because it was more poignant than ever that I was truly alone. The alternate weekend contact arrangement when Tom and Owen spent time away with their father, acted to accentuate my aloneness. I am sure that this was why Moira invited me away from the solitary quietness of my own four walls for the evening.

Having just finished dining on a delicious, wholesome lamb hot pot, complete with dumplings, Phil, her husband, retired gracefully to the front room with a beer, leaving us with the remainder of the red wine and long-awaited girls' chat. Topping up my wine glass, she eyed me knowingly, and without wasting any time in getting to the point, she launched her question.

'I'll bet you've still got that piece of paper in your bag with his number on it, haven't you?'

Smiling sheepishly, I responded by delving into the depths of my bag to retrieve the well-worn, crumpled item.

'Yes,' I sighed, admitting defeat. Moira knew me oh so well!

'You need to do something about it, Jan. Look – Josie and JC have been to see you over here just before Christmas. You know they had a great time, albeit I made the heinous error of offering the French, el cheapo British plonk! I'll never live it down! Bloody 'Poppy Fields' of all things!'

She rolled her eyes in abject horror at the magnitude of committing such a crime. As if in utter disbelief, she repeated herself, accentuating the enormity of it all, her Lancashire accent coming to the fore as she emphasised her mistake

'Bloody Poppy Fields! I still can't believe it! The French arrive! The sister of 'hot lad' you keep going on about, and what do I do? I offer them Poppy Fields! It's like bloody vinegar!'

We broke into shrieks of laughter. Poppy Fields was a far cry from the bottle of Reserve Bordeaux in my hamper from Josie. Moira looked beside herself with embarrassment. It was not the first time that she had recounted this story, and it never diluted in the telling, which was more than could be said for the cheap British wine.

'Seriously, though, Jan. Love indicators are good. On the 'is he interested' level of one to five, five being the highest, course he's bloody interested!'

'Do you really think so?' I asked, already knowing how she would reply because it was not the first time I had asked her the same question over the last month.

'Course he is interested! It's a five! I keep telling you! He thinks of you as Lady Diana, for God's sake! How good is that? Oh, and what about sending that CD by that French singer, the one you both listened to when you were all... Hello... like snuggled up together over there. Err – yes – sending it over with his sister for you when she came to visit. Jan – it's a no-brainer!'

She sat back exasperatedly as if to allow me to digest the information, allowing herself another slurp of wine as she waited patiently for me to process what she had just said.

'Well, I suppose there wouldn't be any harm in phoning him to say thank you, would there?' I replied tentatively, all too aware that I was stepping into risky, unknown territory in doing so. My stomach lurched at the prospect.

'Phone him, Jan, for God's sake, and put me out of my misery!' Moira urged.

'I don't know what to say,' I stumbled. 'I might get it all wrong! It's one thing talking to him when we're in the same room! What about all these 'tus' and 'vous'? I'll probably end up being disrespectful, and what about...'

I knew I was gibbering, and Moira cut me short.

'Jan, you know French better than I do. Look between us, let's sort out what you want to say, and then we can write it down. You can practice it all before you make the call.'

It was my turn now to take a large slurp from my glass. Thank goodness I was able to stay at Moira's that night. Driving home was not an option. Moira reached into one of the kitchen drawers and pulled out a spiral notepad.

'OK. Let's start with the basics. Thank you for the CD.'

She spoke these words aloud while writing them down. She jotted what she had said down, repeating it emphatically as she wrote. Looking up, she continued, 'That's pretty simple, isn't it? *Merci pour le CD.*'

She looked at me with an accomplished smile, only for me to respond nervously, 'He might not know that it's me. I think I had better say 'hello' and say who I am.'

'Jan – I think he is going to recognise your voice, but if it makes you feel better, we'll add it.'

She scribbled above her previous sentence, 'Now – think about what you would *really* like to say to him.'

She leaned enquiringly towards me across the table, a glint of mischief in her eyes, cocking her head, waiting for my response.

'Oh! Oh,' I faltered.

'Oh! Oh, gosh!' she mimicked in reply. 'That is just so 'Jan' Oh! Oh, gosh!' I grinned back at her. It was one of her standard impersonations of me. I did not realise that I used it so frequently as a phrase, but she had picked up on it.

'How about *Je t'aime*?' she persisted. She was obviously on a roll now.

'I can't say that!' I squealed.

'Jan. You are going to have to say something. You come back from France and tell me that you've met this handsome French man. You're all head in the clouds and giggly, which is something I haven't seen in ages. You even tell me that you slept in his bed! I'm thinking good on ya, girl! Ooh, la la! Then in the next breath, you assure me that you were all on your own!'

'OK, OK. Point taken,' I nodded.

Maybe I should be a little more daring after all. I took

a risk and asked, 'Could say "I miss you?" Would that be OK?'

'Of course, it would. How do we write it?'

'Oh, hell. It's a tricky one. Why do I have to choose these complicated phrases? I think what you say is all back to front, so instead of it being "I miss you," it turns into "You I miss".'

I paused, pondering upon it, then adding, 'Or is it "I you miss"?'

I rolled my eyes skyward. How on Earth could this ever work? It was genuinely exasperating.

Having taken the piece of paper from Moira, I spent the next twenty minutes trying to work out which of our alternatives looked the most accurate. Nothing stood out, and I was getting myself in more and more of a state. Time was ticking, and I was tongue-tied with the complexities of French grammar. Every effort had me tangled in linguistic knots.

Moira sensed that my initial frustration had ebbed, feelings of helplessness replacing it as I resigned myself to not being able to make the phone call after all.

'Listen to me, Jan. You will curse yourself if you don't take this opportunity. Just make the call, tell him who you are, not that I think he will have forgotten your voice. Then you simply ask how he is keeping. You can do that bit. Oh, and thank him for sending you the CD. Not too difficult, is it? Get that done, and the job's a good 'un.'

Moira made it all sound so easy, and her enthusiastic cajoling soon made me believe that making a call was worth a try and that I had nothing to lose. Even if Claude couldn't understand me, I'd made an effort to contact him. Life was too short to not grasp it and hold on for the ride.

Moira thrust the landline phone into my hand. With

a racing heart and trembling fingers, I pressed the keys to dial Claude's mobile number, waiting for the pause as the line made the international connection. I listened as it rang out for what seemed like an age. With each drawn-out ring, it dawned on me that the conversation would be shorter than the time it took to connect the call. Was I mad to be doing this?

Just as I was about to lose my bottle and hang up, someone answered at the other end of the line, and a voice spoke.

'*Oui Hello.*'

'Oh!' I squeaked, noticing Moira stifling a snort of laughter out of the corner of my eye.

I had no time to correct my clumsy conversation opener before the rich voice that sounded so familiar to me replied, all too knowingly, 'Ah, Jan! It's you.'

I cringed. It only took a single high-pitched utterance on my part for Claude to instantly recognise who was calling him. I could feel my cheeks burning with embarrassment. My anxiety began to ease as I listened intently to every word he spoke. He told me it was a pleasure to hear my voice and that it had been a long time since we had spoken to each other. Too long. My words stumbled awkwardly back to him as I agreed that several months had passed.

'*Quelques mois.*'

I desperately tried to remember what I was supposed to be saying. The notes in front of me failed to act as a prompt. I went blank. Claude attempted to cover the silence by talking about the weather. I responded with the occasional *"Ah oui"*, hoping I was saying "yes" in the right places, at the same time seeming to be in agreement with what he was saying by throwing in the odd *"Bien sur"*. Confidence growing, I attempted to express how difficult it was to converse effectively over the phone and how it would be easier in person. Getting into the swing of things, I began to feel pleased with myself. However, my sense of accomplishment was short-lived because saying something in my head in English does not guarantee that it would not be lost in translation. The words that I'd rehearsed in my head flew out of the window, only to be replaced with fresh alternatives that popped out in all their uncensored glory to be laid bare and exposed

'It would be better to see you in the flesh.'

There was a spluttering guffaw to my left, and looking up, I caught Moira, both hands plastered to her mouth, her shoulders heaving up and down as she tried to mute her outburst.

The situation was getting worse by the second, and I regretted making the call. I should never have done it.

'Oh, pardon! Pardon!'

I stuttered, this was not at all what I'd wanted to say but my minimal French left me lost for the right words. Overwhelmed with embarrassment, all I could do was attempt to apologise.

Claude laughed. He was amused, but the laughter did not appear to be at my expense. Instead, he seemed to be laughing with an appreciation of how difficult this was for both of us. It was proving a disaster to try to communicate like this, and I couldn't think of how to rectify it.

However, just as he'd come to my rescue, resolving the Halloween torch conflict nearly four months ago, so he saved me from the present impossible situation again by saying, *'Ma chérie. Ecoute moi'.*

Had he just said "Darling – Listen to me?" There was no doubt that I was listening now. His words held me captive. He was speaking slower, far slower, trying to make it easier for me to understand him.

I listened intently, in disbelief at what he was telling me. Moira watched me with renewed interest, trying to get some clues from my facial expressions as I continued to hang onto every word I heard. She found her answer when she saw the smile that spread across my face.

It was Moira that reacted with wide-eyed disbelief when she listened to my voice, as I responded to Claude's declaration with a whispered response of, 'I love you too'.

Chapter 8

I held on to the content of that memorable conversation, keeping it preciously close to me over the many months that followed. Knowing that my feelings for him were reciprocated put a spring in my step as I went about my everyday life at home. Even work had an added sparkle to it in the knowledge that each week in the term timetable was taking me one step closer to returning to France. It gave me hope. It hadn't been a figment of my imagination but an indisputable certainty that there was an undeniable connection between us. The intensity of the feelings was so strong that neither conversational barriers nor geographical distance would come between us. I believed this made our relationship unique because there had to be something exceptional to feel this way. It was a once-in-a-lifetime opportunity that we could not miss.

Time and time again, I replayed what he'd told me on the phone that night at Moira's. He said that he missed me, that it had been too long, and couldn't wait to see me again. He'd voiced what I'd attempted to say in French, but of course, he had the upper hand – he was speaking in his native tongue. I realised that I could understand more words than I could speak.

The weather was warming up as spring gave way to early summer. It felt like the start of a new chapter in my life. I could turn the page to a new awakening. I counted down the days until school finished for the summer holidays, and we would return to France once more.

Chapter 9

Summer 1999

Fellow holidaymakers packed the ferry, keen to cross the channel to start their vacation. We'd booked a day sailing, which meant that we were able to spend the majority of time on the sun-filled deck, watching the rise and fall of the bow as it parted the waves leaving them frothing and splashing in its wake. It was a very different crossing from the one we'd previously experienced. We passed the time, playing pirates in the sun, shopping onboard, and exploring all the levels of the ship. The boys loved the adventure of exploring such a large vessel and finally took up residence in the soft play area for the rest of the journey.

I noticed that the roads heading towards Paris were heavily congested. I thought it must be due to the primary holiday season being during July and August, when many shops and services take long vacations, making the most of the summer months.

Excitement rose as emotional butterflies hurtled in a flutter of activity when we approached the familiar tree-lined avenue of houses that I'd first seen almost eight months ago. This time the plane trees were resplendent in their green leaves, while neat, well-tended lawns lay bordered with colourful blooms. The happy prospect of spending the summer in Paris became even more attractive as I noticed the sleek, pristine Porsche parked with its soft top-down its red leather seats soaking up the sun. It could only mean one thing; Claude was already here.

The greetings were more intense than before, simply because we all knew one another so much better. Josie remarked upon how much the boys had grown in the last eight months. JC was like a big kid, excited to see us, his hips gyrating in hula-hula style while sporting a swimming towel draped around his bottom half, which swung precariously under the overhanging cliff of his ample belly. I noted with amusement that it wasn't only the boys who'd had a growth spurt since we'd last met!

I think JC had been rehearsing his English because he launched into, 'You swim? Toma! O-ven! You swim now?'

Tom and Owen looked at me for permission, and seeing the excitement in their eyes, I grinned, saying, 'Ooh! I think that would be brilliant, wouldn't it, boys?'

'Yes!' they cheered in unison.

Part of the excitement for their holiday had been choosing what to pack and putting things in their new children's cases that had wheels and a pull handle, converting them into trolleys. With news that they could go straight into Josie and JC's outdoor swimming pool, without further delay, they disappeared, towing their belongings through the French doors that led directly onto the large south-facing terrace.

'Armbands!' I shouted exasperatedly to their rapidly disappearing forms.

Tom could already swim, but Owen still needed flotation aids.

'Don't worry. JC is with them. He will help, and he will be there. They are quite safe,' Josie assured me, stepping aside as a familiar figure entered the inner doorway. It was Claude, dressed casually in shorts and a faded t-shirt.

'I will check on the boys and get them a drink. I have chilled lemonade in the fridge for them,' said Josie with a knowing smile. She made her exit, leaving Claude and me alone in the hallway.

Momentarily, my feet felt welded to the floor. I could not move. What was I supposed to do now? So many months in waiting for this reunion, and now that it happened, I was rendered helpless.

Blushing, I ushered a tentative, 'Hello.'

Claude advanced towards me and hugged me to him. All the feelings came flooding back. There was that subtle scent of the same aftershave, the sense of protection and closeness that I had yearned for as he held me, and then there was something else. I had no time to consider whether it was the left or right cheek that I should offer for the first kiss to greet a friend. Instead, Claude kissed me on the lips, sparking a wave of euphoria to rise from deep within. It was a kiss that spoke not only of love but of both strength and desire. The sense of passion took me by surprise. Although not a lingering kiss, its very essence conveyed so much, proving to me that actions spoke louder than words.

Holding my hands outstretched, Claude took a step back. He was smiling like the French version of a Cheshire cat as he said, 'My Jan. My 'Lady Dee.' I have missed you so much.'

I felt his eyes absorb my every detail, a thirst quenched like parched sand, finally satiated by a downpour of rain.

'I've missed you too.' I grinned back at him, adding, 'But I'm here now, and it feels great!'

The sound of a purposeful stomp of little feet over the marbled floor shattered the essence of the moment. A hot-headed Owen appeared, swimming trunks at the ready, one armband in place, whilst the other, held in a furious fist, punched the air in a frantic fashion.

'Mummy! JC can't get my other armband on, and Thomas is *already* in the pool!'

He spoke with such outrage in the knowledge that his traitor of a brother should be enjoying the water without him. Hearing a resounding splash which emanated from the direction of the pool, followed by shrieks of delight, Owen scowled vehemently. I quickly sought to resolve the problem.

'OK, my love. Don't panic. Sometimes it's easier to put these armbands on when they are only partially inflated. Let me take some air out before we slot it onto your arm, and then I'll blow it up the rest of the way.'

I took the offending article from him while he stood jigging up and down impatiently. Speed was of the essence.

'Stand still, Owen! I can't blow it up with you moving about so much. If you stand still, I can do it quicker!' I retorted as I drew another breath before bracing myself to take another enormous breath once again.

'Wait!' I grabbed him by the exiting arm. 'Let me push the stopper in properly, or it'll rub your skin.'

Seconds later, Owen was hot-footing it outside. There was a deliberately loud splash as someone announced their entry into the water, in no uncertain manner, and I knew Owen was waterborne. Next came a squeal of delight as JC's voice coaxed him to gain confidence.

'O – ven *tu peux nager*!' Owen – you can swim!

I looked at Claude. 'I need to unpack and get a change of clothes ready for the boys when they come out. I bet they haven't even thought about needing towels for drying themselves!'

'Bien sur ma chérie,' he replied, and I was pleased that he understood that my priority was to look after the needs of my boys. Grinning from ear to ear because I was delighted that he referred to me as 'darling' in such a natural way, I headed off to sort out the towels and changes of clothing for the lads. I felt happier than I had in a long time.

Chapter 10

Tom and Owen ate their tea earlier than the rest of us before being safely tucked up in bed. This allowed me to sit down on the terrace with a relaxing aperitif.

I'd never tasted Pernod before but served with ice and chilled water, it felt refreshing in the residual warmth of the Parisian evening. The swimming pool sat resting with its cover in place, the previous sounds of splashing water replaced by a gently cascading waterfall that fed an ornate pond. Decorated with aromatic herbs around its edges, the scent of rosemary and oregano floated on the evening air. The setting was idyllic, comparing favourably to the thought of sitting inside at home on my own.

Cornish summers bring their magic, but the warmth soon fades, and unless there is an outdoor fire to sit around, I always prefer to go indoors before it becomes too chilly. But here, however, I could still sit outside in my sleeveless, casual summer dress without the need for a cardigan at nine o'clock in the evening. The sun's heat always feels replenishing, reaching my inner core with its warmth. Summer is the time when my soul blossoms and this particular setting was simply perfect.

Claude was very attentive, and I noticed more than once he'd brushed my hand while reaching for the pot of pistachios that lay on the table. I observed how he opened the shells, setting them aside by stacking them in a neat pile, one within the other. The backs of his hands were tanned, looking both practical and impressively manly.

JC was working flamboyantly on the BBQ, turning a spiral of spicy-looking sausages and swearing under his breath every time a bit of excess fat spat at him. I helped Josie prepare the salad, and we carried all the necessary items for the meal out onto the table on the terrace. This form of eating was informal, and I was grateful for the lack of pomp and ceremony. As the music from the sound system floated through the open French doors, it was almost as if we had a private pianist performing for us. The melody was enchanting with its hauntingly lilting tones. It was so magical that I keenly asked Josie for the artist's name.

'It's Richard Clay-der-man,' she told me as if breaking the surname down into syllables that would enhance my comprehension.

'What is the title of this particular track? It's beautiful,' I asked.

The chair next to me scraped backwards as Claude got to his feet. I looked at him, only to see a complicit grin as he answered my question.

'It is the *Ballade Pour Adeline*. I will show you. Wait, there, my little flower.'

I watched him disappear through one of the open French doors, only to reappear moments later. He was carrying the CD case aloft as if in victory. Placing it in my hand, I searched the inside of the CD insert album cover. It was in French, but I recognised the name of the track, '*Ballade Pour Adeline*.' It was number three on the playlist.

'Thank you, Claude. This music draws me. It's so beautiful.'

Looking across at Josie, who was sitting opposite me, I had to express myself further.

'There is a place for music like this. Sometimes it's a pleasant change not to have any lyrics because the lyrics guide you to what you are supposed to feel about a song. With an instrumental piece like this, you can make up whatever you want, escaping with your feelings for it – your wildest imaginings. It makes it completely open to individual interpretation.'

My words spilt out rapidly, flowing in quick succession without any consideration for Claude, who might be struggling to understand me. I tended to speak with rapid eagerness when I was passionate about something, and of course, I'd reverted to expressing my thoughts in English. Claude appeared bewildered and looked questioningly at Josie for a translation. She obliged, and Claude nodded in agreement.

Turning to me and casually placing his hand on top of mine, he said, 'It's true. Sometimes, feelings are so intense that we do not need the words.'

The pertinence of his words, combined with such an open show of affection towards me, did not go unnoticed by Josie. Viewing each of us in turn from behind the rounded rims of her spectacles, she mused, 'I am so pleased to see you both happy – *mon petit frère* and *ma petite sœur.*'

It felt as if I was dreaming. Had Josie just given her approval? Not only had she said that she was pleased to see us happy, but Josie had just used the same term of endearment for me as she used for her brother. It must mean that she was giving us her blessing. My fingers curled to grasp Claude's hand, and I sensed him turning towards me. Turning my face enquiringly towards him, he answered me with a lingering kiss.

That evening we ate *'en famille'* and I felt entirely at

home. Each time Claude left or returned to the table, he put his hand gently on my back in a loving gesture and an open sign of affection in front of his sister and brother-in-law. The conversation flowed smoothly, and laughter filled the air, especially when JC pointed out that his brother-in-law was now officially seeing a 'lady farmer.' JC, always the stand-up comedian, then impersonated me with my agricultural lifestyle – walking in wellies, milking cows, and driving a tractor. Not only was it hilarious to watch, but equally amusing to see Claude's consternation trying to determine if there was any truth in my supposed farming role.

'Wait,' he said. 'It's true? You have cows and a tractor?'

I laughed, 'No! Not me! Courtney, my next-door neighbour, used to have a herd of cows before he retired. He's still got his old Massey Ferguson tractor, though. I've got chickens, six sheep, and some Dartmoor ponies that I rescued from being slaughtered. That's my lot!'

'Ah, you are still my lady farmer, then Jan,' smiled Claude, 'You must have land for all these animals?'

'Petit frère,' said Josie, 'I already told you that Jan has a large amount of land. Do you not remember that after JC and I came back from visiting her, I told you that she had a big farmhouse and fields for all her animals.'

'I would love to see it,' he replied, looking hopefully at me.

'You are welcome anytime. You must come and visit, and I'll show you my home, and you can meet my friends,' I replied, amused at the sudden thought of Moira, finally meeting the man of my dreams.

'I like open spaces. I like to sit down in the middle of a field, in the long grass, with space all around me,' he said, a hint of wistfulness in his tone.

'That is because my little brother is like an Indian. He is like the North American Indian of the plains!' joked Josie.

I knew what she meant. After all, my initial meeting with Claude had evoked the same image. Maybe there *was* something in it after all. Not only was he incredibly good-looking, but it was increasingly evident that we had a lot in common, the latest being our mutual love for the freedom of open spaces, away from crowds, finding peace in the natural environment. The more I discovered about this man, the more compatible we seemed to be.

Chapter 11

As midnight approached, we decided to continue our evening indoors. Our little social group was not yet willing for the day to end. There was a celebratory atmosphere in the air, one that was almost electric, energised, and positively charged. Claude volunteered to act as our DJ and took numerous requests. The eclectic mix of music introduced me to the gravelly-toned voice of Jacques Bruel, which was a stark contrast to the previous thumping base of an obscure French Techno track. I was awestruck to hear Celine Dion singing in her native French. There was so much more passion, depth, and emotion in her voice than could ever be expressed in English. English love songs ranked a low second best in comparison.

Moving the coffee table to one side, Josie and JC took to the improvised dance floor. Seeing them dancing together reminded me of when we met in Malta. Again, I found myself marvelling at their performance as I clapped and cheered, egging them on. Standing by the stereo unit, Claude continued to sort through a pile of CDs, getting ready to make a new selection. He looked over at me, putting down the small stack of discs he was holding. Skirting the two twirling bodies with a great deal of flair, he bowed in front of me, offering his hand as he asked, 'Mademoiselle – would you care to dance with me?'

'I certainly would, kind sir,' I replied adding, 'But I can't do what JC and Josie are doing! I've never danced like that with anyone!'

Nerves took hold of me as my mind shot back to the last time Moira and I attempted to partner with each other in a jive. It hadn't ended well. Although I could bop around a handbag and had even been banned from a nightclub for 'pogo-ing' too high, these were solitary dance antics for singles, not couples!

'Lady Dee! Has she never danced before? No! This cannot be true!' Claude mocked me teasingly, his brown eyes twinkling and awaiting a response.

With no indication on my part to move from my safe place on the sofa, Claude pulled me to my feet, taking my hands in his and pulling me tightly towards him. Our bodies were touching. He stood a full head height above me, and I suddenly felt tiny. I was potentially on the verge of making a complete fool of myself!

Supposing I stand on his foot?

Supposing I twirl the wrong way?

Oh God, what happens if he attempts to throw me above his head?

Looking up at him with wide-eyed anxiety, terrified of getting it wrong, he smiled down at me, lowering his head to speak into my ear, 'Don't worry. I will teach you everything that you need to know.'

And he did. I found that it was effortless. I didn't have to decide where I was moving next because he steered me, leading me into every turn. I could see that he had rhythm in his soul by the way his feet moved, adding a little extra flurry now and then or doubling the beat just long enough to make it quietly noticeable before relaxing back to the basic steps. My initial worries diminished, and I was now intent on throwing myself into it with as much energy as he did. As we danced, we worked out each other's quirks and uniqueness. Previous shyness and inhibitions left the dance floor, allowing us to move in mutual appreciation of each other.

Time passed, and as one song melted into another, we kept going. Neither of us was willing to end the closeness that we were experiencing with the proximity of our bodies. It was as if we'd discovered a different way of expressing ourselves to each other. It was a place where we spoke the same language. It was where we shared our thoughts and intentions as they communicated through the medium of dance.

Our bodies moved in an intimacy created by our interpretation of the music, and I realised that we were alone in the room. As it flowed, I noticed that it was the sound of piano keys, a familiar melody, playing, and open to interpretation. Claude, sensing that I heard it too, pressed his mouth hard against mine, our bodies intertwined as we sought to embrace the completeness of each other before finally merging as one.

Chapter 12

'So, did you speak to them? Is everything ok?'

Josie enquired as she poured herself another morning coffee, her words puncturing the bubble in which I had been floating. I was so preoccupied and detached in my dreamlike state that I could not answer immediately. Pulling myself out of my reverie, I forced my thoughts away from the glorious past five weeks and back into the present. I needed to update Josie about the possibility of extending our stay in France.

'Sorry, Josie. I was miles away. Yes, everything is fine. Mum says that she is staying over at the farm with our dogs, Millie and Shadow, and I think she is rather enjoying herself. Courtney, our neighbour, the retired tenant farmer, went over for tea last night. Courtney is a real character; he must be in his eighties now. He has so many stories to tell of farming life in his day! They get on well, those two. Between them, they can talk the hind legs off a donkey when they get going! It's really good of them to look after everything at home which means we can stay here longer. I never expected to stay this long! I can't believe the time has passed so quickly! We've already been here for five weeks!'

The significance of my last sentence was having a

disarming effect on me. The implication of the thought surfaced in my mind once more, just as a sudden wave of nausea washed over me, making me sit down abruptly on one of the roundly padded kitchen stools.

'Are you sure that you are OK?' Josie enquired, pausing to frown at me before adding, 'Would you like me to pour you a coffee?'

I knew she sensed that I was potentially withholding something from her.

'Oh – no. I'll have a coffee later, thanks. I couldn't stomach one at the moment.'

I replied, conscious that my eyes would not meet hers and suddenly finding myself fiddling, unwarranted, with intense interest at the top of the salt cellar on the kitchen table. Aware of my action, I quickly jerked my hands away, putting them under the table so Josie could not see their anxious fiddling. I needed to pull myself together and shake off the ridiculous thought that was preoccupying my mind, pointing to the undeniable truth that my period was overdue. It was not something that I had even thought about until now. It was not as if I needed to check the calendar each month. I took my oral contraception routinely and had done so for years, even after my marriage ended. I found it made the whole monthly saga a lot less painful and generally less inconvenient. Then again, who was I trying to kid? My thoughts went back to the frightening discovery I had made a couple of days ago when I found one small white tablet lodged in the torn foil edge of the previous month's discarded blister pack. I had missed a day, and that one single omission on my part could prove to be a life-changer. My stomach lurched.

'You are very quiet *petite sœur*,' Josie commented, scrutinising me over the rim of her coffee cup, her owl-like eyes surveying me keenly through the large circular lenses of her glasses.

I had to share my fears with someone. I wished that either Mum or Moira had been there. They would immediately understand the importance of all this. It was not only the possibility of being pregnant, but all the memories that would come flooding back. The fear of loss, the unspoken guilt that I still felt in believing that I had lost my last child because I was not good enough to be a parent. Only my Mum and Moira were party to these feelings, and now, alone, I felt suddenly vulnerable and scared without either of them nearby.

'Josie,' I started, 'I need to talk to you.'

'Talk to me in French, remember,' she replied, smiling encouragingly at me. I wondered if she would continue to smile with the enormity of what I was about to say to her.

'I can't say this in French. I have to tell you in English. The subject is just too difficult to try and express in French. It's bad enough having to voice it in English.'

I replied, not looking at Josie but preferring to stare emptily at the dull pattern on the ceramic floor tiles instead. I knew that adding a voice to my thoughts would externalise them, bringing the unspoken fear into the open. I felt tears welling up in my downcast eyes and tried hard to blink them away. How would Josie react to my disclosure? Would she think it was a ploy on my part to snare her precious brother? I wanted to run, to distance myself from both Josie and the words I was due to utter. I hoped she would understand.

There was no backing out of it now, so, taking a deep breath, I braced myself, hoping that I could find the courage to divulge my situation in its entirety.

'I have a problem. Well, I don't want it to be a problem. It's not, but then again, you might think that it is. It's a woman's thing. You know – something that ladies have to deal with.'

As the words gushed out, I knew that I was doing my usual prevaricating, making absolutely no sense with my nervous ramblings. I needed to be more precise, and to the point, so I began to try again, only for Josie to cut me short by giving me a nod of understanding as she left the kitchen, calling over her shoulder that she would be back in a moment.

She returned a couple of minutes later and, smiling as if in understanding, she offered me a small box in her outstretched hand.

'Here – take this. I think it is just what you need at the moment.'

With a sense of relief that Josie understood my predicament without the need for me to voice the details in their entirety, I took the florally decorated box from her hand, immensely grateful that she should keep an unopened pregnancy testing kit in the house. She never failed to amaze me with how well she could prepare for every eventuality. The brand name on the box was alien to me, so I turned it over in anticipation of seeing some illustrated instructions for use. In doing so, I faced a colourful diagram, complete with accompanying guidance for the correct usage of the 48 tampons contained within the box. It was funny in a twisted sort of way. God only knows what expression crossed my face!

Whatever it was, it caused Josie to query, 'Is that not what you are talking about, Jan?'

Still, my eyes could not meet hers. But it was too late now. Josie would have to know because she was the only person to whom I could turn. How could I possibly go to a pharmacy on my own to ask for a pregnancy testing kit? My limited knowledge of the French language did not extend that far. Placing the box of unopened tampons on the kitchen table, I knew they were not going to be needed.

'This box won't help Josie,' I mumbled, eyes fixing once again, on the wood grain of the tabletop, before daring to continue with, 'I think it's too late for them.'

Lifting my head slowly to meet her steady gaze, I concluded, 'I think I might be pregnant.'

The words were out. The hitherto unthinkable now voiced openly. I looked at Josie to gauge her reaction to my disclosure. She was not smiling, but perhaps this was because she felt she needed to deal with the immediate practicalities of the situation. As if she needed time to process what I had said, there was a pause before she responded.

'I will go to the pharmacy and get you a pregnancy testing kit. I will be back shortly, and I will help you with what you need to do.'

Taking the car keys from their hook on the wall, she left, leaving me to wait anxiously for her return.

Forty-five minutes later, I emerged from the bathroom, clutching the pen-shaped tester, my eyes riveted to two small windows along its length, waiting to see if anything would take shape in them. A precise vertical line appeared in the first window, just as another pale line began to take shape on the second, like blue ink infiltrating damp blotting paper. Standing transfixed, it gained definition as I continued to stare at it. These solid blue lines, which crossed all language barriers, pointed to the undeniable fact that I was pregnant with Claude's child.

'What do you intend to do, Jan?' Josie asked as each of us tried to absorb the magnitude of the situation.

Good question – would I tell Claude straight away, or should I wait to be sure? Sure of what? I hardly dared to breathe a word to think about it, yet, if I was pregnant, then this was such a gift. The thought that I was deserving of having another child felt incomprehensible. Was I going to be allowed the joy of having a child? It was scary, but an ever-growing sense of delight began to replace my fear.

'I'm going to tell Claude when he comes home from work tonight,' I told Josie decisively.

'It is important to give him time to unwind from his day at work, Jan. Don't rush in too soon but make sure the timing is right,' she replied purposefully, her words delivered slowly to express their gravity. It felt like a beacon of warning.

The hidden meaning behind her response unsettled me. Surely, Claude would be as thrilled as I was? Having never experienced Claude in a bad mood, I couldn't imagine how he could ever be anything other than the person I knew and loved. Admittedly the timing was a bit premature. In a perfect world, we might have chosen to wait before having a child of our own. Maybe this was fate. The Universe was ultimately blessing our relationship. I wanted to celebrate and rejoice, not look for potential problems.

'What about JC?' I asked Josie, 'I wonder what he will think?'

Josie fixed me with a look that startled me with its intensity. I had never seen an expression like this one before. Her glowering stare told me all I needed to know before she even answered, blatantly warning me that speaking of my pregnancy with JC was prohibited.

'No. You do not tell JC. You will say nothing to him. Claude will tell you the same. JC will not understand, and so you must NOT tell him.'

Josie's harsh words carried a veiled threat. Why would the vivacious JC that I knew and loved react so badly to this news? It made no sense at all. He was always so laid back in his approach to life. It was clear that my silence was the only option, but this raised other concerns because it meant I would need to be devious in concealing this secret from him.

Feeling awkward to respond to Josie, I ventured, 'I'm not very good at hiding things. What happens if JC sees that I have lost my appetite or no longer drink alcohol? It won't take long before he puts two and two together. Once he's done that, he is so direct when he speaks. He's likely just to ask me straight out! Then what do I say?'

It was true. JC never beat about the bush. If he thought something, he would say it. His directness often got him into trouble, and he got reprimanded for being tactless, but I rather liked it. His candour meant that I could rely on him to be open and genuine in his response. Whether or not I agreed with him, or chose to take offence, was up to me, but most importantly, I appreciated his unwavering honesty. Regardless of this, Josie replied without any hesitation.

'You will not say anything to JC. He must not know.'

Turning abruptly, she left me to ponder her reasons, all potential exhilaration dampened by her mood.

Chapter 13

I waited for Claude to return from work that evening and was relieved that he was in high spirits, due apparently to his ability to rectify a problem with a client's computer suite. He was looking forward to a relaxing weekend and quickly changed into a pair of swimming trunks in our bedroom. Putting on the same towelling robe that had swamped me on my first visit to France, I noticed how it fitted Claude's taught muscular frame perfectly. Before Claude could leave the room to head for the pool, I decided it was time to tell him I was pregnant with his child.

His eyes widened as a broad smile began to stretch across his face. Looking immensely pleased, he wrapped his arms around me, and in doing so, I smelt the familiar scent of his aftershave, mixed with a tinge of chlorine from the white towelling robe.

Still smiling, he touched my stomach with the palm of his hand as he mused, 'Will our baby have blue eyes? I hope that our baby has blue eyes like its mother.'

So far, the members of Claude's family that I had met all had classic olive skin, dark hair, and brown eyes. Only Claude's eldest son and JC proved the exception to the rule. With JC on my mind once more, I wanted to know

Claude's thoughts on sharing our fantastic news with his brother-in-law. Maybe Josie had got it wrong. I frowned, feeling suddenly vexed that it was Claude's decision, not his sister's.

'Claude!'

I exclaimed, still riding high on the wave of excitement, 'What about JC? Can we tell him? It seems only fair because, of course, Josie knows, and I am so excited that I want to tell my boys!'

Claude reacted like being stung, retracting his hand instantly from my stomach, his physical reaction serving to underline the severity of his spoken words.

'No. You will not say anything to JC.'

His voice was stern and final, but I was not willing to submit to his decision just yet. He needed to see the bigger picture. This ridiculous situation was not just about whatever the problem was with his family, but what about mine? They had a right to know. Undeterred, I pushed him further.

'But how am I supposed to keep this from the boys? I want to tell them!'

I began to dig my heels in. Discovering that I was pregnant was a joy that I very much wanted to share with them from the outset. Being asked to keep it a secret tainted it. Why was I getting a conflicting impression that this news needed to be discretely veiled, forced into a corner like a shameful, shrouded secret; stealthily silenced into submission? It was making no sense at all. I was beginning to feel angry and defiant. I knew the situation was in danger of escalating rapidly. Perhaps Claude sensed this too because he carefully blanketed what he said next by wrapping his words into a gentle warm tone of concern.

'My love. We will not say anything to Jean Claude yet. He does not need to know at the moment. It is too early. It is also too early in the pregnancy to tell the boys.

Supposing you lost the baby? Imagine how they would feel. You'd feel awful for telling them because you know how it would upset them. So we wait for the twelve weeks, and after that, you can let them know.'

Albeit begrudgingly, his words made sense to me. It was true that I didn't want to take the risk of telling the boys too soon in case I lost the baby. He was right. I should have thought more about them than myself and my needs in the excitement of the moment. However, I did feel sad that we would not be able to celebrate openly. If I'd been at home, I know that Moira and I would have been whooping around the table, and the wine would have flowed – I'd have been able to drink it. I had to think about the little life growing inside me from now on. Finding a way to adequately and convincingly explain to JC that I'd converted to being 'teetotal' overnight would be challenging, but Claude was right. I shouldn't have doubted his reasoning. He had the welfare of others firmly at the centre of his decision. I'd simply havt to be patient and wait until the time was right for me to share the unbelievably good news.

The following morning Claude surprised me by announcing that he had booked a medical appointment.

'On a Saturday? Wow! What do I need a medical appointment for?'

I asked, thinking that this was a bit premature to be making prenatal arrangements.

'You will have a scan,' he replied.

'How can I have a scan so early? It's only just over five weeks.'

'We need to be sure,' he insisted.

It sounded like my pregnancy mattered to him, and so feeling very lucky to have such a caring partner, we set off to the appointment.

My first experience of the French medical service

was impressive. It was remarkable how swiftly an appointment could be made and subsequently attended within such a short time frame. Claude seemed excited at the prospect of being a father because he was quick to pay for the scan. Perhaps he also wanted to reassure me that all was well, even at such an early stage. I was grateful to him and completely taken aback by the image that I saw on the ultrasound. The nurse in charge of the scan confirmed that the baby was just five weeks old. I stared in wonderment at the monitor from my lying position on the couch, which revealed a minuscule little being with a gloriously beating heart. This little person was a gift, a complete and utter blessing, and I felt fiercely protective. I blinked tearfully at the screen as I prayed silently to the Universe, fervently seeking assurance that I would not lose this precious new life growing inside me. In that moment I knew I'd do whatever it took to love and keep this little soul safe.

Chapter 14

Several weeks later and I was struggling with eating. The French food was becoming too rich and strongly flavoured for me to bear. Even the cooking aromas made me feel queasy, and as our bedroom was on the ground floor, opposite the kitchen, it was impossible to avoid the smells as they wafted through the lower levels of the house.

There were only so many excuses that I could make for my frequent, sudden departures from the dinner table. I could see that the boys thought it strange, and I'm sure they sensed my quietness. It was neither fair on them, nor me. I was fed up with the cloak and dagger attitude concerning JC. Since childhood, the importance of being honest was something my parents stressed, so I still believed that 'honesty is the best policy.' What could JC possibly say or do that would be so irreversibly terrible? I wanted to enjoy my pregnancy and not keep it a forbidden secret. I thought of my dad, who had been a solid, no-nonsense, tell it as it is northerner. As such, he was similar to JC. Both could be relied upon to speak their truths, albeit at the peril of the recipient. I made up my mind. If my dad were in this situation, he would have spoken out and brought everything into the open. I would do the same.

Once I got JC alone, I would tell him the news. At least it might stop him from making remarks about me "thinking about my waistline," or telling me that I "must be ill" as I "didn't want any wine". I'd fielded all the jibes effectively to date, but enough was enough. It took too much effort to keep up the role of a figure-obsessed, teetotal female. It was ridiculous! There was no reason that I should not put him straight. It would make life so much easier.

The perfect moment arose when Josie took the boys to the park while Claude and JC were working. Having the house entirely to myself gave me uninterrupted thinking time. I considered writing a note to JC to tell him my news but realised that my written French would be worse than any verbal attempt. It'd be far too complicated. At that moment, I heard the sound of the back door opening. Someone was home. No one was due back yet, so it was unusual. Perhaps it was one of the neighbours who'd popped over unexpectedly. They did tend to drop in unannounced. I stuck my head around the kitchen door to find the back door was ajar and someone had left a briefcase on the side of the worktop. I recognised it at once. It was JC's, which meant he was home earlier than usual. Out of the corner of my eye, I caught the movement of a figure in the garden. JC was wielding what looked like a giant shrimping net, intent on fishing debris out of the pool. Not wanting to miss this opportunity of talking to him whilst we were on our own, I hurried outside to see him.

'Jan!' he said as he looked up, hearing my approach as my flip-flops slapped clumsily across the terrace in my vigorous bid to reach him swiftly.

'Jean Claude! Ça va?'

We exchanged our greetings with the statutory

four kisses of the alternating cheek variety, and I told him that I'd something that I wanted to say to him. He surprised me with his gentleness as he guided me to the garden bench overlooking the pond. We sat down companionably. He was now giving me his full attention, and I was grateful for his sudden sensitivity. As he looked at me expectantly, his typical bombastic image had disappeared as if he had consciously tucked it away. It was the first time that I'd seen this side of him. Sitting beside me on the rustic bench was a quiet, patient man with an air of complete calm. Wondering if he was knowingly making it easier for me to speak, I ventured,

'JC. I want to tell you something. I don't *have* to tell you, but you are special to me, so I'd like to share it with you. Josie and Claude don't think I should say anything, and I don't understand why. I have no reason to believe that you would react in any terrible way, and so even if it *is* a risk, I am still going to say it.'

It felt liberating to have sufficient command of the French language to express myself openly. After all, JC was my friend, and from what I knew of him, he was nothing but full of good intentions. I could see he was feeling concerned. His eyes searched for clues in my every expression, and without smiling, he nodded at me, indicating that I should continue. Quickly and silently, I inwardly rehearsed my newly acquired French phrase before speaking it openly

'*Je suis enceinte.*'

There it was, those three words, out there. 'I am pregnant'. Now it was my turn to search for a reaction in his face. He seemed to be taking his time to digest what I had said.

After what seemed like a lifetime, our eyes met as he slowly asked, 'And Jan, are you happy?'

'Of course, I'm happy. I'm thrilled, JC. That's why I wanted to tell you. It is important to me that you know because you are such a special friend.'

'And Claude? Is he happy?'

'I think so,' I paused unexpectedly, surprised at the flimsiness of the words that had come from my lips. Quickly looking to rectify them, I added, 'No, that's wrong. I don't *think* he is happy. I *know* he is happy.'

I was surprised at how much more reassuring that made me feel.

'Then if you are both happy, I am happy,' said JC, but I could see from the tautness of his laughter lines that he was holding back. More than on any previous occasion, it was now that I needed his frankness. I wanted him to be open with me. Yet I could tell by his silence that he was holding something back. What was he not telling me? Why was he so reticent? I pushed him further.

'I don't understand why on Earth they didn't want me to tell you. I knew that you would be fine about it.'

I paused slightly, my eyes seeking clues in his face, waiting for the laughter lines around his eyes to crease as he broke into his toothy smile. There was nothing. Nothing but a coldness, like a shock frozen in time when momentarily the world stands still.

Hesitantly I ventured, 'You are all right about it, aren't you?'

'Of course I am,' he replied.

His body flinched as if startled whilst his eyes blinked a couple of times in quick succession as if bringing his consciousness back into the moment. He indicated that our conversation was over by rising to his feet, but not before I caught a glimpse of concern in his eyes. Making a lame excuse for needing to finish cleaning the pool, he strolled off to resume his aquatic duties. I resigned myself to watching him slowly and deliberately skimming the surface of the water, stopping intermittently to shake the unwanted items from his net. As I observed him, it occurred to me that life could be more straightforward if, just like the discarded leaves and twigs, we could also retrieve the floating thoughts and unfinished conversations by scrutinising them in the mesh of a giant shrimping net.

Once Claude arrived home from work that evening, I waited until both he and Josie were in the kitchen. It was, after all, the heart of the place and if ever I needed to find someone, I first looked in the kitchen.

They were engrossed in an intense conversation, with an unmistakable air of conspiracy about them. I waited until there was an opportune moment before announcing that I'd spoken to JC. Smiling to reassure them, I explained that he'd reacted positively. Josie and Claude exchanged glances. Then Josie shrugged dismissively, but not before I caught the quick raising of her eyebrows to Claude through her round-rimmed glasses.

Half-heartedly she said, 'Well, that is good. You can never tell how JC will react to these things, but I am glad he is happy.'

I thought no more of it, apart from having a sense of growing excitement in the knowledge that I would now be able to tell Tom and Owen. I imagined their reaction to me announcing that they would have a little brother or sister in the following Spring. Perhaps I would have the perfect family, after all.

Two days later, Claude took me to one side and told me that Josie and JC needed to have their space back. The continual rowdy behaviour of my boys was proving too stressful for the couple. They wished to restore some semblance of peace to their lives and home. As a result, we would go to Claude's apartment in Velizy for a few days.

We duly packed our belongings into our cases and left.

Chapter 15

Velizy – Paris

The top-floor penthouse reminded me of a typical bachelor pad. Its whole ambience was well ordered, pristinely functional, and minimalistic.

There was a small kitchen in the corner of the main living area. The two-ringed gas hob and lack of work surface space made it appear ill-equipped to cope with cooking for more than a single person. With its gleaming glass top, the dining table was more fitting for a show home; more a sophisticated exhibit than a practical piece of family furniture. I cringed to think how my sons' inevitable finger marks would, in effect, violate its pristine surface.

Claude pointed to the sleek black leather sofa, which would convert into a bed that Tom and Owen were to share. He told me that we would need to make it up every night. I knew this was going to be a problem as the boys could not go to bed until Claude did. I assured myself that these living conditions were only temporary as we weren't planning on staying there for long.. At least the ceiling-to-floor windows lessened the sense of being in such an enclosed living space. It was far from ideal, but we would make the best of it.

Moving on to the fully tiled marble bathroom, Claude stressed the importance of maintaining the pristine appearance of the glass shower screen and proceeded to show me the location of the cloth and cleaning solution that was to be used immediately after each use. I nodded my head obediently as I absorbed this information.

Although there was only one bedroom, it was substantial given the dimensions of the rooms that I had seen to date. A set of sliding doors opened out onto the roof terrace, and mirrored ceiling to floor built-in wardrobes lined the walls on each side of the enormous double bed, whose covers lay immaculately untouched. Again, this room was a showcase – for display purposes only, and so the state-of-the-art ironing board, standing like a statement piece in one corner, did not appear out of place. Sensing my curiosity, Claude explained that by design, it had an inbuilt steam tank attached directly to the iron as well as the ability to project bursts of steam up through the ironing board itself. I had never seen anything so high-tech before. When Claude impressed upon me the importance of a freshly ironed shirt, I guiltily recalled how I actively avoided having to press anything at home, preferring instead to perfect the timing of taking clothes off the outside line and folding them before they thought about creasing. I'd have to adapt quickly to this new way of doing things.

Just over a week later, it was proving harder than I had imagined living harmoniously in someone else's home and in such a restrictive space. One night, an unfortunate incident occurred for which I accepted total responsibility. In hindsight, I should have been more careful. The sliding patio door to the terrace had been left open and this happened to coincide with Owen entering the lounge through a door with two glass panes. In doing so, he created a through-draft because both doors were open at the same time. A sudden gust of wind caught the interior door, slamming it shut, shattering one of the glass panes with thousands of shards splintering across the floor. I spent ages picking up the pieces while the boys were ordered to sit out of harm's way on the sofa. I didn't want to risk either of them stepping in it. That night I watched nervously for Claude's Porsche to arrive at the entrance to the undercover parking. I was ready with a humble apology for the damage we had caused. It was an accident, and I hoped he would understand. The glass panel was replaceable, and thankfully no one was hurt.

His reaction was not as I'd hoped. Quick to spot the hole in the door where the glass was missing, he demanded to know what had happened. I explained that the accident occurred when the wind had caught the open door.

'I'm so sorry,' I repeated, trying to accentuate how guilty I was feeling. 'I will pay for the damage.'

He threw me a hard, unyielding look, his eyes full of recriminations.

'Your boys,' he hissed, 'you need to control them better'

'I will,' I assured him, 'it's just that we don't usually live in such a small space. It's very different, and we are still adjusting.'

'Children need discipline,' he replied, 'they need to learn respect.'

With that, he walked away to take a shower, leaving me feeling riddled with guilt for damaging his home. I spoke to the boys, impressing on them the need to be more careful in the future, given that we were guests in someone else's house. They nodded in understanding.

Trying to make amends, I carefully prepared a meal,

and we sat down to eat. It was the least I could do to try and make up for what had happened. By doing my bit, I felt I was not imposing on Claude's hospitality. The silence was as palpably cold as the glass-topped table, so it was a relief when Claude showed signs of relaxing after opening the second bottle of Bordeaux. I sensed the atmosphere beginning to thaw and normality was fully restored by the end of the meal. The little living-dining room echoed cosily to the sounds of amicable voices. With a sense of relief, I made up the sofa bed for two sleepy boys, preferring to leave the washing up until the following morning. It was already late, and I didn't want to disturb the lads with the clash and clank of dishes. Wishing them goodnight, I padded along the unlit hallway to join Claude in his bedroom, where his lovemaking was unusually fierce in its neediness; completely selfish and self-gratifying – totally lacking any form of tenderness.

The next day was a fresh start. The sunlight coming through the patio door highlighted shadowy reminders of objects blocking the natural path of the light on the lounge walls. Somehow, I related this to our need for unrestricted space and the freedom found in the natural environment. It reminded me that this constrictive penthouse apartment was a far cry from the expansive fields at home. I cursed the fact that I was without my car. It was left at Josie's house because the parking provision at the apartment block was strictly for resident permit holders. If I had a car, I'd be able to get out and about more easily to explore beyond the bounds of this built-up area.

'Mum, there's nothing to *do*!' Tom whined for the umpteenth time. I was inclined to agree with him.

There were only so many times that we could play

imaginative games on the roof terrace of the penthouse apartment. It was proving a stark contrast to living at Josie and JC's house, where there were always things to keep little minds and bodies occupied. Apart from the undeniable thrill of having a swimming pool, there'd also been an alluring old toy box overflowing with a myriad of entertaining items. On the rare rainy days, Tom and Owen passed many an enjoyable hour rummaging through its contents and some cartoon books depicting the adventures of Tin-Tin proved a particular favourite. This apartment just wasn't suitable for young children. The garden at Josie's had provided hours of entertainment with its assortment of bushes providing the perfect backdrop for battles enacted with a well-used set of plastic cowboys and Indians. The penthouse terrace's grey flagstones were as devoid of vegetation as they were of inspiration.

'I'm bored,' said Owen.

'Me too,' echoed Tom.

Eyes implored me to provide some suitable form of entertainment. An idea came to me.

'Let's go and see if we can find a park. I know we can only see endless rows of rooftops when we look out from the view on the terrace, but that's just one side. Let's go and see if there is anything in the other direction. There must be a park or some green space area where all these residents can go and relax.'

We set off, each step proving to me that we were in the suburbs of a large city. Preoccupied with their agendas, pedestrians did not attempt to make eye contact, let alone smile. It was ironic to find that being in the midst of so many people could feel so isolating. Apart from the vehicles passing us in this street, I heard an endless buzz of fast-moving traffic in the distance. We must be close to a part of a major road network. Planes passed directly overhead and started their final descent into Charles de Gaulle Airport. The noise was alien to the three of us. In rural Cornwall, there was only the occasional spinning of rotary blades as the air ambulance passed across an unpolluted sky. This Parisian sky was a milky blue as if someone had diluted it with a water-laden paintbrush before streaking it with cirrus clouds that hung motionless in the stagnant air. I wondered how many people had breathed it before me. It was warm to inhale, a blend of exhaust fumes and hot tarmac. A familiar wave of nausea swept over me. I felt tired. Over the last few days, I'd noticed that my energy reserves felt depleted by the afternoon, and I yearned to put my feet up and rest. It was not an option, though, because Tom and Owen were bursting with an energy that needed to be handled with care until it could be safely unleashed in an appropriate open space.

'Look!' I pointed across a road to a long line of chestnut trees, behind which appeared to be the green of open space.

'I think we have found the nearest park!'

We quickened our steps, eager to confirm that our quest had been successful. A plot of green, bigger than a football pitch, stretched before us, chestnut trees standing sentinel-like around the perimeter. Both boys yipped with joy before running in wild excitement at the thrill of our discovery. It was not long before the skills of passing the football to one another absorbed our thoughts. I watched in loving amusement at Owen taking another feverish swipe at the ball with his foot. He threw himself into everything. Tom was beginning to try out some nifty footwork, probably something that he'd seen on the television and was determined to re-enact.

At least it wouldn't be long now until we could go back home to Cornwall. We were only staying on so Claude could visit the clients he'd already scheduled to meet. He'd then be moving to Cornwall with us on a permanent basis. I was thrilled by the idea, although I realised that it would be a vast cultural upheaval for him. Life in rural Cornwall would be something of a culture shock for Claude. However, he assured me that he was making the right decision for all of us. He preferred open countryside to the built environment and was in no doubt that he could continue to run his business from our small Cornish hamlet. Being the co-owner of a computer firm gave Claude the freedom to locate wherever he chose. His brother, also his business partner, had given his blessing.

Claude spent long working hours in front of a computer. The powers of the internet would enable him to work from home. He could also commute back to Paris as and when required. It sounded like a perfect solution. We would be able to live together as a family at last. I was counting down the remaining three days. Boxes of his possessions neatly lined the sides of the bedroom, sealed and labelled with their respective contents. My vehicle was far better than his Porsche for transporting bulky items, but I was concerned that we might still find ourselves short on space for the journey. I asked him if he planned to transport the smaller boxes in his car. He laughed, dismissing my suggestion by stating that he had already sold the Porsche and would use his 'other car' instead.

'Your other car?' I asked, 'I didn't know you had another one as well.'

'It's an old Mercedes,' he had replied, ' bought it off Josie a few years ago. I won't be needing the Porsche in

Cornwall, so it made sense to sell it.'

I couldn't argue with that.

'Come on, boys. Time to head back to the flat. Tom – when we get near the road, you must pick the ball up and carry it.'

Sensing that I needed to lift their spirits for the walk back to the confines of the apartment, I called out, 'Who's the best football team in the world?'

'Newcastle,' they chanted back.

'Who?' I teased as if I had never heard of them.

'Newcastle,' they shouted back as loudly as they could. As I led the way, my little brood of Brits marched happily onwards once more.

If I'd only known then the direction that I was leading them in, we would have taken a very different path.

Chapter 16
Back to Mithian – Sept 1999

'So – you're going to be Mrs Campait in November! Who'd have thought it!' grinned Moira, as we sat together in the September sun-filled conservatory at Mithian Farm. The citrus scent of the lemon geraniums emanated from their pots on the window sill and I had the feeling of utter contentment being at home. It meant that I could discuss wedding preparations, now only a couple of months away, with my great friend who shared my excitement.

'I know!' I exclaimed as if still hadn't sunk in, 'I suppose it just seemed like the natural thing to do, especially after our heart-to-heart conversation I told you about.'

Moira looked at me and, checking for confirmation that she'd understood, asked 'You mean when he dropped the bombshell that...'

I cut her dead in her tracks as she caught the scowl I sent in reaction to what she had just said. She reworded it and carried on

'Ok – well, not a bombshell – but let's face it, you didn't know about the fourth child, did you?' she continued. 'I mean, you knew he had three children from his first marriage, but you didn't know about the *other* son from another relationship.'

'We were honest and open with one another, Moira," I impressed upon her and continued, 'I'd been open with him and told him that I'd always struggled with the fact that I was born out of wedlock. It's always been something I've felt passionate about. These poor children do not choose to be illegitimate!'

I could feel I was already jumping on my soapbox, and I was not going to stop. Instead, I was going to take ownership of my feelings on the subject

'I still believe that there's a label attached to illegitimate children today. People are so quick to make judgments, to waggle the finger. I know I was so lucky to have been adopted, and I couldn't have chosen such an amazing mother and father, but it's about identity. I would love to have had a surname to which I belonged – a surname that reflected my roots. That was the conversation I'd with Claude. I just want our baby to feel that he or she truly belongs.'

Moira nodded in understanding.

'And you managed to express all this in French, did you, Jan? Wow! Good for you, girl!'

'It was so important, Moira. I had to make sure that he understood. You know me, if I feel it strongly enough, I have to say it,' I replied, 'and I think because of that, he was able to tell me about his son.'

'Tell me again what Claude said. Sounds awful from what I remember – something about paying not to see him?' Moira queried.

'You're right Moira! It was awful! He had a relationship with this girl, and she became pregnant. He wanted to stand by her, but her father had none of it. When the baby was born, he went to the hospital to discover he had a son. He told me he was thrilled. But his potential father-in-law refused to allow Claude's name to be entered on the birth certificate! Can you imagine that? How dreadful!'

'And then he paid Claude off, you said?' said Moira incredulously.

'Yes! He paid Claude to ensure that his name wouldn't be on the birth certificate. Can you imagine how terrible that must have been for him? Imagine being forbidden to have anything to do with your child! It beggars belief. So, when he told me, he had tears pouring down his face. If it'd been me in that situation, I know I would have too. My heart went out to him.'

I paused as I re-lived the moment before adding, 'Oh – and that is why I said that if we have a boy, I think he should take Claude's name as his middle name.'

'Aah, that's sweet. What a lovely idea. Typical you, Jan, making it OK. You're such a caring person.'

I chose not to dwell on her compliment as I always struggled with accepting praise, so I moved on with my story instead rather than lingering.

'So that's when we decided to get married. It seemed the best option for both of us. Claude took me to a jeweller in the large hypermarket complex nearby and chose this sapphire and diamond engagement ring.'

I looked down at my left hand, the ring glinting in the now paling sunshine.

'Oh, and I know what I haven't told you about!' I added, my words sounding like an unintentional afterthought, 'I met his other three children from his first marriage! I thought it would be good to invite them over to meet each other. I had to ask Josie to make the arrangements because I didn't have any contact details for them.'

'Oh – so they met their stepmother to be, eh? Go on – what were they like? Did you get on with them, OK?'

'Well, it turns out that Manu, who is the eldest, grew

up with Claude from a very young age, and he lives nearby in Paris. The other two, Gael and Raphaelle, live with their mother in Bordeaux. Claude is particularly close to Manu. It's because he was a single parent for many years.'

'Good on him. There's not many fathers I can think of that'd do that! So, you still haven't said what they were like!'

'Raphaelle seemed quite reserved, she was at ease with her brother, but I couldn't help but notice her large brown eyes watching me from across the dinner table. She didn't look completely at ease with her dad either – moody almost. Still, I don't know, who knows? Maybe it was just a one-off. Her brother Gael is easy-going, ready for a laugh. I liked them both, but I think it would take a while for Raphaelle to feel comfortable around me. They were both great with Tom and Owen, so that was a real bonus.'

'I'm so pleased for you, Jan,' affirmed Moira. 'Where is the groom anyway? I thought he was supposed to be here.'

'Oh, you're right. Claude *was* supposed to be. He's set up his office in the corner of the living room. Everything fits in perfectly. He's been working from home but had a call and had to go back to Paris. A client had a problem, and only he could fix it. I took him to Newquay airport this morning. Thank goodness for that airport. It makes things so much easier. Gives us quick access to the outside world!'

'And how are you in yourself, Jan?' Moira asked as her gaze shifted to fix on the front of my sweatshirt that now concealed a small expectant lump.

'I'm feeling great, Moira. I'm so glad to be back home. It was lovely being away, but it was quite a struggle in that rented apartment of Claude's in Paris. We were too big for the place. It was fine for a bachelor but not for a young family!'

I laughed slightly awkwardly, embarrassed by the memory.

'Particularly a family with inquisitive boys!' I added, 'I didn't tell you about the waste disposal unit escapade, did I?'

'Err, no. Go on. What are you going to tell me now? There's always something happening with you!' Moira leaned towards me in a conspiratorial manner, keen to learn more, and chuckled in anticipation

'Well, there was this chute type thing, on the wall above the kitchen sink. Weird it was. Anyway, if you pulled the lever, it opened out towards you like a large metal dustpan. You put your rubbish in it, closed it up, and all the waste shot down the chute into enormous waste bins in the basement.'

'Sounds like a good idea to me,' replied Moira, 'typical of the French to have something like that.'

'Oh, great idea,' I agreed, 'Great idea until a certain young Thomas decides to slot his brother's action man into it and to show his brother how it can vanish!' I laughed. 'I know it was naughty. Claude didn't see the funny side at all. We did though! It took us ages, ferreting around in these huge bins.'

I couldn't stop laughing as I recalled the horror on Claude's face, which made it all the funnier. 'Oh, it still tickles me, Moira. I wish you had seen it! The joy of having boys, eh?'

'That is SO funny, Jan!' Moira was aghast. 'So you had to put your hands in other people's rubbish?'

'Yes! Amazing what you could find down there. We had to take torches – one person held the torch while the other put their hands in. I mean, some bits were decaying and a bit soggy and...'

I was goading her now. I knew full well which buttons to press to get a rise out of Moira.

'Oh! And the nappy...' I started, but Moira was having none of it. Showing her disgust, she stuck her neck forward, filling her cheeks with air, as with mouth tightly closed, she resisted the urge to vomit.

She screeched as she made a desperate signal in the air with her hand to make me stop. I paused to let her get herself together before finishing my tale of triumph in a way that would not be offensive to her.

'Anyway, the main thing is that we found him. Action Man and Owen were reunited.'

Moira looked up, demonstrating that my words were now acceptable to her sensitive stomach and ears. Stifling a laugh whilst avoiding any eye contact with her, I mischievously added, 'It took some time to wash him, mind you.'

Chapter 17

On our wedding day, a small group of friends witnessed the civil marriage ceremony at Truro registry office.

The inimitable Moira rose to the challenge and volunteered her catering services, placing herself in charge of the wedding buffet. Moira was in full swing; her final preparations were underway. An apron covered her wedding outfit, her high heels tapped busily over the slate floor of the old dairy as she went about her culinary preparations.

As I stood with her in the kitchen in my purple velvet shot dress that I chose to wear as a bride, we reminisced over memorable highlights that had cemented our friendship over the years. Moira featured strongly in my past, and I hoped that she would always be there in my future; real friends are few and far between. She felt like family to me; she was the sister that I never had. For whatever reason, we found ourselves talking about our shared past. Perhaps it was the story of why we found ourselves together that day.

We recalled the first time that Thomas was invited to Christian's for tea after school. Christian, or Chris for short, was Moira's eldest son, and he joined the same Year 1 class as Thomas when Moira and her family moved to Cornwall from Lancashire. I remembered going to pick Tom up from Moira's at the agreed time, only to be met on the doorstep by Moira, who was brandishing a coat hanger with Tom's school uniform placed on it. It was secretly horrifying because I realised that it was something that I'd never done when my boys had friends back to play. Once the young guest had changed into 'play clothes,' I put their school uniform into their backpacks, so they would not be left behind. Had I got it wrong all these years? The pristine uniform that Moira now handed me was so uncreased that it convinced me she had carefully ironed it before placing it on the hanger! However, it took several subsequent meetings with Moira before I dared to mention the subject. When I did, she took me by complete surprise, assuring me that it was because I spoke in such a posh voice that she thought I would expect high standards. I've never let her forget it! Her notion of me being 'posh' was fondly waved farewell on the night of the dreaded 'jive' practice. Momentarily, my mind fleeted back to how that memory had come dangerously close to stopping me from dancing with Claude all those months ago. I was pulled out of my reverie as Moira took up the story.

'Do you remember when the Miners was hosting one of its winter theme nights? You remember the ones they used to do to try and raise a bit more revenue in the winter months. Something to keep the locals spending in the pub?'

I nodded sheepishly, knowing what was coming next.

'That bloody '60s night! Do you remember? We hired out those costumes. Even the blokes were in skirts! We decided to practice before the big event, so I came to yours one evening. We chose a bit of Chuck Berry. You said you would be the one to catch me. I was to run into your arms, and just as they do in the films, you would swing me from one side of your body to the next.'

Moira eyed me distastefully, and I quickly tried to justify the thought process by saying, 'Yes – well, that's because you are smaller than me. You would never be able to lift me, and so I thought it best that I did the lifting.'

We caught each other's eyes and dissolved into hysterics as we pictured what followed next. True to form, entering the spirit of the moment, Moira launched into the start of our dance routine with her usual vim and vigour. She threw herself off the floor towards me just as Chuck Berry urged Johnny to 'Go Johnny go!' So Moira went. She went and continued to keep going as I made a frantic grab for her. It was too late. Her momentum carried me back with her, crashing into the table and sending the stack of '60s CDs toppling to the floor. The conservatory come dance studio now looked more like something out of a disaster zone – a pot plant, unearthed from its pot, lay with soil and roots exposed to the unruffled tones of Chuck cheerfully urging Johnny on from the side-lines.

We laughed at all these memories as I topped up Moira's wine glass, and she insisted that I was not to roll up my sleeves and help as it was 'my wedding day.' I felt blessed that I had such a great friend and that we'd shared so many times, both happy and sad. With a Moira in my life, I was grateful that sad moments could be turned on their heads. Moira had an uncanny knack for finding humour in the darkest of places and that meant there were always blue-sky moments to be found on the darkest days.

On the whole, Moira had the glass half full mentality to life, but, when a wedding guest exclaimed that a vehicle with a French number plate was pulling up outside, her usual optimism. This was totally unexpected – as far as I was aware, none of the French contingent had been able to accept our invitation. I dashed to the window in the conservatory to see who had arrived. To my surprise, I spotted Josie stepping out from the passenger side of their Mercedes.

'Surprise, surprise *ma petite sœur*!' she smiled as I embraced first Josie and then JC.

'I can't believe you came after all! It's so lovely to have you here! Wait until Claude sees you! Come inside. He's in the lounge, sorting out cocktails for everyone.'

After I'd reunited the pair with Claude and made some introductions to other guests, I returned to the kitchen to see how Moira was progressing. I found her manically mashing garlic on the chopping board before scraping it with shaking hands into a bowl containing the ingredients for her secret marinade recipe.

In a sheer state of panic, she hissed what appeared to be an urgent confession, 'It's years since I was at catering college. OK – so I worked in Switzerland and the Lakes, but that was ages ago!'

She proceeded to baste her speciality of 'sticky chicken wings' with the dark mixture from the bowl in a fraught and frantic manner.

In a broad northern accent that came into its own at times of stress, she added, 'And now I'm supposed to impress the French Fuckers!'

There was a pause as we both digested the enormity of the situation. I could feel gurgles of laughter rippling up inside me, threatening to explode at any time. It was one of those occasions where, if I know I'm not supposed to laugh, it makes it even more impossible not to do so. With wide eyes, Moira was doing a good impression of a stunned rabbit in headlights.

Her voice squawked in urgent tones, 'Jan! What shall I do?' Her eyes implored me to somehow come to her rescue in a bid to switch from 'blinding beam' to 'dipped heads' to release her from her frozen trance.

Attempting to calm her, I grabbed the nearest bottle of Bordeaux. I offered up a silent prayer that the bottle would at least bear the label of *'mis en bouteille à la propriété.'* After all, we now had the French contingent in our midst, and I dreaded the thought of being caught red-handed with my usual 'flat bottomed bottle' of bargain-basement quality.

'I guess we'll just have to wing it!' I grinned, smirking at the pieces of glazed chicken in the baking tray.

'Cheers,' we said in unison, before taking a couple of nerve-calming gulps from our glasses, giggling like a couple of schoolgirls.

It was no surprise that Moira, aided by several hearty glasses for good measure, breezed the buffet to such an extent that JC even asked for her secret chicken wing recipe. I breathed a sigh of relief. All was well. Franco-English dining passed amicably, and both friends and relatives alike now turned to top up their cocktails, one of which had earned the distinguishing title of 'anti-freeze.' This was due to its splendid blue hue. It was undoubtedly proving its ability to warm the frostiest of moments. The highly contentious subject of England beating France in the Six Nations rugby final on the afternoon of our wedding became duly quelled by the fruity combination of grapefruit, curacao, and lichee liqueur.

By late afternoon, Moira was already fluent in her 'Cab Savs' and 'Tarte au Citrons'. Fuelled with alcoholic confidence she had imparted the sum of her Lancashire culinary expertise on the accommodating ears of Josie, who was now, after all, my new sister-in-law.

The celebrations continued late into the night as music and laughter echoed around our large living room and the shadows of people dancing rippled to rhythms across its walls. I felt pure joy to think that I was lucky enough to have found love and that this was just the beginning of an extraordinary life for us all. In my heart, I felt content in knowing that by marrying Claude, the child that I was carrying could never be classed as a 'mistake' or feel unwanted. By sharing the same surname as its parents, this baby would grow up with a sense of belonging.

Chapter 18

April 2000

For the umpteenth time, I hoped that I was doing the right thing, but, as I stood under the flowing bough of the blossoming cherry tree in the front acre garden of Mithian Farm, labour pains advancing all the time, I realised that it was now far too late to change my mind. That boat had already sailed! My child was going to be born British.

Claude had been adamant that I should return to France for the birth. He impressed on me the benefits of staying in a hospital bed with a nurse who would tend to my every need for the first couple of weeks. In his opinion, it was too risky to contemplate giving birth in England, let alone wanting the baby to be born at home.

However, I was adamant that I would not return to France. On a practical side, I could not leave Tom and Owen behind, and it would have meant far too much upheaval taking everything that I could have needed with me. Then there was the emotional side. I had the support of friends in Cornwall, and my mum, who had already witnessed the birth of Owen at home. I wanted those people I could rely on to be on hand. Not only that, but I did not want to delay introducing Tom and Owen to the latest addition to our family. They were very much a part of this, and I didn't want us to be isolated from one another. If I went to France, they might think that I'd abandoned them in favour of the newborn. It could harbour resentment and that wouldn't be a good start. Even the thought of being amid painful contractions while exasperatingly trying to communicate with a French health team was hideous. I had no idea what the French equivalents were for 'contraction,' 'forceps,' or 'umbilical cord,' and I had no intention of needing to find out! No. I'd made the right decision to stay in England. I'd met the team of midwives that would be on call. I was particularly fond of one who I later discovered was known locally as Mrs Tiggywinkle. She was a common sight in the local community, bustling down Cornish lanes in her age-worn red Beetle, on a mission to serve the needs of mothers-to-be.

Looking up through the boughs of the cherry tree to the blue April sky, I felt so blessed. Today my baby and I would meet each other. Smiling at the thought, I set off in the direction of the back field, keen to keep moving because felt more comfortable. The sheep were frolicking about, enjoying the early warmth of the Spring Day and at that moment, it felt as if the whole world was echoing my sense of excitement.

Our son, Morgan, entered the world four hours later. The birth was uncomplicated, and Claude finally started to relax. He stood awkwardly in the corner of the bedroom, and I wondered if he felt that he'd be in the way. Perhaps this is what they did in France. It seemed odd for someone who could be so tactile, to physically distance himself, making it clear that he was more comfortable gripping his whisky glass in preference to my outstretched palm. How could the single malt in his hand merit more attention than mother and new-born?

Staring into the tiny face of the infant, wrapped in his swaddle of blankets that nested in my arms, I smiled at his shock of black hair, and I wondered if he would take after his father in looks. My mother, who arrived at the last minute, had not long departed to do the school run, collect the boys, and tell them all about the arrival of their little brother. They were going to be so excited. I was glad that my mother would be there to share the moment of witnessing their reactions.

'How about a cup of tea?' asked Jane.

I smiled at her, thankfully.

'Oh, that would be superb, Jane. Thanks. And thank you for coming over today too and helping out. Was it how you expected?'

Jane smiled, 'It was amazing, Jan. Thanks so much for letting me be part of it. I had always wanted to be present at the birth of a child. It's very different from your own birth experience, I can tell you! A lot less painful for a start!'

I remembered the terrible time that Jane had in the hospital with her firstborn, Alice. We'd met at the local ante-natal class and ended up in the hospital together. Our firstborns were only two days apart. We'd been friends ever since.

Jane cast her eyes across the room towards Claude, and with a puzzled frown, she asked, 'Are you OK now? I must admit I've never heard of anyone spring cleaning a house while their wife is in the throes of giving birth! At least you can't accuse Jan of squeezing your hand too hard! Brian said I cut off all circulation to his hand – I gripped it that tight when Alice was born!'

There was a momentary pause as if she was letting her words sink in before adding, 'Must say, though, you are a dab hand with a duster and a bottle of Pledge! You can come and clean my place if you want!'

And with that, she strode out of the room in true Norland Nanny style to make me a much-needed cup of tea.

There was a sudden bang that echoed up to my room from downstairs. It was the familiar sound of the rear stable door being flung open in excitement. A series of shrieks and then thundering footfalls followed as Tom and Owen raced each other up the stairs, competing to be the first to see their baby brother.

I was just in time to see two red faces appear around the side of the bedroom door, about to launch themselves through it, when Claude yelled an elongated '*Stop!*'

The boys stopped dead in their tracks, a look of momentary puzzlement crossing their eager little faces. They were within twelve feet of the bed. I was holding Morgan and all eyes were on the tiny bundle swaddled in his blanket. They strained forward, trying to get a better look

'Tom, Owen,' demanded Claude, obviously wanting their full attention.

Dutifully, they turned to look at him, and so he continued, each word spoken with deliberate repetition so that there could be no scope for misunderstanding.

'Tom and Owen. You will go back downstairs. You will walk quietly back downstairs. You will both go and wash your hands. If you are going to see the baby, your hands must be clean. I will not let you see your brother until I have checked your hands.'

They turned and left the room. I could hear the boys meeting their Gran on the stairs. Perplexed to find them descending the stairs so quickly, I heard her ask, 'Gosh! That was quick! Have you seen your brother?'

Tom replied, 'No. Claude says that we've got to wash our hands.'

Owen repeated the same sentence, like an echo, although his tone was one of undisguised, disgruntled indignation.

On their return, Claude stood in the open doorway, and the rigorous hand inspection got underway. Finally, the boys were allowed into the bedroom to see their brother.

Tom's face broke into a gappy grin, which indicated that the tooth fairy had recently been very active in the collection of two baby teeth.

'I am a big, big brother now aren't I, Mum?' smiled Tom, and I nodded.

Owen looked awestruck. He extended his chubby index finger to touch the tiny hand of his baby brother only to find Morgan tightly curling his fingers around it.

I could almost hear the cogs turning in Owen's head, and he said, 'It is real, isn't it?'

He was still staring at the tiny form in front of him. He frowned as if he was working through a process and then looked at me.

'So this is the one that kept kicking me when I put my head on your tummy, Mum?'

'Yes, Owen. I think he was keen to know you even then! Perhaps he was trying to tell you that he'd like to be a member of our football team!'

It was the right answer. Owen looked satisfied and, putting his head closer to Morgan, who squinted at him from his dark blue eyes, whispered, 'I'm your big brother. I will always look after you.'

And when Owen spoke those words, I believed his every word. The testimony of those words was to be put to the test sooner rather than later.

Chapter 19

One year later

Morgan had just celebrated his first birthday. I wondered if he would spend any of his future birthdays in England. After all, it was not going to be that simple now that we had decided to move to France permanently.

Over the last year, Claude continued to work from home and commuted to Paris as before. However, I noticed an increasing edge of sadness and frustration tipping into his life and this was affecting our relationship. I tried to get him to come out and socialise because I thought it would help him to feel settled. Instead, it made him even more reclusive. I could only recall him going out once with me in public and that was to push the pushchair down the seaside high street in Perranporth. He rejected offers of meals with friends, preferring to work late into the evening on his computer. This meant that I rarely left the house for social events because he asked who would look after the children if I was not there. It felt daft to resort to paying a babysitter when one parent was already in residence, so in the end, I decided it was just easier to stay at home.

I was worried about how isolated Claude must be

feeling. Now and again, he attempted to speak in English, but most of the time, it was down to me to converse in French. Tom and Owen were expected to do the same.

He was also becoming progressively stricter with Morgan's brothers. Small things that hadn't bothered him before began to cause increasing irritability. Routines were put in place to try and avoid any confrontations and I was the one to impart these new ways of doing things to the boys. Shoes had to be stacked neatly inside the doorway and sand washed from wellies, before putting them away. Even socks had to be folded correctly to ensure contents of drawers were orderly. I'd been taken aback when Claude pulled apart all the socks that I'd so carefully paired, telling me that I'd folded them incorrectly. He then proceeded to show me the 'proper' way to do it. From then on, I painstakingly paid great attention to how I folded socks. It was worth doing it his way as it avoided causing further irritation on his part.

Claude's parenting style was also proving to be far more authoritarian than I'd seen before. The man who'd played endlessly in the swimming pool with Tom and Owen in France now avoided spending any time with them. The relaxed, carefree man had been replaced by someone who swooped on misdemeanours with an eagle eye, and who demanded respect through a strict and regimented approach.

However, sometimes it felt as if the flow of respect didn't have a return valve. On one occasion, I'd been struggling to juggle the needs of three boys, whilst preparing dinner. An offer of help would have been appreciated. However, Claude continued to sit, smoking a cigar and drinking a whisky, which was his preferred aperitif, as he chatted nonchalantly to a client on the phone. He knew when dinner would be ready because I had told him. The conversation he was having didn't sound particularly technical but seemed to focus on the antics of a memorable skiing vacation.

Tom and Owen were sitting impatiently at the dinner table and Morgan was in his highchair. I poked my head around the lounge door for the fifth time and gesticulated that dinner was now on the table. It was a lovely roast and there was no point in it going cold so we started. There was still no sign of Claude and in a sudden wave of anger, I picked up his plate and dumped it defiantly directly under the nose of the delighted dog. What was the point in making an effort, only for it to go unappreciated? Having polished off their food, Tom and Owen were still grinning at my act of defiance. As they departed, they turned, giving me a secretive thumbs up signal as a sign of solidarity.

Some twenty minutes later, Claude strolled into the room. He frowned as he looked expectantly towards his place at the head of the table. In a fleeting moment, the frown was replaced by disbelief as it dawned on him that a few smears of gravy on an otherwise glistening plate, were all that remained of his roast dinner.

'Too late,' I snapped, shrugging my shoulders in an act of defiance. 'Your dinner is in the dog.'

He looked at me as if he was struggling to believe that I would dare to do such a thing. I levelled a look straight back at him, determined that I was going to make my point. My act of defiance lit the blue touch paper within him. He acted with the speed of a hunter chasing down its prey, and in a split second his face was less than an inch from mine. Slamming his fist down with full force onto the farmhouse table, making the plate jump, he yelled at me in a spiel of French that I did not understand. I did not need to comprehend the words. The meaning came across loud and clear in the intonation of his voice and was fuelled by the depth of unfathomable hate reflected in his hard obsidian eyes. In that instant, the man that I'd always thought of as my protector, had become the oppressor. He saw my fear and turning, stormed out of the room, slamming the door closed behind him.

I pulled back a chair and sat with my head in my hands at the empty table, berating myself for my childish behaviour. It was all my fault. I'd driven him to behave in that way and I was ashamed of myself. I wanted everything to go back to how relaxed it had been initially. I wanted to see the smiles and hear the laughter again; to have the easy-going camaraderie back that we'd once shared. It must have been something that I wasn't doing right that was causing the problem. I yearned to rediscover the man who could love so deeply, not this apparent stranger, devoid of compassion; the man who the previous week, forbade me from going to console our son crying relentlessly in his cot.

'Leave him,' he'd ordered 'You cannot go to him every time he cries out. He has to learn.'

I wanted to point out that I'd already waited the five minutes as advised by the health visitor, and that I knew my son's crying better than anyone. I knew it was a cry for help – that he needed his mother's attention. It was not because I was a first-time mum and therefore over-anxious. I'd already had enough practice with Tom and Owen to distinguish between the different types of cries. In fact, I would have described myself as quite laid back and I hoped that this would impart a sense of calmness to my baby. Claude was adamant that I should leave the baby to cry as he instructed; apparently, it was all part of the wider picture. He pointed out that had I left Tom and Owen to cry for longer as infants, they wouldn't be so needy and demanding now. There was no point arguing; perhaps he was right and I was wrong. I knew something needed to change and it dawned on me that perhaps Claude was struggling with life in the southwest of England. Could it be this that was causing his negative attitude?

I decided that the situation could not continue and when a few days later, I suggested that I sold the farmhouse and that we move to France, Claude seemed to gain a new lease of life. The smiles returned. He became more tactile and considerate, and the mood in the house lifted to one of expectation and excitement.

It would be an emotional wrench for me to leave my mother behind and we both sobbed when I told her the news. However, she said that I should do what was best for my family and my tears flowed even more freely in appreciation of the love of this beautiful selfless soul who stood before me. I would miss her so, so much. And so would the boys.

'You must visit though Mum. It's only the south of France after all. It's not the other side of the world. In fact, you can get there quicker than you can get to Scotland! It's a small village where Josie and JC have bought a holiday home. They are planning on moving down from Paris permanently when they retire. We will rent first and then buy. Josie has already found us a property on the same residence as them. Promise that you will come and see us!'

Mum nodded, 'Of course, I will. You try and stop me!'

I hugged her tight. My mum was such a huge part of my life. The pain of leaving her behind was unbearable, but I had to think of what was right for our family and I believed that our only chance of a happy future together lay waiting across the Channel.

Chapter 20

All that remained was an empty shell. It reminded me of the body of a person discarded in death as the soul moves on. Strange that a house emptied of all its belongings could feel that way too, but not surprising given that it had witnessed so much laughter, tears and birth over the years as it had housed my family, and borne silent witness to both our private and public lives. Mithian Farm had been so many things. Initially, it had been the dream house with land, even surpassing the estate agent's description of being a sought-after property within dog walking distance of the north Cornish coast. As our family home, it had been the place where Owen helped me bottle feed the orphan lambs we rescued, the four of them growing up to share the fields with the Dartmoor ponies. They'd also been saved from the clutches of the meat market at the annual Tavistock livestock auction. The large sash window in one of the back bedrooms had been the setting for one of Tom's experiments. It was here that he'd hurled his favourite Buzz Lightyear toy out of his bedroom window with an excited yell of, "To infinity and beyond", convinced he was going to witness him fly!

In bleak contrast to the blissful times however, its

rough woodchip walls had absorbed the wails of my splintering, all-consuming grief when I'd lost the baby that would have been a brother or sister to my two sons. As I stood there in the emptiness, I reflected on the emotional void of the past; a place where unresolved emotions culminated in divorce proceedings as neither myself, nor my husband, father to Tom and Owen, could move past this insurmountable obstacle, each locked in our own grief.

Catching my thoughts, and reminding myself that this was a part of our history in this house, I walked over to the window seat in front of the large sash window, not yet ready to separate myself from all the memories, but wanting to recollect happier times before I locked the front door for the final time. Sitting down, with my back to the window, I could imagine the shapes of the armchairs, the large bookcase, and Claude's desk in the corner. I could almost convince myself that I could see the outline of Milly, the Labrador, spread out in her favourite pool of sunshine that streamed in over my shoulder. I smiled. I reminded myself that I was prone to all sorts of imaginings, especially in this room. It was here where I had glimpsed my friendly apparition, whom I subsequently named 'Alice', for the first time after Claude altered the configuration of the staircase to make space for a fourth bedroom upstairs prior to Morgan's arrival. He inadvertently put the new staircase in the position of a previous one that must have been in situ in the late 1800s according to the historic records of the place. This was at the time when Mithian Farm was in fact one large farmhouse before it was split into two dwellings many years later. I remembered that I was quite convinced that 'Alice' had shown herself to us when the work to alter the existing staircase was underway. It was as if 'change' prompted her to appear.

It was near midnight and I was looking at the empty void that was now opened up in the far corner of the lounge – the place that would be filled with the new staircase, but at that time, showing wooden structures that pointed to the fact that a previous staircase had been in that very spot. Out of the corner of my eye, in my peripheral vision, I saw a young lady with a black, flowing floor-length skirt with a white apron over the top. The apron was ruffled at the edges. This was the only part of her outfit that looked remotely ornate. She wore a white mob cap which partially concealed her dark hair that was arranged in a bun. She looked at me shyly for what must have been a matter of seconds, before she disappeared through the doorway into the main entrance hall and vanished.

I grinned to myself as I recalled that I felt her presence on various occasions until the time the building work was completed. Was she been trying to tell me something I wondered? It was unlikely. I preferred to think that she was in some way pleased that the farmhouse was being restored in part to how it was when she worked there.

So that was Alice, but what about the 'Butter Lady' as we referred to her? I suppose that if you are open to the idea that the walls of a home can hold the energy of its occupants over the years, then it's possible to believe that these energies could manifest themselves when the time is right. I'd been in unfamiliar buildings in the past, not necessarily those steeped in history and the ravages of time, but that were comparatively modern and I could still sense different feelings exuding from their walls. Some were welcoming, radiating a comforting warmth, even when there was no source of heating, whilst others with central heating and double glazing remained hostile and cold. There were definite 'pockets' of feelings at Mithian Farm.

The second sitting room was one such place. In this room, I'd discovered a huge hidden fireplace, complete with a clome oven, when I'd embarked on what was supposed to be a simple DIY effort to remove the unsightly, outdated Formica units that covered one wall. They'd been been more precariously pinned together than I'd thought. Perhaps the dust that had accumulated over the years, made the joints between the units invisible to the naked eye. I remembered how unscrewing one singular panel, prompted the complete collapse of the whole structure, sending it tumbling from left to right, like a stack of giant dominos. I'd watched in amused horror as the whole edifice fell apart around me. In doing so, it revealed an enormous slate mantelpiece underneath which, after several hours of hard graft swinging a sledgehammer, I'd discovered the old walk-in fireplace and oven. There were small fragments of blue and white china in the hearth as well as coal dust and remains of crows' nests from the now disused chimney. I felt like a modern-day explorer, an apprentice of the 'Time Team'! I never really liked history at school; I failed to see how anyone could be remotely excited about things that happened so many years ago. The only thing about history lessons that excited me was my ability to duck out of them by hiding in the school grounds to avoid the 40 minutes of pure tedium.

However, in this instance, intrigue got the better of me, and the Butter Lady brought history to life. It was not the history of textbooks with their yellowed, time-faded pages. No, the Butter Lady was another past occupant of Mithian Farm. I sensed her when we first moved in. Mainly she frequented the old dairy that we made into the everyday kitchen. I never actually saw her, but very often, I would walk over the stone-flagged floors and the scent of cream and butter would fill my nostrils. Somehow it gave me a warm feeling. It was cosy and homely, just as I am sure she would have been. It seemed I was not the only one aware of her presence, for Thomas told me quite matter of factly one morning, that the Butter Lady had visited him in his bedroom and quite unperturbed, he'd enjoyed chatting with her from his bed. There were numerous occasions when we could smell what I can only describe as a 'warm cream' type of scent, either in Tom's room or in the dairy and we'd smile knowingly to each other and say 'It's the Butter Lady'.

Curiosity eventually got the better of me and I asked Courtney if he knew anything about the previous occupants as they were, after all, his next-door neighbours. He told me that he had vivid recollections of a man who he described as 'pure evil'. I was astounded and shocked to hear that this neighbour had been cruel to his livestock and on one occasion, speared Courtney's pet cat with a pitch fork out in the front yard! Courtney told me that there'd been many neighbours over the years and that he did recall an elderly lady who resided at Mithian Farm when he first moved in there to look after his ailing mother. The lady had lived on her own due to a tragedy having struck and that she indeed did make the butter and cream in the dairy for the neighbouring hotels. I asked him if he could find out any more about her because I was enthralled to know more. He promised that he would let me know. The tale of the Butter Lady, brought history to life for me and I was intrigued.

I wondered, if the Butter Lady missed us? How would she feel about the new occupants? Would she be as happy to share her home with them just as she'd been with us? I'd miss the comforting aroma that her presence brought. Her presence had never scared me; it was more reassuring than anything else. I would miss her. For a brief moment, it even entered my head that it would be incredible if she could visit France. It wasn't as if she'd need to go through passport control.

Was it really only a year previously that Mithian Farm had witnessed the joy of Morgan's birth? So many memories and now the only possession that remained was the red fireside rug that was rolled up and awaiting collection in the conservatory. Every other item that was going to France had already gone. It was a difficult decision as I knew that I had to take the things that meant the most to me, as we didn't have room to take any 'just in case' items. I had been ruthless and given away a lot of household items. Electrical goods had been sold as the voltage was different in France. In addition, we held a sale in one of the outbuildings and people came and bought the brush cutter, lawnmower, chain saw and childrens' outdoor equipment. I sold my car because Claude assured me that we would only be needing one vehicle and it made more sense to keep his, which was, after all, a left-hand drive.

A friend of mine was expecting her third child and so I gave her the precious wooden crib that had been used for all my boys. I was sad to see it go as it was very precious to me but practicality trumped sentimentality.

I had packed my most treasured possessions. These included the baby photos of Tom, Owen, and Morgan, as well as their First Year books in which I'd meticulously documented their 'firsts' – there were cuttings from the newspaper of birth announcements, samples of hair, dates of first teeth appearing, invitations to christenings and all the sorts of things that you would expect a proud parent to want as a keepsake to pass on in years to come. I also put the old blue suitcase out. It was a hard case with a patchwork of labels on it that told the history of my parents' travels around the world when they were first married and before they realised that they could not have children of their own. It was special to me because I remembered it from being an infant and the excitement that it generated on the sight of it. This case housed the Christmas decorations. My mum had carefully conserved the decorations that I made whilst at Primary school – the paper angel, the cardboard wise man and even the salt dough star, whose glitter had long since dropped off. It was a collection that had been added to over time and now held Thomas' and Owen's festive works of art as well. There was something incredibly traditional about it and so it was certainly going to make the journey with us and I looked forward to decorating our first French Christmas tree with its contents.

'I am just going to have a final check around the house for one last time. I need to make sure we haven't left anything and that all the windows are closed and the back door locked' I told Claude. 'Then could you drop the key through Courtney's letter box?'

I simply could not face saying goodbye to my elderly neighbour of eight years. I knew he was feeling as upset as I was and the thought of actually having to see him to say goodbye was too much. Courtney had been my rock, especially when Nick and I split up and I was left on my own to maintain the house and land. It had been quite a challenge; especially as old properties tend to always need ongoing maintenance. However, he helped with the ongoing chores such as cutting the grass, and mending the Cornish stone wall that divided the strip field from the back field. He was also present on the day when we witnessed the excitement of seeing what appeared to be a black panther jump over the hedge before disappearing into the coppice at the very back of one of the fields.

Somehow, the fact that we both experienced this most amazing occurrence, cemented our friendship even more – it meant that if one of us was labelled as crazy by the neighbours, then so was the other and we spent many an evening discussing the reasons why we could not dispute what we saw. Having reported our findings to the police, we were both stunned that ours was not the first sighting in the neighbourhood. It was thought that our 'panther' could well have been living in the wild from when circuses had to get rid of their animals and many were turned loose to fend for themselves. Neither of us ever saw it again but Thomas and Owen took great delight in warning their playmates "don't go into the back field or the panther might get you!" It was certainly another memory from my time at Mithian to take with me.

'On y va,' said Claude, which prompted me to take one last look at what had been my home.

It wouldn't be long before dawn was breaking. I could tell by the odd twitter of a bird as if it was doing a solo in preparation for the main dawn chorus in which it would be accompanied by a fully feathered orchestra. I called the dogs who were waiting, knowing that something was afoot and they leapt eagerly into the back of the car. I climbed into the passenger seat of the Renault Scenic with its French number plate, closed the door and took one last look over my shoulder as we edged our way up the gravelled driveway, the car tyres spitting the tiny stones aside, underlining to me that this was final. We were truly leaving.

I closed my eyes briefly and offered up a prayer to whoever might be kind enough to listen, "Please let this be OK. Please make it better for all of us now that Claude is going back to his home country. Don't let him be angry anymore."

And with that I turned my eyes to the road as we took the first of many turns away from Cornwall, away from England and away from everything safe and familiar; the distance from these things increasing with every kilometre or mile.

I wondered what might lie in wait on the other side of the channel and hoped fervently that I had made the right decision.

There was no going back.

Chapter 21

The first month was spent trying to settle into our new surroundings as well as dealing with the practicalities. We unpacked only our most needed possessions, whilst others were left in storage in a purpose-built facility near Perpignan. Tom and Owen were enrolled in the local Primary School and we registered with the doctor.

The name of the estate, the residence, itself was welcoming, 'Les Maisons du Soleil' – the houses of the sun. The complex consisted of just over one hundred bungalows with a secure gated entrance off a minor road that meandered through the vineyards to the Mediterranean. I later discovered that it was a short cycle ride of 10 minutes at the most. The residential complex was backed by one of the many salt lakes of the flood plain, known locally as 'les Etangs'. The pink flamingos that paddled in the sunlit shallows were a sight to behold.

Our little bungalow was a tight squeeze for all of us. It had only one bedroom and a mezzanine above the kitchen-living space, despite stating in the rental details that it suited up to six people. This was a property that was primarily suited to the tourist industry, a temporary holiday home, but not suited to being a permanent dwelling. As it was situated in the south of France, there was a lot of demand for this style of property. It appealed to visitors from the north, especially Parisians, who wanted to holiday in the south during July and August when the whole country kicked back and relaxed.

However, I was glad that we'd found something near to Claude's sister that we could rent on a long-term basis until we found somewhere more suitable to live permanently. Thanks to the Mediterranean climate we were able to dine outside. This gave us the extra living space that we desperately needed, especially with two dogs that were keen not to miss out on meal times. In the heat of the day, they would happily laze in the shade of the mimosa tree – a beautiful delicately leaved species, but one that I cursed in terms of the flower heads that it dropped. I was continually wielding a broom to sweep up the wispy foliage to stop it from entering the bungalow. Often, I thought I was fighting a losing battle and whilst I loved the appearance of the tree, vowed to never plant one in my own garden.

Tom and Owen were loving the on-site sporting facilities and were already beginning to hang out with other local children of the same age. Although I'd pictured living in a detached villa with a swimming pool, in retrospect I was glad that our current environment allowed the boys to mix socially and begin to integrate. They seemed quite popular and I wondered if this had something to do with their collection of Pokémon cards. The cards seemed to be a universal ticket to acceptance. As soon as the Easter holidays were over, Tom and Owen were going to join the local primary school at Vic. Hopefully, the youngsters with whom they had already forged the foundations of a friendship, would be at the same school. I knew that it would be challenging for my sons, but at the same time, if we were to really embrace living in France, it seemed pointless to send them to an

English-speaking school. So, although they were in effect being thrown in at the deep end, I hoped it would prove to be beneficial in the long term. It gave Tom a couple of years before he was due to go to secondary school and so it would allow him time to settle and conquer the language barrier before the onset of exams.

One of the biggest obstacles for me was the fact that I had to learn and apply the French medical terms for managing Owen's diabetes. Owen had been insulin dependent since the age of four and a half and this required ongoing monitoring. He was now nearly seven years old and I had to get the English prescriptions converted into their French equivalent. I also had to sort out which consultant he would see on a regular basis.

Given that my French extended no further than O-level, I could see this would be a potential obstacle. Understanding French medical terminology, coupled with the need to report blood glucose readings and subsequent doses of insulin, would be essential in order to manage his diabetes effectively. The whole idea petrified me, especially as I have always had a fear of numbers and am prone to reversing the order of them.

So, I was relieved when Claude returned from his three-week business trip to Paris, a trip that he'd taken within two days of our arrival in France. However, I was terrified that both Owen and myself were booked into a specialist residential children's hospital at neighbouring *Pavolas les Flots* for a week in order that Owen could be assessed and a new insulin regime started.

This meant that I was going to have to try and understand whatever the medical staff told me and apply it accordingly. I begged Claude to come with me as he would be best placed to understand what was going on and how to best support Owen. I even asked him to drop me off and collect me later each day, just so I could spend some time away from the hospital and see Tom and Morgan. He refused point blank. It seemed that he had a lot of work to do regarding his internet business and he could therefore not afford to take any time off.

Hence, if Owen was to get the help that he needed in terms of his diabetes in France, the only option was for us to be dropped off one week and picked up the next. What would happen to Tom and Morgan in the meantime? Claude assured me that he could look after them as he would be working from home, before adding that if I cared about my son, I needed to be with him. I tried to explain the difficulties that I felt I might encounter, but he did not listen. So, Owen and I were dropped off at The *Institute St Pierre*, with our luggage. It was a superb beachfront location and the hospital resembled more of a holiday apartment-style building. On each of the five floors were large wooden terraces that contained an assortment of toys, varying from table tennis and football tables to tricycles. After the children learnt about their medication and attended their morning school lessons, they could take part in the usual beach activities, including volleyball.

I knew that I had to be strong for Owen. I did not want him to sense that I was uncomfortable as I knew that this would permeate to him. We needed to present as strong and upbeat, British but nice, nonetheless. This was because I was already getting a sense of being disliked by a lot of the French people with whom I'd had contact. Several took great delight in saying *'Ah British – aah c'est la vache folle!'* In other words, they took great joy in saying 'British – it's the mad cow!' It was after all at a time of the outbreak of BSE in the UK.

Thankfully, the professional conduct of the hospital staff meant they didn't make derogatory comments and I was impressed by their conscientious attention to all medical details relating to my son.

On the third day, however, I was taken to one side and told that in France it would be up to Owen to gauge what amount of insulin he needed on a daily basis. I felt frantic. In England, we had been extremely lucky in having a designated 'diabetic nurse'. In our case, it was a lady called Anita and as far as we were concerned, she was both a modern-day saint and a life saver. She had been at the end of the phone 24 hours a day. This meant that we were hugely reassured that, should we need help, we could rely on her. The situation that I now found myself in was a far cry from what I'd been used to. I was being told that Owen would need to check his blood glucose levels himself and depending on the reading, adapt the dose of the two different types of insulin accordingly.

On the inside, I was screaming in full technicolour English, "This is a six-year-old boy! My six-year-old boy. How can you let him take responsibility at such a young age?"

My internal outburst and cry for help were silenced by the Staff Nurse who told me, 'You are his mother. You will oversee it.'

I felt like I was being asked to walk a frayed tightrope. One slip and it could prove fatal. Teetering tentatively, putting one step in front of the other with the loss of balance threatening every move, knowing that to look down would be paramount to losing my grip completely. How on earth could I be sure that I was understanding the numbers of the doses correctly and what would happen if I got it wrong and gave him a fatal dose?

Where was Claude in all this?

How dare he leave me to play what felt like Russian roulette with my son?

Why had he abandoned us?

Would I have left him to deal with it if the situation

had been reversed? I could never imagine deserting a parent whose child needed medical help. It felt even more scandalous when neither parent nor child could speak the language sufficiently. We were rendered helpless; held hostage by a language barrier!

Finding ourselves in a geographically isolated location we just had to get on with it, knowing that there was no contact with the outside world. It was a sink or swim situation stranding us high and dry beyond the tideline in the sterility of a strict hospital regime. Either I had to conquer my knowledge of numbers and apply the formula to Owen's insulin medication, or we would be staying indefinitely until I did so. The fear of getting it wrong will haunt me forever, I think. It was almost as if I was being granted permission to play God.

As the days progressed however, I became more confident in my decisions and Owen adapted to the new pen-style insulin system as opposed to using a syringe to mix up his short and long-acting dose accordingly.

By the end of the week, we were confident in what we were doing, to the extent that it felt quite liberating. It put us in charge as opposed to relying on being spoon-fed every step of the way by a nurse at the end of a telephone. This was actually more empowering for Owen. He felt more in charge of what he was doing to his body. He would analyse the readings and respond accordingly and so take responsibility himself, albeit at a young age. It was a positive experience for the long term but nonetheless, we were relieved to be collected by Claude at the end of our week's stay. The experience proved to both of us that we were tougher than we thought.

Little did we know how important the seeds of these realisations would be in the months to come.

Chapter 22

July 2001

The feeling of initial homesickness was beginning to diminish; it was now nearly three months since we'd arrived.

We were still in the same bungalow and despite looking at various properties, we couldn't agree on one that suited all our needs. I'd seen the most superb places that were affordable with the profits from the sale of Mithian Farm. The foothills of the Pyrenees were beautiful and I was particularly taken with one farmstead that offered acres of land, some of which crossed the border into Spain. It was an isolated property but it had all the space we could possibly have asked for. I felt that it would have been well worth the inconvenience of having to transport the boys down through 15 minutes of hairpin bends to school each morning. But it was not to be. Claude seemed increasingly reluctant to move away from the immediate area and found any excuse to remain in close proximity to members of his family. Despite my offers of undertaking any redecoration work that might be needed, he was never suitably convinced. Therefore, as June gave way to July, we were still in the same rented bungalow. I was beginning to wonder if we would ever find a home for ourselves or at least one that Claude would deem appropriate.

In the meantime, I was conscious of systematically paying out for the ongoing monthly rental for the bungalow. I became increasingly concerned as the rental cost rose extortionately for the summer months in order to make maximum profit from the tourists in peak season. We needed the money to be put into our own home. Our little bungalow was not ideal for the boys either. They needed somewhere where they could organise their belongings and do their homework undisturbed. Although it was currently the long school holidays, September would soon be upon us and so with each passing day the pressure to find somewhere increased.

Time progressed and I continued to support the family, paying household bills and putting food on the table. When I perused the statements from my French bank account, these living costs were accumulating and it annoyed me to think that I was paying for the rental of a property which was money that could never be recouped. The lump sum that I'd banked from the sale of Mithian Farm, was diminishing, like a trickle of sand unnoticed between the fingertips. Claude had taken care of setting up the *allocations familiales*, in other words, the Child Benefit. However, this money was now being paid directly into his bank account. He hadn't signed the papers necessary for us to open a bank account in joint names.

Then there was the question of the visits to the local doctor. Thomas had a severe bout of tonsillitis which necessitated three trips in quick succession, followed by an appointment with an ENT specialist. I found myself praising the NHS system when I realised that just to shake the doctor's hand cost the equivalent of fifteen pounds and that was *before* the consultation!

There is a system in France whereby an individual can claim back a proportion of the costs as well as the prescription. Claude set it up so that he was the beneficiary and was therefore reimbursed each time either myself or the three boys needed medical attention. I dared to broach the subject with him a couple of times but there was no sign that he would transfer any funds to my account.

Chapter 23

It seemed amazing that Tom and Owen had completed a term at the Primary School and were facing the long holidays that Europeans relish. They'd done really well in terms of both their learning and socialisation, spending most of their after school hours mixing with children from the village.

I remember Tom being astounded on the first day of his new school. When he arrived home, his eyes were still wide with disbelief as he exclaimed, 'They give us pieces of baguette at break time! The teachers put on rollerblades and skate around the playground with a huge basket on their arms. In the basket are the pieces of bread! Can you imagine it Mum? Teachers on roller skates?!'

'Wow! I can't imagine Mr P doing that at Mithian!' I replied, a smile rippling across my face at the sight of his obvious amusement. I had never warmed to the head teacher at the boys' Primary School.

'Not only that, but Mum, you should see the dinners! We have a three-course meal at lunchtime! *Three* courses! And not the horrid typical school dinners that we had in England. These are proper meals. No wonder we have a one-and-a-half-hour lunch break.'

Although the school day was longer than in England,

both Tom and Owen seemed to enjoy it and even headed off on a Saturday morning for their grammar lesson. In return, they had Wednesday afternoons off. From what I'd seen on the occasions that I'd been to school, it appeared to be very formal in terms of teaching. There were no bright displays on the walls and nothing that really impacted visually. Instead, there were long lists showing all the different tenses and I wondered how I would ever cope with writing correctly in terms of being accurate grammatically. It was enough to conquer the *'tu'* and *'vous'*.

As I spent most of my time with other family relatives I was used to using *'tu'* as they were familiar and it was deemed OK. I still struggled with applying the *'vous'* formula to strangers as I was not so practised in this part. In order to overcome this, I decided to join Tom and Owen in the Saturday grammar class at school in order to try and learn how to use the tenses correctly. I sat at the back of the class, hoping to be inconspicuous. It was a silly idea really as I was surrounded by 10-year-olds so I stood out like a sore thumb. The teacher challenged us with questions and we had to write down what we thought was the correct answer. I found the whole experience humbling for want of another word.

Having been a teacher, I was suddenly plunged into the world of being a student and one who was struggling at that! I'd no idea what the answer was supposed to be but I had to write something on the tiny chalkboard that I had been given. When I'd written my answer, I had to hold up the chalkboard like all my other classmates for the teacher to see. It was horrifying! I was twenty-five years older than the rest of the class and I was up the proverbial creek without a paddle! In desperation, I did just as I'd scolded my pupils for in the past, and copied the person next to me! I was not sure how my fellow student ranked in terms of academic ability and so it was taking a real risk to copy him. I just hoped to goodness that he happened to be gifted, but to be on the safe side, I copied what he'd written in the smallest chalked writing that I could muster, in the hope that the teacher wouldn't be able to read it from the front anyway!

Thankfully, I got away with it but I realised that I'd one hell of a way to go until I could be sure of writing accurately.

Chapter 24

I was elated.

Phil and Moira had just confirmed that they would be arriving the following day as expected and with their sons, Chris and Jake. It was like a breath of fresh air passing through the room. To think that I'd be able to chat away in English for a change instead of having to sit through meals in silence for the most part as I lacked both confidence and knowledge to communicate in French. On the quiet, I was feeling gleeful that I was going to be spending the next 10 days with my closest friends and that we could joke between us and perhaps even mock the French. After all, I'd had enough of the 'mad cow' cracks and the *'fièvre aphteuse'* accusations – blaming the English for foot and mouth disease as well. For a change, it would be *my* turn to mock the Frogs instead. And without doubt, if I could rely on anyone to bring a sense of humour to the mix, it would be Moira.

'I can't wait to see Chris again,' said Tom.

I knew how precious it felt to Tom to be able to see his best mate. I felt the same excitement at the prospect of catching up with Moira too. I wondered if young Jake had grown and if he still had that mop of unruly blond curls. The Wright family were like our extended family and I was thrilled that they were coming to stay. There would be guaranteed laughter waiting just around the corner, or to be more accurate, upon the arrival of their flight from Stansted. It struck me that could actually be myself again. I could be the *real* me. I could relax in the familiarity of cherished friends. Hopping from foot to foot impatiently, I watched the arrivals board at Montpellier airport and was elated when I saw that the plane landed on time. It was just a question of waiting for them to clear customs and then I'd see them. I was so impatient. The coolness of the air-conditioned terminal belied the heat that waited outside. Moira would no doubt be thrilled by the impact of the wall of heat that would meet them as we exited the arrivals building and headed for the car park. We could spend the next week, working on building her Mediterranean tan!

People started to stream through the automatic sliding doors as they wheeled their baggage through on trolleys having cleared customs. It wasn't long before I caught sight of the Wright family. The boys were scanning the room for faces to recognise, Phil was pushing the luggage-laden trolley and Moira was very much in control, sporting a pair of Sophia Lauren sunglasses and looking as if she had just flown in from Monte Carlo.

"Always a flair and a sense of glamour has our Moy," I thought with a flood of affection. I dived through the line of expectant people and dodging a few trolleys, came to a halt in front of the new, pale-skinned arrivals.

'Oh! It's so good to see you chuck,' said Moira as we flung our arms around each other; I noticed the male contingency roll their eyes skywards.

'Hey Phil! How's things?' I asked as I threw my arms around him in welcome.

'All the better for seeing you little Sis,' he smiled as he poked his glasses with one finger back up towards the bridge of his nose.

'Wow! Can't believe how you boys have grown!' I exclaimed as I bent to embrace Chris and Jake.

The familiarity of seeing the whole family was quite overwhelming. 'Welcome to France!'

The chatter was endless as we drove home towards *Vic La Gardiole*. There was so much to catch up on and it was as if we were cramming in as much talk as we could muster in the time that we had. Moira brought me up to date about my mum; I was so relieved to hear that she was alright and that Moira visited her regularly, taking her for trips out to various places. If all went to plan, Mum was going to come over for a holiday later in the season when it was not quite so hot.

Chris and Jake stared out of the window at their surroundings, taking in the parched soil of the mellow, rocky, thyme tufted terrain of the scrubland known locally, as the *'garrigue'*. In the distance they could see the sparkling deep blue water of the Mediterranean and the soft horizon, indicating that the weather would remain settled.

'Bloody hell Jan. No wonder you wanted to move here! I hate to say it but I think it does beat Cornwall', declared Moira as she scanned the scenery through the passenger window, 'Bet the wine's OK too eh?'

'It's all good in terms of wine and weather Moira. Hey! See that place over there on the left? That's an ostrich farm. It's only a couple of minutes' drive from where we are and they sell the most amazing ostrich steaks. You'll have to try it while you're here. We've got so much to do and see, and talk about. I feel exhausted before I've even started! Anyway boys – I reckon the first thing that you might like to do is head off to the pool with Tom and Owen and have a dip. What do you reckon?'

'Yessss!' came the chorus from the back.

'Whilst the boys are doing that, we can have a coffee or an early aperitif on the terrace and you can get yourselves settled.'

'Sounds perfect' said Phil 'I could do with checking out the French lagers.'

'Am sure we can accommodate you.'

We turned off the main road and onto the French equivalent of a minor road that took us into the little village of *Vic La Gardiole*. It was a mellow stoned village with basic amenities. There was a tabac, a hairdresser, a tourist office, a doctor, an estate agent and a boulangerie. It was graced with a market every Tuesday which sold fresh fish, fruit and vegetables, leather belts and bags, authentic Laguiole penknives with their bee emblem and bowls and boards made out of olive wood.

'This is home,' I said as we drew up at the gates of the residence and I 'beeped' the infrared button on my key ring to activate the gates to open and allow us access.

Once parked, everyone tumbled out of the car. Tom and Owen launched into view as they hurtled towards their friends. There was an initial moment of shyness between all the lads in which it seemed awkward to voice anything. However, this was soon overcome when Chris and Jake heard the echoing shrieks of a child's enjoyment coming from the direction of the swimming pool.

'Fancy a swim?' asked Tom.

'Yeah,' chimed both boys.

'OK. Let's get your trunks and towels out of the cases and off you go,' said Moira.

With cases thrown open and swim gear grabbed, Moira and Phil were left to calmly sort out the rest of the contents of their bags whilst I waited with Claude and Morgan on the terrace. When they came to join us, Morgan was happily waddling around in his nappy, picking up toys and taking them to Phil and Moira who had become his new audience.

'Where's my little Morgy-noos?' said Moira, scooping Morgan up in her arms and putting him on her knee. His chubby little fists held her hand and he looked at her and gave a one-toothed smile. I wondered if it was possible that he recognised her from three months ago or whether she just had a natural way with youngsters.

'Phil, Moira – *voulez-vous quelque chose à boire? Pastis?*' Would you like something to drink? *Pastis* was another name for Pernod. This was always served with water and ice. Claude was obviously into his hosting duties and I was pleased that he was showing a warm welcome to my friends. For a brief moment, a small part of me whispered "wish he was just as attentive to me" and then the thought took flight just as quickly as it arrived and was replaced by a Mediterranean sun with an all-encompassing blue sky and company that had been longed for. This was neither the time nor reason to feel any form of resentment, however slight.

And so, one day merged into another. Memories made from dipping in the warm waters of the Med, mingled with the scents of pine trees whilst cycling home, only to be greeted by the aroma of fresh sardines grilling on the barbecue. There was song and laughter, togetherness and deep-rooted friendship amidst the evening call of the cicadas. I retired to bed on one such night, feeling a brimful of happiness and blessings.

As I turned to plump my pillow, Claude whispered, 'Don't kid yourself that it's you that they've come to see. It's a cheap holiday, that's all. Sleep well *ma puce.*' I always thought *'puce'* was a term of endearment but the sting in his previous sneering sentences told me those words were devoid of genuine affection.

The words chafed; bitter and twisted, belittling and hurtful. How could he say such a thing?

'I don't understand,' I said. 'What do you mean?'

But all I heard in response was silence. A silence due to sleep or a silence that couldn't be bothered to answer, I don't know, but a painful silence nonetheless. Wounded by his words, I lay staring into the black stillness of the night, alone and somehow vulnerable. Despite knowing my friends were close by, I was aware that Claude was intent on putting a distance between us. Perturbed, I lay awake, willing the promise of the new days sun, to bleach away the dark words of the night.

Chapter 25

It meant an early start. Claude and his sister and brother-in-law had friends that had run safaris in Africa. As a result, they had a Land Rover that was kitted out with all the gear needed for survival in the great outdoors. It had been decided that we should form a convoy and go together to the famous Camargue, an area where the musicians, 'The Gypsy Kings' had originated.

It was near the town of St Marie and meant that we would leave the road, to travel on unmade tracks with the intention of spending the day at a remote beach. I loved the passion of the music of The Gypsy Kings and Moira and I had spent many a Friday night shimmying around the kitchen at Mithian, with *'Bamboleo'* blasting out of the music system at full throttle. Teaspoons were the perfect replacements for castanets as we whirled like dervishes on the Cornish slate floor, stamping our heels for maximum effect. And now, it seemed we had the chance to visit the place from which our idols had originated. Similarly, Phil, Moira's husband, was an accomplished guitarist and was keen to see more of the area for himself. Eagerly, we had accepted the offer of going on the trip; it was too good an opportunity to miss.

There were four cars in total. Leading the way was the

Land Rover, followed by Josie and JC in their Jeep with Moira and Phil on board with their boys. Next came Claude's friend Henri and his friend, who we'd been told was a dentist. Claude, me and our boys brought up the rear. We departed at six in the morning and I knew it would be a long day.

Finally, we arrived in the Camargue area. This was the furthest east that I had been. I remember having a poster when I was little of white horses galloping through the Camargue and my vision through the window, seemed to bear a strong resemblance to the poster. We passed through an area where there was a gypsy encampment with caravans and dogs running loose. I wondered if we were welcome to pass through.

The location was off the beaten track and I doubted that they were used to tourists driving uninvited through their midst. We kept going. I could now see that we were blocked by sand dunes on our right-hand side and the low areas of swamp land had disappeared. It was impossible to see beyond the dunes because they were too high. However, as we progressed, so the gap between the dunes widened to reveal the sea beyond. It was as if each gap between the dunes was a secret cove, some of which were inhabited by caravans and some that weren't.

We finally came to a standstill at a place where there was no sign of any other people. The sand shelved gently down to the sea where the tide tickled the shoreline. It was here that we would set up our camp. With everyone helping it did not take long for the awning to be put up to shield us from the blaze of the cloudless sky. Various cool boxes were plugged into the Land Rover's 12-volt supply so that the food items for the day and the Rosé wine were kept nicely chilled.

Jean Claude came up to me brandishing something that could only be described as a cross between a shrimping net and a rake. I asked what it was and he told me to follow him down to the shoreline. Fascinated, I watched with eager anticipation as he began to drag the rake through the area where the water was lapping the sand. As it raked up the sand, it passed the contents through the net as if sifting it for something. A moment later JC raised his net victoriously to reveal a load of very small shells that look similar to our cockles in England.

'Les tellines! C'est bon – il faut les les mettre dans une poêle à frire avec du beurre and et un peu d'ail. Quelque minutes - c'est tout!'

Apparently, these cockle equivalents tasted delicious when put in a frying pan and cooked briefly with some butter and garlic. It was not long before all the boys were crowding along the shoreline to gather tellines which would be cooked fresh to have with an aperitif on the beach a couple of hours later.

Another source of great excitement came in the form of a jet ski which, having been taken off its road trailer, was now being filled with fuel and was bobbing enticingly in the shallows. Moira and I sat with our glass of rosé and surveyed the scene.

Moira gave me a nudge, dipped her head to peep briefly over her sunglasses, a cheeky smile on her face, as she said 'Oooh la la! He's right good looking that French Dentist! Wouldn't mind tearing around on the back of a jet ski with him!'

The French Dentist as he was known, as neither Moira nor I could recall his first name, was finishing preparing the jet ski. He turned to face his audience in order to ascertain who would be the first to accompany him on today's virgin voyage. Moira had no sooner opened her mouth to respond than JC eagerly leapt up and pounded down to the shallows like a little boy about to try out a new toy.

'Seems like you'll have to be patient Moy! At least this gives us chance to see how it all works.' I grinned, seeing the sudden disappointment on her face.

We watched as the jet ski bounced its two passengers as it accelerated through the wake of a passing speed boat. It certainly did look fun. We walked down to the tide line to see what the boys had achieved with their latest telline pickings – their findings being dumped into Morgan's bucket – a place of safekeeping for their treasure. I smiled as I watched Morgan enjoying prodding at the sand with his chunky spade.

It reminded me of how I played on holiday as a child in Cornwall, making sand pies and sticking sand flags into crumbling sand castles. Such simple things and yet the seaside could always weave its spell of magic for old and young alike. I crouched down and chatted to Morgan, passing him halves of bivalves which he scrutinised and then following my lead, threw into the water with a whispering splash. He giggled and we repeated the process.

'He's back! He's back!' Moira was pretty much hopping from foot to foot with excitement and a *Colgate* smile as the Adonis-like vision of the French Dentist brought the jet ski to a showy halt in the shallows in front of us.

'Would either of you ladies like a ride?' he called as JC jumped off the back into the water, leaving the rear seat vacant.

'I think Moira would love to have a go,' I replied mischievously.

The French Dentist nodded and signalled for her to go out to join him as he waited. Moira rapidly dropped the shorts she had been wearing, passing them to me to hold, before wading out in her navy-blue one-piece swimsuit to the patient dentist. JC was making for the shore and they passed each other en route. He seized the opportunity to soak her with splashes of seawater and she screamed some northern expletives in his direction which seemed to amuse him greatly. He joined me on the sand to perform an impromptu impersonation of Moira getting a drenching. We continued to laugh as we watched Moira attempting to get herself onto the back of the ski and failing abysmally, falling sideways into the sea and creating a scene. Eventually, the ski was brought further inshore for her to climb aboard, by now all grace and glamour exited stage left. JC, still beaming, nodded his head as if in mock despair, before turning landward and strolling back towards the sun awning where the rest of the group were sitting.

It was not long before I could see Moira on the back of the jet ski, speeding out across the bay. The odd scream carried back to shore as they hit a particular bit of swell and the ski lifted before landing heavily, sending up a flume of white spray. From what I could see, Moira appeared to be holding on for dear life! I could not help but chuckle. My crazy flirty friend. To be honest, I think she deserved a bit of adventure – Phil was still seated under the awning, yet another beer in his hand. He hadn't moved!

We made our way back to the awning to discover that the French contingent had taken all of the deck chairs, leaving the rest of us to sit on the sand. It didn't bother us; we were just happy to sit together. It was a long leisurely lunch and for once the dominant voices had been those of the English. Moira and I were recounting our antics of when I'd been allowed to pilot the jet ski and we'd taken off together over the ocean. I was in my element. I was relaxed and revelling in being able to just let go and allow my humour to surface. It was a welcome change to make a 'play on words' in my own language as I was not yet thinking naturally in French to be able to do so. Raucous laughter reverberated around the enclosed cove and both Moira and I found that the French, who were sitting in their own little group, had stopped their conversations and were eyeing us in a disapproving manner. I felt like a naughty school child that had been given the warning glare by a parent, only in this case, it was my husband whose eyes and set of his jaw, were telling me to behave myself. I could not understand why he was not pleased with my obvious enjoyment of being surrounded by friends. I heard him mumble something, that was too quiet for me to catch, to the rest of his little group. Then I heard knowing sniggers and the phrase 'Les Anglais' and I sensed that it was derogatory. Not wanting to continue to be sneered at, I chose to remove myself from the situation. I stood up, brushed the fine white sand off the backs of my legs and looked appealingly at Moira.

'Hey, Moy – how about we take the boys to have a look at that lighthouse?'

'Good shout Jan. Tom, Chris, Jakey boy, Owen – come on! We're going exploring! Let's go and find it; the one we saw in the distance when we arrived. Who knows what we might discover!'

The huddle of boys got up eagerly from around their sandy mound that had been chiselled into an imaginary stronghold against attack from the plastic soldiers which had been tactically deployed around its base.

'We can sort out the attack when we get back,' said Tom, already trotting towards us, the rest of his troops following dutifully behind.

I scooped a young Morgs up onto my hip and our mixed team of adventurers set off.

The lighthouse had appeared to be relatively near to where we were based but as we marched in single-file through the scrub wasteland, we were not gaining any noticeable ground. Instead, we were hindered by the sudden appearance of large pools of water in the salt marshes and were having to make numerous detours, to our 'as the crow flies' route, that we had set out on. Moira and I exchanged glances, knowing that we needed to keep morale high as we marched our little soldiers forward. I changed hips umpteen times as I had to resort to carryingMorgan throughout. This was because the older boys complained that he was holding everyone up by walking too slowly and also because Morgan got a better view of his surroundings, perched on my hip. He was too small to contend with the spiky grass of the marshland.

'Hang on a moment,' I panted, 'I'm going to put Morgan on my shoulders. It's a more even dispersal of weight if I do that.'

Everyone halted whilst I stood Morgan on the ground in front of me, before then squatting down to lift him up over my head. And we were off again. This was much easier and I wished I'd thought of it earlier. I remembered that my dad carried me in exactly the same manner as we'd made our ascent back up from our family's favourite cove, when I had been Morgan's age. I felt decidedly more balanced and, holding two rather sweaty little hands for that added feeling of security, I lengthened my pace.

The walls of the lighthouse with its black and white stripes were shimmering in the sizzling heat of the afternoon sun, making the structure of this landmark appear like a giant, 36-metre, two-tone blancmange. It almost took on the air of fragility as the heat rose from its surface and it wavered before our eyes. We were certainly closer, but we were nowhere near being able to touch its sides. By my reckoning, it would be at least another half hour, without stops, to cover the final distance needed and I could see that the boys were getting tired, thirsty and frustrated with the endless twists and turns of the route. We'd already dealt out the water rations to the group and the little plastic bottles had now been collected and put back into Moira's backpack, with a view to re-filling them from the large water container, stored on the Land Rover, when we got back. The idea of a long cold drink was extremely appealing and the more I thought about it, the more I thought it would be a better option for us to turn around and head back. We were not prepared for every eventuality because we'd not anticipated that it would be such an arduous journey. I wondered for a split second if that was why Jean-Michel, the owner of the Land Rover and subsequent safari expeditions, smirked when he heard my suggestion to visit the lighthouse. Had he let us set off with the boys, knowing that we would fail? The French could be a funny lot at times, almost with a natural resentment and scorn for the English. I felt suddenly annoyed. Perhaps it was just the heat that was making me feel this way. Morgan felt the lift as I physically shrugged my shoulders in response to my thoughts and I squeezed his little hands in mine, in a gesture of reassurance. I needed to alert Moira to my concerns, but would have to do it in such a way that the boys wouldn't be aware. A sudden idea came to mind. From what I knew of my dear friend, and judging by her gritted teeth demeanour, I ventured, 'Moira – here's a challenge for you, not that what we are doing right now isn't challenging enough! Do you know the French for 'lighthouse'?'

She looked across at me as we strode in step, side by side, 'challenging question Jan, challenging question, err, can I phone a friend?'

She grinned back, wiping the sweat from her brow, before swiping at the damp wisps of dark brown hair that had escaped from her ponytail and were now tickling her reddened cheeks.

'Problem is Moira that I don't think you could phone anyone out here,' I replied emphatically, hoping that she was picking up on my unspoken words.

'Good answer Jan, good answer,' and she momentarily flashed a pair of widened eyes at me, before shouting, 'Troop halt!'

She got everyone's immediate attention, 'Change of plan boys, change of plan.'

They eyed her expectantly, 'You have all done so well, haven't they Jan?'

'They've done remarkably well,' I replied, as her second in command, smiling approvingly at the little band of bedraggled boys who surrounded us.

Whilst Tom and Owen's skin had already become more accustomed to the Mediterranean temperatures and were glowing a healthy bronze, poor Christian was beginning to turn beetroot as his face clashed with the intense tones of his ginger crop of hair. Moira had repeatedly slapped factor 50 sun cream on him, but I could see that prolonged exposure in this heat was going to give rise to sunstroke if we did not find shelter soon.

Moira took a deep breath as if it was a mighty decision that she had been lumbered with making and informed the boys, 'You have done so well because I think that you are probably the first ever explorers to have gotten this far! I don't think anyone will have managed to do what you have done. So, let's quickly mark how far we have come with our own flag and then we'll head back.'

She pulled at a couple of long swaying wetland grasses and tied a rough knot in them before laying them in the centre of the path. I fumbled in my pocket and placed a couple of shells, that I had collected from the beach, on the sandy ground either side of the makeshift knot.

Moira nodded in acknowledgement of my gesture and carried on, 'and, to celebrate your victory, if you all choose to march back without a single complaint, there'll be an ice cream in it for each of you!'

The entourage cheered, suddenly revived by Moira's subtle yet effective bribery, appropriately disguised as a reward for their endeavour and bravery in the face of such adversities.

'Ice creams with the toy in the bottom?' asked Jake who was obviously trying to strike a mean deal, while the offer was still open to potential negotiation.

'Yes! The ones in the plastic tub with the toy!' added Owen, with a sense of importance, wearing a contrived spur-of-the-moment smile and cockily turning his head to and fro for additional effect.

'Is it a deal boys?' shouted Moira in rousing tones.

But she had no verbal reply as a swarm of little bodies had made an about turn and were charging back down the path up which we had just walked.

'Mission accomplished,' Moira smiled, raising her hand in readiness for the 'high five' gesture of success.

'I'm glad you got the message Moy. I was getting worried. We've been getting nowhere for ages! I did actually have something quite cryptic up my sleeve you know when I asked you about the French for lighthouse.'

'Yeah – what is the French for lighthouse after all that?'

I tittered to myself before replying, 'La Phare. Only in this case, it was too far away!'

Moira groaned at my wit. Feeling refreshingly uplifted by this, my steps gathered an energetic momentum.

Chapter 26

The notion that the return journey often seems shorter that the outward one proved to be true and we marched back into camp with a sense of relief.

Phil was still dozing in a low-slung beach chair, unaware that the sun had moved round making him only partially shaded by the large khaki awning that extended from the side of the parked Land Rover. The rest of the party had successfully invaded the central part of the awning and were arrogantly guarding their territory with an impenetrable circular fortress of chairs. They cast us a few glances before returning to whatever their riveting conversation had been before we had so rudely, distracted them. Claude seemed oblivious to our presence. I wondered if any of them had even remotely thought to rouse Phil who'd been abandoned on the battle field. I gave him a nudge and suggested he shuffled his chair out of the scathing sun. Collecting our empty water bottles, I flounced over to the water tank on the side of the Land Rover, pushing my way between the chair occupants in order to reach it.

'You want water?' asked Jean-Michel rather scathingly in an attempted English accent that had undertones of clipped South African. His eyes stalked my every movement, making me feel like one of the 'big game' that he claimed to have hunted on the lighthouse savannah.

'Yes please, we do. The boys are really parched after all that walking in the heat.'

He nodded, consenting to my request and with an air of unveiled contempt, added, 'So, did you get to your lighthouse?'

I knew, by his derisory sneer, he was expecting me to admit defeat. I was sure he'd have taken gleeful enjoyment to have made me confess that we had not succeeded. I took a big breath and was about to answer him when Moira intervened.

'Yes. It was great.' She accentuated the 'great' whilst looking him in the eye as if to defy him to challenge her very words and then continued victoriously, 'we found the lighthouse and completed our mission! Now Jan, I think we need to get these bottles of water to our heroes, don't you?'

She turned her back on him and we strode away, chins held aloft. One nil to the English!

'Good on you girl!' I whispered through clenched teeth.

'French knob,' she muttered under her breath. 'I didn't lie to him. We did 'find' the lighthouse. Let's face it, you can't help but *find* the fucker! You can see it for miles around. It's just getting to touch it that's the difficult part, but he doesn't need to know that!'

Chapter 27

'Don't you *ever* show me up in front of my friends like that again!' Claude hissed at me, his hands clenched to the sleek leather steering wheel.

Having re-joined the autoroute homeward, Claude floored the accelerator with forceful *puissance*. His action felt like an extreme bid to distance himself both physically and mentally from his memory of the day.

With dawning horror, I realised his fit of fury could erase more than just memories and we were in very real danger. His speed felt like an extension of his anger and I questioned whether at this point in time, he was capable of controlling either his rage or the vehicle. I was terrified. All three boys were in the back, thankfully sleeping through it, exhausted after their antics of the day. Was Claude not aware he could kill us? Was he even bothered? The speedometer topped 200 km/hr and was still rising as we hurtled down the outside lane. Driving as if he was on an emergency call out, he blared his horn at anything that got in his path as he weaved in and out of the lanes. Combined with his pent-up silence, this made it all the more petrifying. He was behaving like a maniac. I wanted to close my eyes but I was somehow transfixed on the road ahead, silently pleading that other road users would take evasive action to save us from the unthinkable. It felt like there was a distinct possibility we were going to die and I wanted to be forewarned if that was going to happen. If I closed my eyes the fear would be worse as I wouldn't see it coming. My hands had turned icy cold and I was wringing them uncontrollably in my lap. I had to get a grip, I needed to pretend that this was just a fast car chase that was happening in a film and that I was simply watching it, not taking part in the action. My mouth was dry and my heart was fighting to break out of my rib cage, almost as hard as I wanted to fight to get my three boys and I out of this vehicle of death.

I had to say something.

I could not understand what I'd done to cause such extreme wrath. If I understood, if we could talk about it, then maybe he would calm down.

'I'm sorry but what have I ...' my question cut short as a pair of arrow slit eyes glinted from their deranged human bastion. Before responding, he squeezed down on the accelerator, the impact of the turbo kicking in, pushing me involuntarily into the back of my seat.

'You come here with your friends and you drink all the rosé wine! Moira is a bad influence on you! Who do you think you are?'

We were now doing 220km/hr. I must have angered him more by trying to speak. I fell into silence. There was no reasoning with this man when he was like this and so I didn't dare say anything else. I knew in my own mind that his words were a direct attack on Moira and I. The content of his outburst was completely irrational. It felt as though he resented that I'd had such a good time with Moira and was finding any excuse to destroy my happiness, by implying that my behaviour had been shameful.

I also knew that we were all Claude's captives. I was powerless to do anything; held ransom to his madness. He had complete control.

Mutely, I turned my head to look out of the passenger window, salty tears running in rivulets down my face and into my mouth. I felt sick as the scenery faded into oblivion behind us and we raced westwards, headlong into the ever-deepening, blood-red sunset that threatened to engulf us.

Chapter 28

It was difficult to believe that the sky of the night before had cleared to make way for a calm beautiful day. I was sitting on the terrace having an early morning cup of coffee before the rest of the household awoke. I cherished the peaceful moments and today I felt particularly grateful because we had made it home in one piece.

'*Tu veux boire quelque chose?*' asked Claude tenderly, stepping out onto the terrace to walk up to my side and plant a kiss on my cheek.

It threw me.

He could see that I had two-thirds of a cup of coffee left, so why was he asking me if I wanted something to drink? His complete mood change perplexed me the most. I'd half been expecting him to pick up where he'd left off last night as he had stormed indoors, leaving me to gently rouse the sleeping boys from their car seats and put each of them to bed. Today, however, his caring question almost hinted that my breach of etiquette yesterday was almost forgiven.

I thanked him for his offer of coffee hoping his gesture was a means of offering an olive branch. I didn't want any further antagonism so decided to follow his lead and pretend that it had never happened. Maybe 'least said, soonest mended' was the best way forward.

It was the last day of Phil and Moira's holiday and it had all passed too quickly. I wanted it to be a holiday that was full of happy memories for them. I wanted to spend the precious last evening together with my English guests but I was disappointed to discover that Claude had prearranged that we should dine with Josie at their home just a short walk away. JC was going to conjure up one of his paellas which was rapidly becoming his trademark dish in the south of France. He was particularly proud of the huge pan, fired by a gas burner, on which he cooked his mix of paella rice, fish, prawns, mussels and chicken. I'd witnessed his culinary skills in the past and knew that he would spend about three hours in preparation and cooking time. I could picture him now, an apron thrown over his shorts and vest, wielding a large spatula – *Monsieur Le Chef*!

And this was exactly how it had been. The table had been set on the terrace with its rustic olive decorated wipe-clean cover. *Saucisson* had been cut and the boys eagerly devoured the slices that were offered to them, keeping the hunger at bay, until the main pièce de résistance was ready to be served.

As we sat down to eat together, I was grateful to Claude who was being the perfect host and paying particular attention to the needs of Phil and Moira, whose glasses he replenished without hesitation. He seemed particularly jovial and was even making an effort to talk to both of them in stilted English.

Phil tapped his glass to gain everyone's attention before delivering a speech in which he formally thanked Josie and JC for their hospitality and Claude for making his 'little sis' happy. Everyone clapped and I smiled back at them all, just as I knew I was expected to.

The previous day was probably a temporary blip, a

misunderstanding. After all, I couldn't expect everything to be harmonious *all* the time. Every now and then a disagreement was bound to happen. It was, I told myself, just part and parcel of being married. Tomorrow, my friends would be gone but for now, I needed to make the most of the time we had left.

Chapter 29

Josie was speaking so quickly to Claude that I could only catch snippets of what they were talking about. I heard the words "sale", "residence", "two bungalows" and that was about it. As they came to the end of their animated conversation, they turned toward me.

'*Petite sœur*! I have good news! Tell her Claude,' said Josie.

Claude told me that Josie had heard of two bungalows that were side by side on the residence in which we were already living. They had apparently been converted into one larger property by the current owners installing an internal interconnecting door. They were not yet on the open market and Josie had taken the liberty of making an appointment with the owners for us to view them. Claude thought this could be an ideal opportunity for us, as the boys were already settled into the local school and we would be close to Josie and JC.

The element of 'affordability' figured strongly in the equation too. I was very much aware of this, having been put in a position a couple of weeks previously in which Claude had asked me to lend his great friend Henri, a considerable amount of money. He needed to borrow the equivalent of £30,000 for an investment in a property development opportunity in Northern Spain. My initial response had been one of shock that it was such a large amount and I was loathe to lend it as I felt that we, as a family, should have taken priority in terms of being able to buy our own property. Lending this amount to Henri would limit our choices considerably. However, I finally relented when Claude accused me of not trusting him sufficiently as my husband. He had yelled that there was no point being married to someone who did not trust the other person, so if I did not trust Henri, it meant that I didn't trust him either. He created such an atmosphere that I dutifully surrendered, knowing that it would be the only way to restore any semblance of peace and well-being.

As a result, when the two properties at *Vic La Gardiole* came up, they had the added advantage of being something that was readily affordable. So, in my mind, they were well worth visiting.

Bungalows 113 and 114 were located directly across the residence from Josie and JC, away from the tennis courts and swimming pool but within easy strolling distance. I opened the side entrance gate and walked through. As I rounded the corner of the building, an impressively large sun terrace opened out before me. There was no garden as such, just a few borders, perfect for planting with Mediterranean plants, and I could even picture the bougainvillaea that would grow up the arbour. It looked sunnily inviting. There was a little gate directly onto the road, with a makeshift bridge that spanned the small *fossé* (stream). This would be ideal as it meant that I could walk the dogs from here more easily than having to traipse through the estate to get to the gated entrance. I'd be able to get them out into the fields in no time. The vendors were very accommodating in showing us around their cherished property which they said that they'd bought so they could bring their large family on holiday. Now their family had grown up and flown the nest, they no longer required such a large space as it was only the two of them. The interior layout was such that there were four bedrooms in total, two current kitchens and two bathrooms. Although they had made the bungalows interconnecting, they had never altered it, but left them as the original apartments. I could see that we'd need to get rid of one of the kitchens to make that into the family lounge. I knew Claude was very practical in this way and could not see it being a problem. We agreed to go away and discuss it between ourselves before calling the owners back with our decision later that day.

By the end of the day, Claude had made the necessary appointments for us to see the *Notaire* in the working town of *Sete* – a town where the *Canal du Midi* meets the waters of the Mediterranean Sea. We had agreed to pay the full asking price for the two properties as Claude said that it was a superb investment opportunity, one that we could not afford to miss. I was relieved to think that my capital from the sale of Mithian Farm would now be put to good use as we forged a new, permanent life for our family in the sun-blessed region of Languedoc. I was looking forward to the day when I could finally bring all the boxes out of storage and open their contents in my new home. They had after all been my most precious possessions, not in terms of monetary value but more in terms of the sentimental value attached to them. I felt sure that these items would help in my yearning to feel finally settled.

The legal process of buying a property in France was very different to the UK and I had to rely on Claude to guide me through the process. I was particularly grateful to him for suggesting that we sign an additional clause that he told me would protect my future interests if he were to die. The legal document which we dutifully signed in the interim period was to safeguard my right to the property, should his children decide to lay claim to it. I thought it was rather sad that we needed to make contingency plans such as that and couldn't imagine any of his children that I'd met behaving in such a way. It was inconceivable to think I would ever be suspicious of my own boys in that way. Still, regrettably, I realised Claude knew his offspring better than I did and so I was led by his greater wisdom.

We were heading towards our completion date on the 24th August, a couple of weeks away and the days seemed to slow in their passing as my excitement levels peaked, matching the heat of the Mediterranean sun.

Chapter 30

I sat on the cool of the tiled floor, surrounded by packing boxes, their labels making me smile in eager anticipation of unwrapping the memories that lay cradled in their depths. I found a china swan that'd been given to me when I was five years old, a souvenir that a friend had brought back from a holiday. It was heavily made, not fine porcelain, its form symbolic of a solid friendship, withstanding the test of time, something to be treasured. I was glad to be reunited with some of my favourite kitchen utensils – a particular vegetable knife that I'd habitually reach for, a reliable friend for meal preparation, an old egg whisk that had belonged to my granny, my mother's old blue leather recipe book, the pages marked with spillages, the ink blurred in places where cake mixture had inadvertently landed over the years. Firm favourites, holding sentimental significance to me, greater than any monetary value. Each one now giving me the building blocks to create a sense of home and belonging.

I had already hung some of my watercolour paintings on the wall. I smiled to see Godrevy Lighthouse, a familiar Cornish landmark, now displayed on the white wall of the dining area. It made me nostalgic for home which now seemed so very far away; it was a beacon of familiarity, symbolising that Cornwall still existed and I could bring it closer just by looking at it. It also brought back memories of hunting the sea sculpted cliff for bits of china exposed after storms. The small blue and white fragments held a haunting echo of a bygone era when a little tea room perched precariously on the edge of the cliff. Memories of many a day spent spotting seals gathered on the sands at low tide.

There was also the painting of Falmouth Bay. It reminded me of the day we'd walked through the gentle, leafy woodland with its May blanket of bluebells. We wove our way to a hidden cove where we'd picnicked after searching the rock pools for crabs. In the afternoon, we'd settled ourselves on the edge of the shoreline, to paint. The boys had seen me use my little watercolour set before and were intrigued to watch the wash of colour blend across the paper. I always had a fascination with seascapes and their salty horizons. I'd bought each of the boys their own set of paints. Using little plastic containers of saltwater to wash our brushes, precious time together, sitting, painting and chatting about our individual compositions. It had been one of those occasions whereby the outcome of our efforts had not been important. Rembrandts were not essential. Instead, it was more about the process and the quality of the time that we spent together. Moments like that make the 'glow on the inside' type memories.

What I didn't realise as I decorated our new home with the warmth of memories past, was that someone had other thoughts in mind and would paint a masterpiece layer by layer, in detailed, carefully executed strokes of destruction.

And so, he began.

Chapter 31

The first brush strokes were applied within a month.

Our home was, in a lot of respects, a blank canvas. We needed to get a proper kitchen installed as the property was geared only to people spending their holidays there. As a result, I was struggling with a solid two ringed hob and grill as the only means of cooking family meals. I longed for an oven and a flow of worktop space. It was proving really awkward when it came to meal preparation because I had to juggle everything around on the eighteen-inch gap between the hob and the draining board. I'd got my skills of execution off to a fine art, but it remained a chore and a challenge. I was looking forward to being able to spread out and cook properly. Claude and I went to look at some of the local stores to see what was available. I was thrilled when we found nautical blue kitchen units as well as a self-cleaning oven. I was overjoyed at the thought of not having to scrub and scrape for hours upon end in an effort to get the racks and linings gleaming. I'd also found an induction hob and so I purchased this at the same time and we stacked all our purchases into the back of the car and headed home. In no time at all we would have a new kitchen which in turn would help us feel more settled in our new home.

Another couple of weeks went by and still there was no change and no sign that Claude was going to embark on putting the new kitchen units in place. Instead, they stood stacked together in their flat pack cardboard wrappings, cluttering up more space and emphasising my sense of being a nomad each time I saw, or tripped, over them. I offered to help Claude in any way that I could, hoping this might encourage him to make a start on the task. He finally agreed only to inform me the following day that he'd received a phone call from the office and had to go to Paris for a fortnight. He left that evening. I spent the next two weeks using the stack of cardboard boxes as temporary extensions of the work surfaces for which I longed and being taunted by the picture of my dream oven, emblazoned on its heavy-duty plastic wrapper; tantalisingly close, yet out of reach.

September made way for October and the trees that overhung the border of the garden, dipped in an Autumnal breeze as they waved farewell to the departing season with finger-like fronds of reds and burnished yellows. I too said my goodbyes to thoughts of a homely kitchen. Instead, I was beginning to sense that the more I spoke to Claude about it, the more he was finding excuses not to do it. There was never any conversation about him not being capable of undertaking the work. In fact, I knew he was a dab hand at DIY. He was more than capable of problem-solving too. He proved this when he moved the huge staircase at Mithian Farm.

As time drew by, I began to sense it was more about him being able to control the situation and by choosing not to do the kitchen, it kept him firmly in command.

I resigned myself to making do with the makeshift kitchen that I'd been using for the past two and a half months. What Claude didn't know was that when he was away, I used the top of the cardboard boxes as improvised work tops! It actually became more of a relief each time he announced that he had to go away for a week as it meant that I could spread out and no one would reprimand me for my unconventional methods!

In some ways, it seemed quite humorous, but the reality was dawning on me that I needed to behave in a certain way in front of Claude. I couldn't actually relax because I was worried I might inadvertently do something to annoy him.

It was very much the same for the boys. Bit by bit, it dripped into my consciousness that the four of us could only truly relax when Claude was absent. There was a tightness simply in the way Tom and Owen moved. It was as if they too sensed the need to be wary. They waited until Claude left the room, before they'd relax and allow their natural outgoing selves to show. Claude was becoming more and more regimental in his approach to all three boys. Respect and discipline were paramount but they were alien to my style of parenting. Rightly or wrongly, I'd always come from the belief that if a parent can build a positive rapport with a child, generally this generates respect as the child is keen to please the parent. Having achieved respect, the discipline falls naturally into place.

My beloved furry four-legged companions became reserved and edgy. Millie, the middle-aged Labrador and Shadow, the Collie I'd rescued fourteen years ago and who'd been my family long before the birth of my eldest son, were quieter and subdued. Milly's natural exuberance and love of life had faded and it was a feeling that appeared to have been passed on to Shadow. Milly was the one who instilled the older dog with a new lease of life and a natural ability to find joy in all things. It worried me to see my loyal companions so forlorn. They deserved to be happy because they gave of themselves so unconditionally, placing their trust in me to look after them. And I was letting them down.

Now, for the first time since I'd homed them, they were no longer classed as part of the family. Claude slammed all thoughts closed when he shoved the dogs outside, shouting they would remain outdoors from now. With the animals successfully barred, he'd taken his place at the meal table, rubbing his palms together, before blowing on clasped hands in a gesture of needing to generate warmth. We'd eaten in an icy November silence. I watched two black noses streaking the outside of the glass pane, their features indistinguishable in the reflected glare of the internal light. Shadow's eyes, faded with the cataracts of old age, searched beseechingly, uncomprehendingly, as if asking what she had done that was so wrong. Milly regarded me though puzzled eyes, waiting in anticipation of some new game we were about to play, the rules of which she'd yet to understand. They'd placed total trust in me and my inaction was letting them down.

Ashamed of myself, I turned away, despising myself for being such a coward. Owen eyed me in raw disbelief from his corner on the oak pew. Thomas was helping Morgan to finish his last remaining spoonfuls of food. Maybe it was a way of was distracting himself from the situation. Discarded plates and the scattered crumbs of a baguette lay on the table. Owen was on cleaning up duties and waited, dishcloth in hand, for me to make the first move. I knew he was willing me to speak up but the words never came. Claude continued to observe me through slitted eyes as if biding his time, stalking a prey, waiting for it to break cover. I sat motionless and the air hung heavy with anticipation.

Suddenly, the silence was broken as Owen leapt to his feet, slamming the dishcloth onto the table and heading defiantly for the door, he yelled 'You can't leave Shadow and Milly outside! They're family!'

'Sit down!' shouted Claude.

Owen sat abruptly back down again, but I could see as he took a deep breath, swelling the chest of his eight-year-old stature, that he was not yet ready for submission.

'But...' he started.

'*You* will listen to me!' Claude snarled, slapping the flat of his hand so hard against the oak table that the crumbs scattered to the floor and Morgan startled, hit his knees on the food tray of his high chair. Everyone stared at him and he lowered his voice to a serpent's hiss.

'They will stay outside. I will not have those dogs in my house. The door will stay closed and they will know their place.'

A sickening feeling coursed through me and with it, an indescribable heaviness descended, weighing me down, rendering me helpless. I'd betrayed everyone precious to me. Owen was relying on me because he believed I'd make everything better, just as a parent waves the proverbial magic wand or puts 'magic cream' on the hurt; but I said nothing. I did not challenge Claude. I did not retaliate. I did not open the door. I'd already learnt on previous occasions that if I said anything, it would only make matters worse. I could put up with my punishment, but I couldn't bear the thought of my boys being punished and it would be them he'd take it out on. Perhaps he knew the way to inflict the greatest hurt on me would be through everything I loved, whether it be my boys or my faithful dogs. I was beginning to learn that the best way was to keep quiet.

Claude was proving relentless in his ruthlessness and that no one in the household was exempt.

Chapter 32

The Dr Jekyll and Mr Hyde characters were so well orchestrated, with the precision that was inevitably expected of someone who obsessed, like Claude did, over details. He conjured the cloak of whichever guise best suited the situation. The charm of a doting father and courteous husband only took centre stage when entertaining an audience. I was beginning to wonder if Claude found it difficult to summon up such a kind and loving personality, especially when neighbours or family dropped in unexpectedly. I could not understand how someone's demeanor could fluctuate so easily. Was I responsible for triggering his unreasonable responses?

Uncertainty added to the growing sense of unease. I never knew where I stood with him or how he was going to react at any one time. It was important to make a conscious effort on my part to avoid any potential situation that might cause him to react negatively. I needed to shield my boys from his outbursts, but it was easier said than done because he was so unpredictable. As time passed, behind closed doors, the well-intentioned Dr Jekyll was cast to one side, and Mr Hyde awoke. A deeply shrouded veil descended on the house and as the storm brewed, charging the atmosphere with an ominous foreboding. In this mood, tiny irregularities which might otherwise be of minor significance to others, captured the attention of Claude. Eyes irrationally fixated, the predator swooped in for the kill. Whether the death was short or tortuous depended on how the mood took him. Sometimes he'd play for a while by involving himself in stealthy manoeuvres. At other times he would simply pounce unannounced. However, one thing I could rely on – there would never be any sign of compassion or remorse.

One particular day, there was great excitement in the house as Claude had promised to take us all out for the day. We were going to the safari park, *'The Réserve Africaine de Sigean'*, home to some three thousand eight hundred animals. Whilst Tom and Owen had seen large game and mammals at Newquay Zoo, they had no idea what to expect from a safari park. But with the adverts we'd seen splashed on local advertisement hoardings of lions and rhinos in particular, the day promised to be an epic adventure. Picking up on the excitement, Morgan was practising his lion roar in eager anticipation. I was proud of the way Tom searched for picture books to show Morgan the animals of the African plains, explaining to him what we might encounter on our trip.

I made a packed lunch, sorted out all the necessary paraphernalia needed when going out with a toddler for the day. I'd walked the dogs early that morning and arranged for our neighbours to come and feed them at tea time in case we were late back. We stood in the kitchen waiting, brandishing our backpacks. I was relieved when Claude appeared because it was getting too exciting to have to wait for him much longer.

However, instead of heading out of the door, he said that he needed to check how clean and tidy the house was before we left. There were some unmistakable, 'under the breath' type sighs from Tom and Owen as Claude strode towards the direction of the staircase leading to their bedroom. Owen reassured me that it was already tidy as if to endeavour to speedily dismiss anything that might halt the beginning of our adventure. In an orderly procession, we followed Claude as he mounted the stairs, unaware that the unrelenting shadow he cast on the wall, was that of an emerging Mr Hyde.

The hawk-like Mr Hyde circled Tom and Owen's bedroom and it passed the scrutinising, fault-finding eyes of the predator. Both boys had carefully made sure that everything was scrupulously clean and in its exact place to be sure we'd be allowed out. Their spirits were rising with anticipation of getting away from these four walls and in the hope that Claude would relax in a different environment. Away from here, perhaps we could almost pretend that we were a real family of five, enjoying ourselves.

But it was not to be.

Having passed the bedroom inspections, I'd not countered that Claude would then turn his attention to the whole of the ground floor. In the bathroom, he checked for water marks around the bath, soap scum on the shower screen, the cleanliness of the toilet and the state of the toilet brush. It appeared that everything was in order and so we followed him with baited breath as he continued his inspection.

Nothing was out of place in the living room; this was probably down to the fact that apart from Claude, it was seldom occupied. He'd assembled a long desktop which ran the length of one wall, housing all his computer equipment. The space was now exclusively for his use only. This was the room where he worked on a daily basis and so we knew to keep away to allow him to concentrate, leaving the rest of us to congregate in the kitchen instead. This was the last room on his tick list.

He smiled as he looked around and sidestepped the flat pack units that still lay dormant and untouched. I was relieved. He looked pleased. Everything was in its place. I knew I needed to set a good example to the boys because Claude had reprimanded me for not washing up immediately and for leaving things out. It made sense to tidy as I went I suppose, but sometimes it made the kitchen feel less lived in and more like an operating theatre.

'Ah!' exclaimed Claude, jabbing his finger pointedly and triumphantly where the tiled floor met the upright mushroom-coloured plinth of the kitchen base unit. Four sets of eyes followed the line of his extended finger. He nodded his head as if to stress how disappointed he was. His gesture was a direct contradiction to the look in his eyes.

'Such a shame,' he sighed in deliberate tones, enjoying the imminent fear he was creating as we realised what was coming next. 'I was looking forward to going out *'en famille'* but your mother has not cleaned properly and so...' he paused for effect, then continued, 'so, we stay at home.'

Turning the metaphorical knife blade, he planted it, purposefully wounding as he looked directly at me through his black corpse-like eyes.

'You expect me to put up with your mess? You have ruined it for all of us.'

And without further comment he walked out of the kitchen, shutting the door behind him as he went back to his computer lair in the lounge, leaving us to stare at the three tiny crumbs on the kitchen floor.

Three crumbs in a neat linear formation.

Three crumbs lined up in order of size.

Three crumbs were all it took.

I stared at them.

The first crumb took away our chance of freedom.

The second took away any sense of hope.

The third crumb, the tiniest of all, mocked us as I realised that whatever we did, it would never be good enough.

We were at the mercy of the persona who lay in wait on the other side of the kitchen door. The creature that had just added another layer of paint, thinly stretched like skin, to his canvas and who, no doubt, smiled as he hung it out to dry.

Chapter 33

I couldn't believe that it was the day before Christmas Eve. It's significance meant I could open the ancient hard-topped blue suitcase, with its peeled and faded travel stickers reminding me of how my parents travelled the World, prior to my arrival. I recalled the story that my mother had told me repeatedly over the years, on occasions when we were running late for an appointment somewhere. It was a phrase she called upon in times of need, "better not dead than dead on time."

It related to the plane journey my parents took when my dad was sent as chief engineer to establish a smelting works in New South Wales, Australia, in the 1950s. They were crossing the Atlantic Ocean at the time on route for America as their first stop. I recalled Mum recounting the details avidly, pointing out that they were "just past the point of no return", in other words, just over halfway. Looking out of the window, she noticed that one of the propellers had stopped spinning. Apparently, the steward made an announcement, apologising for the fact that this delay might cause an inconvenience, given that they had to divert to Newfoundland. He then added the now infamous words of "better not dead than dead on time".

I smiled. Mum always had an uncanny way of looking

on the bright side. I wished that I could conjure up her same inspiring spirit and I realised just how much I missed her. I wondered if she was missing me or if the Alzheimer's had taken hold and that she'd perhaps forgotten she had a daughter and three grandsons.

My hand slid lovingly over the smooth navy top of the suitcase that housed all our Christmas decorations and I hoped that on opening the lid, the room would be filled with the smell I associated with Christmas over the years at home, a mingling of mothballs and mustiness from being stored in the loft; a direct contradiction to the sparkling festive contents of the case that lay inside. I wished I was back in Cornwall and that the boys and I would be spending Christmas with their Gran. I knew it would be the most terribly lonely time for her and that no festive phone call could ever replace actually being there in person. We'd always spent Christmas together and this would be the first one we'd ever been apart. I'd chosen a life in France and so I'd chosen to spend Christmas with my husband who was due back from his travels the following day. I wondered if he was looking forward to a season of good cheer with his family.

I was jolted from my thoughts by whoops of delight as Tom and Owen entered the room to find the familiar suitcase, and all they knew it entailed, waiting for them on the floor. I'd promised not to start decorating the tree without them. We all pored over the contents of the case, Tom and Owen exclaiming each time they found something they remembered from past Christmases. Morgan, keen to be involved, poked a chubby fist into the colourful nest of tinsel and pulled out a salt dough star. Some of its glitter had dropped off but Owen immediately greeted it like a long-lost friend.

'That's my star that I made at Mithian school!' he smiled, gleefully holding it up out of reach of a perplexed

Morgan.

'Have you still got your man in the Mexican hat figure?' asked Tom earnestly.

I laughed.

'He's probably in here somewhere,' I replied, 'but I really don't know why he's classed as a Christmas decoration! I think I must've made him during a 'making figures out of paper' art lesson at school at some point and Gran just put him in there with the rest of the things! Still, somehow it wouldn't be Christmas without him, would it?'

'I like him,' said Tom, 'We need to find him. I like the way his head nods up and down under his ... his...'

He searched for the words.

'His sombrero,' I filled in the missing gap.

'Yes,' he smiled.

It took hours to decorate the tree because we couldn't come to a mutual agreement as to how it should look. Tom was keen on a particular colour theme whereas Owen wanted a spectacularly multi-coloured, all singing, all dancing tree. There'd been a few heated exchanges as Tom got annoyed when Owen placed a couple of the decorations that Tom didn't like on the already heavily adorned boughs, but a compromise was amicably reached. We'd sung our festive socks off and, for a moment, I wondered if there was a French equivalent of Jingle Bells. Perhaps there was, but I was sure they didn't know the alternative version which the boys had sung unreservedly, peals of laughter flooding the room.

'Jingle Bells, Batman smells, Robin ran away!'

Our little tree stood like an emblem of warmth and hope in the corner of the lounge. I felt an eagerly anticipated excitement rising as I thought of the presents that I'd wrap and the stockings that I'd place gently on the beds of my sleeping sons tomorrow night. It was lovely to see them relaxed and happy. This was what

Christmas was about I thought to myself; a time of joy. Smiling, I looked at the assortment of Christmas cards from England, standing like sentinels of good spirit on the book case that ran the length of the room. The card from Courtney was gratefully received because within it was a handwritten letter, bringing me up to date on all the latest happenings in the day-to-day life of his small community. I was relieved to read he'd visited my mum on several occasions and that they'd actually ventured out for Sunday lunch together. However, the most exciting part of his correspondence was learning that he had news on the infamous Butter Lady of Mithian Farm. With his arthritic hands he wrote:

"I paid my old friend Dr Henry a visit last Tuesday because I wanted to talk to him about one of my Muscovy ducks – I've only got two left now since that bugger of a fox had one the other night. He never ate it, just left a mess of a trail of white feathers. They kill for no reason, those foxes! Anyway, Dr Henry and I were talking about the old days, about the war effort. A time we ploughed the fields to plant tatties, and about how we had an evacuee come stay with mother and I, all the way from London. Dr Henry turns round and says 'Mrs Evans, next door to you must've been some pleased to have a young lad around the place again'. I can't say I remember, but then he says 'That poor soul lost all her men folk in the Great War – a husband and two sons killed in France'."

There wasn't much more in Courtney's letter, but it echoed on in my mind. It was more than just being able to put a name to the 'Butter Lady' who I now knew had been a 'Mrs Evans'. It suited her. My heart lurched as I put myself in her position and I felt a wave of sadness flood over me as I tried to imagine the degree of suffering that she must have encountered. For someone to lose just one person in their life was unthinkable, but the pain of losing all three men on foreign soil was intangible. It also struck me what a coincidence it was our sharing a connection with France. I wondered if this was the reason that she'd made herself known to me.

Such a tragedy.

'I'm so sorry,' I whispered to her, knowing I'd never be able to adequately verbalise such a terrible feeling of loss.

Lost in my thoughts, she began to manifest in my mind's eye. Appearing to me at first through a thin veil of time, the vision growing progressively more defined, as she made her presence known to me. I could see her now. Her rounded face held a comfortable soft, milky complexion, contradiction to the intensity of and eyes that. I stared back, mesmerised but, try as I might, I could not understand what she was trying to convey. Then I blinked and she was gone. All that remained was a sense of unfathomable unease at the back of my mind, nothing I could pinpoint, but the seed of something nonetheless.

Claude arrived home late on Christmas Eve. Apparently, it had been a particularly difficult time for him with one of the clients in Paris who demanded that his computer system be restored prior to the festive break. Claude's mood effectively lowered our spirits and 'Papa Noel' was barely mentioned. The evening ended abruptly with Claude announcing that he was overtired and needed to go to bed. This left me with the daunting task of wrapping all Morgan's presents on my own. I'd deliberately left them so that Claude could see them and I hoped, be involved in the excitement of wrapping parcels and placing them around the tree. It was his son and I thought it would be a precious memory. The reality was that once I finally got the two older boys to bed, I sat amid a sea of snowmen, roundly smiling at me on their rolls of paper and strings of Sellotape that became permed curls as soon as it was cut. It was going to be a long night and I knew I'd have to be up early in the morning, whenever the first cry of excitement from a waking child heralded the start of the day. Still, I was not going to be perturbed. Nothing would prevent me from making our first Christmas in France as enjoyable as possible. As I wrestled with the latest parcel, so I caught the opening of the lounge door out of the corner of my eye. I panicked knowing that it meant that either Tom or Owen was about to walk in. I didn't have time to move anything out of sight, as a tousle-headed Tom peeped around the corner.

'Tombo! What are you doing still up? You're supposed to be fast asleep by now you know!' I exclaimed, wondering how on earth I was going to explain the myriad of parcels that were strewn about me, all colour coded so I knew which ones belonged to which boy.

'Mum,' said Tom, in a placating tone that almost had a kindly finger wag attached to it, 'I know who Father Christmas is. I've come to help. I can be your elf.'

So, it was Tom who worked with me into the early hours to ensure his little brother would wake to a magical morning. It was my precious, thoughtful Tom who helped me assemble the parts to make a ride-on tractor and trailer that had been delivered as a flat pack. Meanwhile, Claude slept, oblivious to everything.

It was Tom, when the last of the gifts were placed around the tree, who whispered, 'Can I be the one to put the stocking on the end of Morgan's bed?'

I would love to recall details of a magical Christmas

Day, spent with family. I do remember that Morgan was thrilled with his ride-on toy and propelled himself continually from room to room with loud shouts of "Watch me! I'm going fast!"

I do remember that Tom and Owen were more excited to see their awe-struck little brother, delighting in the fact that Santa knew to deliver to his home in France and not Cornwall.

I do remember that when I gave Claude his gifts, he gave nothing in return apart from the excuse of being too busy with work to have time to shop.

And I do remember the ordeal at the dining table when the boys were faced with salmon and new potatoes as a poor substitute for roast turkey and all the trimmings. No democratic vote. Claude's decision. We ate in silence. Scowls and spat fish bones were a far cry from the usual merriment of pulling crackers. No one was in the mood for frivolity, wearing paper hats, or telling jokes. Instead, with every forced mouthful my appetite shrank as it became satiated, fed by large helpings of despondency.

Chapter 34

I needed to get out of the house. I was feeling more and more trapped within its walls and so when March arrived with the *Mistral* wind bulldozing the grey skies, southward, leaving a carpet of blue overhead, it cleared a path for me to get outdoors. Whilst Tom and Owen were safely at school, I used the now more plausible excuse of a beautiful day, to walk the dogs to get away from the confines of the house and its brooding occupant.

I set off on numerous treks, taking Morgan with me on many an adventure, along the lanes that bordered the vineyards. On other occasions, the boys and I would explore *'les etangs'* – shallow salt water lakes that were graced with an ever-increasing presence of pink flamingos just returned from their winter migration. Just as I'd always associated seeing wild daffodils blooming on the waysides in Cornwall as an announcement of spring, so the flamingos of the salt lakes held the same symbolism for me now.

It was a time of fresh beginnings and new life which reminded me that Morgan was soon to reach his second birthday. His first birthday in France. It felt significant to me and I wondered how and where he would spend his future birthdays and how he would choose celebrate in years to come. I was also aware that my mother, his gran, would not be present and I felt a wave of yearning for my previous home life in Cornwall. A life is precious and deserves to be celebrated. As I thought about it and reflected on the Christmas we'd endured, I was not sure Morgan's forthcoming birthday was going to receive the special attention it deserved. My mind was whirling, thinking about how I would like things to be and how the reality we were experiencing was such a stark contrast to everything I hoped for.

Who was there when Morgan learnt to swim and dive in the pool on the residence?

Who witnessed the uncontained laughter that pealed around the salt lake as Owen excitedly hooked his first fish, endeavouring to land it with such enthusiasm that both line and fish got tangled in a nearby mimosa tree?

Who taught the patient tying of shoe laces or the changing of a puncture on Tom's bike?

Had Claude been involved with any of the children's visits to the doctor for tonsillitis, earache or chest infections?

I knew the answer.

So far, my husband had profited by receiving the reimbursements for the boys' medical fees directly into his own bank account. Along with the *'Allocation Familial'*, the equivalent of Child Benefit, he was assured of supplementing his income on a regular basis.

I have always been someone who is willing to roll up my sleeves and work. When we first arrived in France, Claude insisted that my place was in the home and tending to my offspring. To begin with I was quite happy with this arrangement because I wanted to make sure that the boys felt settled and I was content with being both mother and housewife. However, I'd envisaged it as a temporary state of affairs and as the boys became settled at school and had made friends easily, I felt surplus to requirements. To add to this, Claude told me Morgan should start attending 'L'école maternelle' when he was two years old. I was not keen on this idea because I felt he was too young to be sent off to a formal educational establishment. However, Claude arranged an appointment with the head teacher and we went on a tour of the place. I was taken aback by both the orderly environment and its staff. Little tots followed a strict, regimental programme that even extended to the placing of their blankets in strictly regulated ranks, prior to their statutory 30-minute rest. Despite feeling uneasy about the whole idea, I agreed to let Morgan attend and so a place was reserved for him. On the positive side, I thought it would be good for him to be surrounded by French speakers as I spoke to him in a mix of both languages and was worried about the possibility of developmental delay. It would also give him the opportunity to socialise with children his own age and make some playmates.

With the opportunity of finally having some time to myself, I broached the idea of taking up teaching again, perhaps teaching English as a foreign language. Claude was singularly unimpressed. I stressed that it would add to our joint income, especially as I was aware that the surplus funds from Mithian Farm were being depleted on a weekly basis with all the household bills. I needed to generate my own source of income to compensate. A heated argument followed in which Claude told me there were too many hurdles to overcome, in terms of paperwork and I was not entitled to employment in France as I'd not been in the country long enough. He dismissed the whole idea by emphatically explaining that additionally, I was not qualified enough to work in any capacity in France, let alone as a professional teacher.

Rightly or wrongly, I'd always allowed my occupation to influence my sense of self-worth. It gave me the opportunity to prove my ability to myself. His cutting derision sliced me apart, leaving me in downtrodden fragments on the floor. I was becoming more and more useless. I was now being cast aside as a mother, continually criticised for failing my household chores and rapidly becoming a worthless nobody.

All these thoughts took centre stage in my head to perform a technicolour tragedy. Where had I gone? Had the person that I'd been, simply vanished overnight?

No.

The process had been skilfully manufactured over a prolonged period – barely indistinguishable, a malignance in the background, like the slow drip of water from a leaking tap. The realisation it had been there all along and once heard, could never be unheard. Like Japanese water torture; a relentless drip, drip, drip.

I deliberated as I pushed the now sleeping child in his buggy over the uneven ground of the meandering pathway, the dogs oblivious to my thoughts, distracted by sticks and new scents. I scanned into the middle distance as if searching for understanding. I was preoccupied by my thoughts.

As each frame passed in my mind's eye, it depicted a woman, familiar and yet a stranger that I didn't recognise. I saw a stooped person, unsure if her next step could be relied upon to support her, burdened by life itself, endlessly struggling to please, but never succeeding. I watched helplessly as she strove so hard to get every ten out of ten perfection life score, as she gave of her best, only to be told to try harder next time. 'Never good enough' would be the words on her epitaph. From the damp, dark silence of her cask, she pictured the landscape of the burial ground that lay above her, a place so close and yet beyond reach.

Long ago, the words 'positivity' and 'praise' had been meaningfully inscribed on the face of the tombstone, as if holding some sort of significance. Now, simply forgotten, discarded by the earthiness of time, she saw a tired granite surface with an indistinct inscription and raised her hand as if in a gesture to trace their cold outline with her fingers. She felt the uneven texture brought about by the roughness of the pale lichen that clung to the stone and from her resting place, below the heavy earth, she began to weep. Stricken by the loss of all good things in the world, she mourned for what might have been, her sobs silenced by the unyielding tomb.'

With a sudden realisation that my imagination was becoming all too vivid, I caught my thoughts before I stumbled completely into an abyss of self-pity. It would be far too easy to be consumed by these feelings, but I needed to fight them off. I could not allow them to take over. I had to keep strong. Three boys and two dogs relied upon me and regardless of how I felt in myself, I was not going to let them down. Spinning the pushchair about in a one-hundred-and-eighty-degree turn, perhaps a subconscious movement to turn my back on my previous thoughts, I whistled for the dogs to follow me. I needed to change tack.

Remembering an advert that I'd recently seen in the window of the local paper shop, I strode out purposefully in the direction of the village centre.

As a plan began forming in my mind, I smiled as I recalled the defiant lyrics of a song, *"I get knocked down, but I get up again"*.

Grinning, I increased my pace.

Chapter 35

A victory, however small, is still a victory. That's how it felt. In the grand scheme of things, it would most likely be classed as unimportant, but inwardly I was celebrating my small triumph. It had even involved what I chose to call 'strategic planning' on my part, to ensure the best possible outcome. By waiting until I had an audience before I made my announcement, as well as ensuring that the audience would be likely to respond in a positive way, I told everyone my intentions and awaited their response.

'What a good idea!' said Josie and her other guests, who'd been invited to dine with us, also nodded and smiled approvingly. 'And where did you say you saw this?'

Smiling inwardly I replied, 'It was an advert at the local newsagents. It's for anyone who wants to learn English. The lessons are to be held in the room above the tourist information office every Wednesday from 7.30 – 9.30 in the evening. It will be ideal for me because as Claude has pointed out that apparently I'm not in the position to teach English at the moment so it will give me the valuable opportunity of seeing how it is done.'

'Get yourself out of that one,' I simmered to myself, casting as genuine a smile as I could muster in Claude's direction. He smiled back in a show of approval to

his unwitting audience, but not before I glimpsed his other self, as Dr Jekyll fought momentarily to regain his composure.

I eyed him defiantly, knowing that just for once, just in this moment, *I was in control*, not him.

'I've spoken to the lady who runs it. She works in the tourist office during the day. She was really pleased to have what she called a 'real' English student and so I am starting next Wednesday.'

I looked pointedly at Claude and added, 'It will be so nice to chat to people who want to speak English!'

Claude mastered a forlorn expression for the benefit of his audience, before responding in true thespian limelight.

'My poor wife. She has to make all the effort to speak French because my English is so... so... how do they say in English – terrible. I am not a good student.'

He was playing the victim and everyone sympathised with his linguistic inadequacy. He was so convincing, just as he'd been when I first met him. Everyone believed this polite, quiet man with his gentle humour. There was nothing about him to hint of a darker side which stepped out from the shadows in the quiet of our own home.

With this in mind, I decided to lessen the risk of the monster appearing and so I invited Josie and JC to come over for dinner the day after my first language class. They were pleased to accept my invitation and I was equally relieved.

I knew I was now assured of being able to attend the lesson because it was now public knowledge that I was planning to go and no doubt, they would ask me about it when I saw them.

I'd also safeguarded us from any backlash from Claude. He wouldn't dare to expose his rage in front of our visitors.

What I hadn't banked on was that in his quest to

regain control, Claude was already plotting a revenge attack.

And like an ambush, it came when I least expected it.

Chapter 36

I thoroughly enjoyed my first experience of the English class and met some lovely members of the local community. Although I felt very nervous at the outset, the group soon put me at ease and before the end of the lesson, I became some sort of star attraction helping with the intonation and correct pronunciation. It was a two-way thing – mutually beneficial as I felt sufficiently relaxed to ask questions of my own.

I immediately warmed to one gentleman in particular who was of retirement age. I sensed he might be ex-forces given his grey, tight cropped hair, the fact that he was clean-shaven and wore an immaculately pressed shirt. He spoke with a quiet air of authority and was not afraid of asking for further clarification on aspects of English grammar. He continued to ask questions until he understood a concept. By the end of the evening, I'd learnt his name was Jacques and he lived in a neighbouring village. In his free time, he was particularly eager to learn English now he'd retired from his position as the Chief Police Commissioner for Sete. I could imagine him in his uniform, although I doubted it was his appearance which earned him the respect he deserved. He had a manner about him that made me feel safe. He was someone I could trust and I realised I needed a friend, someone who was beyond the reach of Claude's family.

The following evening, as we sat around the dinner table, I shared my experience of attending my first 'English' class with Josie and JC, who were delighted to hear how successful it''d been. Claude hadn't mentioned the subject since my announcement the week before. He'd not even inquired about it when I'd returned from the first session. Now he listened attentively, as if genuinely interested. He'd not put any obstacles in my path to prevent me from attending and so I concluded that all must be well and I dared to relax.

In retrospect, he was simply lulling me into a false sense of security.

Two days later, he struck.

Out of nowhere, Claude challenged what I was doing going to the English classes, accusing me of having an ulterior motive, of no doubt meeting a man there. I thought of the fatherly figure of Jacques, the policeman and wished he was here now because I was suddenly feeling very afraid.

It was not just the anger in Claude's voice, knowing there would be no reasoning with him, but the way he was physically intimidating me. My fear increased as the menace of his very close proximity shut off any options for escape. With my heart pounding, I knew I needed to run. I knew I needed to get away fast.

Before I could translate my thoughts into actions he grabbed me by the wrists, throwing me against the door frame. My head slammed backwards as the edges of the wood gouged into my shoulder blades. Then just as suddenly, he let go, throwing my wrists away like a fox spits out discarded chicken bones.

Turning to look at me with vile abomination, he spat, 'You are nothing but a whore! Let's see how tidy the sons of a whore can keep their room,' and he sped up the stairs, taking two at a time, to Tom and Owen's bedroom.

I ran after him, screaming for him to stop and wanting to physically put myself between him and my boys. But I'd already heard the sound of furniture being overturned, paper being ripped, my children's screams and then a thud.

I reached the top of the landing to see Claude with his hands around Owen's throat as he threw him hard against the pine rail of his bed. Owen stayed motionless where he had fallen, fear coursing out of his beautiful blue eyes. My beautiful boy's eyes. Tom was cowering in a corner by the open window. A curtain was flapping wildly across a teddy bear. It looked as if it'd tried to jump, only to be caught last minute, by a singular padded paw which had tangled in the tail end of a departing duvet. Pokémon posters were ripped from the walls, chests overturned, school books scattered.

Their room had been violated and it was my fault, just as it was my fault that as Claude turned away to walk down the stairs, I saw the red finger marks, the pattern of pressure points screaming at me on Owen's neck. They pointed their raw fingers at me, blame planted firmly at my feet. This was all my doing. How could I have been so naive to think that I could defy Claude?

Footsteps retreated into the distance and although it felt like a lifetime of waiting, I could not allow Claude to see my emotion. I would not give him the pleasure. Instead, I waited, motionless, scared I might do something to inadvertently escalate the situation further. But he'd gone. I could hear him whistling quietly in the distance as I ran to my son, squatted on the floor beside him and drew him close. He was sobbing now, the type of heavy uncontrollable sobs that sudden relief brings. I cradled him and rocked him as a mother desperately wanting to take away the pain. Aware of Tom, I looked up and extended my other arm to him, indicating that I wanted to hold them both close and ease their suffering. I'm not sure how long we sat on the floor in silence, with me just rocking and cradling my children, long enough for the fear to subside little by little.

We were still sitting on the floor amid the remnants of their bedroom, when Owen raised his head from my shoulder, looked at me and whispered imploringly, 'It was only a sock mum. Everything else was tidy. There was just one sock on the floor.'

I squeezed him close.

'None of this is your fault Owen. It's not your fault and it's not Toms either. It will be all right. I promise you that it will be all right.'

Glancing down at my own reddening wrists, I wasn't sure how anything would ever be alright again and I bit down hard on my lower lip, swallowing and fighting to hold back the tears that threatened to engulf me. It was down to me now.

We were effectively stranded in the southeast of France. The gravity of our situation dawned on me. There was no one we could genuinely rely upon. There were miles of driving distance separating us from a ferry port which could take us home and I realised in all probability, we'd be stopped before we got there. Claude would waste no time alerting the appropriate authorities. Access to the phone or internet was guarded making it difficult to raise a call for help. Our passports were locked away inside Claude's filing cabinet and I didn't know where he hid the key.

Could the situation get any worse?

Chapter 37

To call it an emotional roller coaster ride would indicate an element of thrill was involved and that couldn't have been further from the truth. There are no words to adequately describe the extremes of uncertainty we faced. Claude appeared quite normal after his outburst. He was jovial, attentive and relaxed.

None of us was fooled.

I wonder whether Owen's classmates were fooled when he insisted he was only wearing his roll neck jumper because he felt cold?

Like Owen, we covered things up too. It was easier that way. I pretended to be the perfect housewife and mother when Claude's family called round. We nodded in all the right places, we went out of our way to keep the house that was no longer a home, immaculate.

In a moment of insanity, desperate in my bid to find help, I asked Owen to peel back his jumper to show a neighbour the finger marks and bruising. The elderly gent was aghast, but even more horrified at the notion of being complicit when I'd asked him where I needed to go to report it. Bidding a hasty retreat, he waved his hands in a dismissive gesture, making it clear he'd absolutely no intention of getting involved. It was as if they closed ranks to form a barricade against their ancient enemy, leaving us targeted for being English and consequently classed as social outcasts.

It was a couple of weeks before I dared to return to the English class in the village. I wanted to be sure Claude was feeling contented which meant allowing him control. For this reason, I asked his permission to attend and this was duly granted with the nod of a head as he paused from his work on the computer. On this occasion, the display on his computer screen confirmed it to be work related, unlike the porn I'd been privy to seeing the previous week. Claude hadn't attempted to hide what he'd been feasting on. On the contrary, he'd probably *wanted* me to see it, to underline how inadequate I must be in the bedroom, how incapable I was of meeting his needs. Did he brand these women as whores, or was it a title he reserved exclusively for me?

The English lesson ended promptly at nine o'clock just as the church bell in the village square started to chime. Jacques, who seemed to be watching me intently over the course of the lesson, got up from his seat, bid the others farewell and started to escort me to the door leading to the staircase.

'You have missed some lessons,' he said in a never miss a trick, matter-of-fact voice.

'I, I know,' I replied, looking down at the dark marbled floor of the landing. I couldn't meet his eyes.

'I was wondering if you were OK,' he said, tipping his head to one side in a questioning gesture like a crow.

'Oh no – everything is fine Jacques, thank you.'

Still, I couldn't look him in the eye because I knew that of all people, he'd detect the deceit immediately.

Trying to sound convincing, I added, 'Just the boys. You know how it is. They haven't been very well and so I couldn't leave them.'

'Of course, of course,' Jacques smiled back. 'And your husband? He does not mind you coming here?'

Gently spoken, but I sensed that he was about to ask some more of his typical clarification questions if I wasn't careful. I couldn't speak to Jacques, not yet anyway. It was too risky. If I disclosed what had happened to anyone, I had to be sure of the consequences and in particular, I had to be sure that we could be as far away from Claude as possible. If I spoke our truth and we were left under the same roof, I dreaded to think what might happen. I had to be careful. Very careful.

I took a deep breath, 'I think he might be glad to see me out of the house for once!' I replied, trying to be light-humoured. 'Probably glad to see the back of me!' I added.

By now we had reached the bottom of the stairs and Jacques pushed open the external door with one arm in a gentlemanly fashion, to let me out.

'I rather doubt that,' he said and went on, 'In fact, I would not be at all surprised if he comes to collect you.'

I looked at him in surprise and not understanding why he should make such a comment and as I did so, I heard the long press of a car horn. Looking up, I saw Claude in the Renault, waving at me to get in the car.

'Oh!' I exclaimed staring at Jacques in disbelief, wondering how on earth he'd been so accurate in his prediction. 'Jan. Trust me. I have worked with many people over the years and I have met your husband's type before.'

He gave a simple, expressionless acknowledgement in Claude's direction, before turning on his heels and walking away in the opposite direction. Little did I know it would be many months before I saw Jacques again, and that when I did, it would be under very different circumstances.

That night as I lay awake in bed alongside a satiated, sleeping, husband, I wondered what Jacques meant. Was it possible that he knew what happened in this house? Did he know that behind its golden exterior with its sunny blue shutters and array of colourful plants, lay a tortuous prison, where a dark fury strained as it snarled to be unleashed? I doubted that even Jacques could have known what was going to happen that night.

It would never make sense to a normal human being, but then Claude had just proved that he was as far removed from anything that could be called human. He was an animal. He had devoured the very last piece of me, drooling in anticipation at the taste of raw, red meat.

I'd gone to bed before him, leaving him downstairs to watch whatever intrigued him on his sacred computer screen. I guessed what he was watching because of the sound of women's gasps and groans of ecstasy coupled with the fact that he'd taken gleeful deliberation in telling me that he got more satisfaction from watching porn on the screen, than he had ever experienced with me. Climbing into bed, I hoped desperately to quickly fall asleep. I wanted to be oblivious to the man who would lie beside me. He revolted me and I couldn't bear to endure his physical being so close. I willed sleep to take me to a place where my mind could rest and my body relax.

But sleep evaded me, just as I thought it would. There were some nights when desperate for sleep I went to bed, only to hear the sound of the music system being turned up as its bass notes thumped up through the floor from below. No piano lilting melody, no 'Ballade Pour Madeleine', but the harsh, heart-thumping beat of Techno music. I pictured Claude, cigar in one hand, whisky in the other, tapping his feet, smiling contentedly. I knew it wasn't his passion for music which pleased him so much, but the knowledge he'd be keeping me awake.

I knew sleep deprivation was a form of torture. It was one of Claude's favourite methods to inflict hurt. He employed the technique on numerous occasions. It was at its peak of effectiveness when I'd been suffering with a fever and flu-type symptoms. The speakers hummed as the bass notes pounded out and the feverish beating of my own heart, sought to outrace it. Weakened by illness and exhausted, I'd hauled myself out of bed every day to tend to the needs of the boys as Claude exhaled peacefully, his breath sending wafts of stale whisky around the bedroom. I don't know how I survived.

But this night I lay in the stillness and after about twenty minutes, I was aware of padded footsteps coming ever nearer and then the bed dipped as his weight sat on it. I had my back to him and made an effort to keep my breathing as natural as possible as if I was already asleep.

Perhaps my breathing hadn't fooled him.

Perhaps he wasn't bothered whether I was asleep or not.

I did not move.

I did not move as Claude grabbed me by my hair, tugging it downwards into the pillow.

I did not move as he used his free hand in one swift move to push my legs apart with such force that I'd no time to gasp before the pain I felt as he drove himself into me.

He was panting excitedly, saliva dribbling onto my cheek, as he swore, 'You bitch! You little bitch! That's what you like isn't it, you whore!'

And then the physical flood of his release was felt far away in some distant place, somewhere I'd never visit, a remote island where all suffering dwells. I willed it out of sight, forcing it over distant horizon in my mind, rendering it invisible to the human eye. If I couldn't see it, maybe one day I'd believe it never happened.

Satiated, physical constraint lifted as Claude pushed himself away from me, rolled on to his other side and quickly fell asleep. Shaking in the darkness, I realised I'd been holding my breath and I fought to regulate a sudden, continuous need to gasp for air. Frozen into a tightly curled foetal position, I blinked into the dead of night.

And I was still in the foetal position, as I gave into the overwhelming, giant wave of nothingness and the oblivion of numbness.

Blinking silently.

Blinking silently.

Blinking silently.

And all the while, begging the blackness to come to dissolve and extinguish my very being.

Chapter 38

I functioned.

In the months that followed I functioned because I needed to for the sake of the boys. It remained a blur, the nothingness keeping it that way and the numbness helping me to cope with each day. It helped when we had visitors, especially staying guests because it meant Claude was put under pressure and I liked to think he suffered whilst trying to maintain his Jekyll character. I liked to think that he'd had an inner battle with himself which would consequently inflict some element of pain on him. I hoped he'd crack and show himself to others in his pure evil glory, to let the world see what he was really like, to let his doting sister in particular, experience what he was capable of. She'd already accused me of being overly sensitive so I knew anything I said would fall on deaf ears.

Hoping I might receive a more empathic response, I approached JC when he was busy sorting out the pool water chemicals in his garage. However, it seemed that I'd completely misjudged him. With a cold bluntness and scathing tone, he dismissively told me that Claude was a difficult person for anyone to get on with and I should have thought of that before marrying him and having his child. Perhaps he'd already known about Claude's extremes of behaviour. Did this explain why Josie and Claude were so adamant I should conceal my pregnancy from him? Why had he not been so brutally honest with me on that occasion, as he had so many a time, with so many others? It made uncanny sense now. The odds were against me. At the end of the day, loyalty was the clear favourite but betrayal was there at the photo finish.

I'd like to have given him the benefit of the doubt. I wondered if his reaction might have been different had he witnessed the scene that unravelled one tea time.

As Owen was diabetic, it was vital that he followed the strict regime of eating twenty minutes after his insulin injection. To not adhere to this could prove fatal. On this occasion, for no reason at all, Claude swooped in to victoriously remove Owen's plate as it was placed on the table in front of him.

Would JC have continued to be a bystander when Claude said, "Now let's watch you go into a coma"?

I knew that as his mother, I would make matters worse if I intervened. Bitter experience had shown me that if I stood up to Claude in defence of my boys, their punishment would double in its intensity. So, paralysed by this fact, I stared mutely watching with increasing horror, as the fear mounted in my son's eyes. I knew he was beseeching me to protect him, to do the job a mother is supposed to do. I hated the man who could be so cruel but I despised myself more for being such a failure. The winning card was weakness and we needed to play it for all it was worth, despite inwardly battling with the premise that it would be our saviour. Claude was feasting on the horror in our eyes as he starved my son of life-saving food.

The clock on the wall chanted a solitary death march, marking time and punctuating the eerie silence as if prompting a 'flip a coin' gamble with my son's life.

Tick – life.

Tock – death.

Tick – life.

Tock – death.

It echoed in my ears, swirling into the winding tunnel deep within my thinking, where a voice was already planning practicalities. She was like a stranger – calm, composed and ready to act. The other person within me had already thought about the essential glucose gel and its exact location. She had already calculated the number of steps it would take in order to reach the fridge and the time it would take to twist the top off the bottle and squeeze its liquid contents into the mouth of the little one. She had processed what would be needed, faced with the possibility that she would be dealing with her child's convulsions as he first fitted uncontrollably, prior to losing consciousness. She knew she would need the orange plastic box that held the emergency glucagon kit. She rehearsed in her mind how to mix the content of the syringe with the powder in the vial. It would save valuable time which would otherwise be wasted by reading through all the instructions that were folded neatly inside the box. All the while, the person within me was secretly plotting my next move. The eyes that met Owen's across the six feet that separated us, silently communicated to him, vowing vehemently, *"I've got this. I will not let you die."*

I would not let him die, just as I would not challenge Claude and make matters worse. I would be quiet and subservient.

The noise of the clock was now resonating urgently louder.

Life, death; life, death.

Tom's knife made a scraping sound, cutting across the china glaze of his plate as he lifted the morsel of meat to his mouth. His action was Owen's salvation. He knew how Claude's psychopathy operated and that this move was an indication of his conformity. It recognised the perpetrator's unchallenged superiority by which we were rendered mute. As if satiated, having feasted on our fear, Claude topped up his wine glass and left the room, closing the door behind him, signalling an end to his latest attack.

Relief flooded over us and I rushed to get Owen's tea placed in front of him and to tell him how the word *brave* would never be enough to describe what he'd endured.

I wondered what JC would have said when he saw Morgan being force-fed in his high chair as we stared in undisguised horror, as Claude pinched his nose, the effect forcing Morgan to open his mouth and Claude ramming the food-laden fork into it mercilessly.

Mealtimes were the only occasion when we met as a family unit. They should have been a relaxed and social affair with the sharing of news – something to look forward to. Instead, we faced the meal table with a sense of impending fear and dread.

Would JC have lost his usual appetite for food had he been a guest, sitting at our table? Of course, Claude would never hit Morgan repeatedly around the head in the presence of a visitor. No one witnessed Claude's intolerance of the eighteen-month-old infant's inability to hold a knife and fork properly. Instead, lashings of deceit smiled radiantly to the world outside, whilst the truth was reserved for our eyes only. Numbed to each unravelling, we were conditioned to remain gagged and unresponsive.

No longer reactive to the raised hand that found relief in its pent-up frustration, each slap to Morgan's head echoed around our holding cell. Only the stark walls bore witness but remained the silent, insentient keepers of secrets. Bricks and mortar don't talk!

No longer reactive to Claude hurling Morgan from his highchair and through the open doorway onto his cot bed because he was banging his fork on his food tray.

No longer reactive to the fact that any inaccuracy in Claude's throwing technique could prove fatal.

Resistance was futile. Over the months I learnt that no reaction proved to be the best reaction. The consequences of reacting would be considerably graver and this meant Claude was confident that the torture within, remained exclusively a family affair.

Morgan was programmed to expect the worst when he inadvertently got his hands dirty. Had no one ever thought to question his screams when he found he had sand on his palms whilst playing on the beach? Morgan's experience of the beach was devoid of the joy of building sandcastles. Would JC or anyone else ever know that those screams came from a deep-seated fear of what would happen to him next?

Claude sniggered when I asked that we install a stair gate. He openly laughed when Morgan fell down the wooden stairs. Oblivious to the coldness permeating up from the tiled floor, I sat rocking him cradled in my arms. Despite every effort to comfort and console my son, I felt an overwhelming sense of defeat on my part. Sickened by my shortcomings as a mother. Nothing but a wretched failure. The moment for protecting and shielding my son had long since gone. Left only with a metaphorical comfort blanket in which to wrap him like an afterthought woven with remorse. An indisputable weave that read; my culpability; my cowardice; my fault.

'He has learnt now,' smirked Claude, 'he won't do it again.'

JC had always affectionately referred to Owen as *O-ven* when pronouncing his name. It was because of this mischievous gentleness that I thought about JC now.

Why would he ignore his obvious love for my son by saying nothing? For all his bravado, was he just a coward underneath, incapable of doing the right thing? Why would he not breach family loyalties to stand up for what was right?

It reviled me to recall the obscene abuse inflicted on Owen when he had simply asked Claude to pass him tomato ketchup at the dinner table. A simple request with a polite 'please'. Claude did more than simply pass him the bottle. He took it upon himself to upturn the sugar-filled contents all over Owen's food, before proceeding to oversee the clearing of the plate, each mouthful sending my son's sugar levels rocketing out of control. The inane suffering he inflicted on my child, deepened my sense of self-loathing, as I detested myself for being so pathetically useless. All I could do was to ensure Owen had an additional dose of insulin to compensate for the sugar which was already dangerously surging through his little body. Another injection piercing his skin that in normal circumstances would never have been needed. But these were not normal circumstances. Stranded in a foreign land, control continued to invade and flourish, allowing fear to gain an ever-increasing territorial stronghold.

How would my potential ally JC have reacted if he'd witnessed nine-year-old Tom being forced to clean around the u-bend of the toilet with his bare hands? All the while, Claude smiled in the satisfaction of knowing that he had debased Tom to a level of feeling he was worth no more than the excrement that his small hands wiped from the toilet's walls. When Tom allegedly failed to meet the expectations of the task, what would JC have thought on seeing him forced to stand for twenty minutes fully clothed, under the relentless sting of a high-pressure shower, leaving him shaking with cold and self-loathing?

On the other hand, I did not matter. I was the ragdoll he could play with at his convenience, shaken, hit or with a fist held to my face as he exercised his greed for authority and lusted after my fear response.

There were dark nights when he'd wait for me to haul the chest of drawers across the door to the downstairs bedroom I'd moved into to sleep, hoping that the physical barricade would keep me safe. Dry-mouthed, I hovered shakily on the other side of the door, listening in anticipation for the words I knew would follow. Slithering as they were spoken, they infiltrated my temporary sanctuary.

Laced with venom, they hissed, 'Yes. I would do that if I were you. You certainly have every reason to feel scared.'

I wondered how JC would react if I told him that I'd lost my self-respect, that it was submerged somewhere alongside my self-worth in a musty discarded pile of yesterday's news. I'd replaced it by mastering the art of masquerading like a wanton tart as a pitiful means of obtaining Claude's approval. I could attend functions with him, pimping myself, knowing I'd get the flirtatious attention of other men. It was guaranteed to get Claude's attention. I paraded the 'Lady Dee' look to perfection with the tilt of the head and the shy upward glancing eyes. At gatherings, everyone apart from the green-eyed females adored Lady Diana and I shamelessly played the part to my advantage.

Weight was dropping off me and having been a size twelve, I was now wearing clothes for a size eight and some of those were hanging off me. Beneath the phoney smile, I felt nothing but contempt for the arrogant, flirty French men who vied for my attention. They disgusted me and I despised Claude for making me feel that way.

I wondered how an onlooker would have responded to the events during the evening when Claude spent three hours on a slow drip, drip technique, as we were forced to sit, huddling together on the sofa listening to him. He paced up and down the sitting room, a carving knife gripped menacingly in his right hand. Surreptitiously I whispered to the boys to sit still, to not make any sort of response and to just let him rant unchallenged. It was too dangerous to provoke the tirade of this deranged figure. Whilst we sat in watchful silence, he told the boys what a terrible mother they had, how she was a whore that slept with any man, and how she was psychologically disturbed. I noticed Tom shot a look at Claude and opened his mouth defiantly to say something. I squeezed his knee with my hand as a gesture to keep quiet and thankfully he did. Although, Claude's words were scathing, I was not unduly perturbed because as long as his anger was aimed at my failings, he was leaving the boys alone.

However, perhaps due to lack of reaction, he changed tack and raising the carving knife above his head, he sunk it with full force into the top of the nearby work unit. Everyone jolted in terror of his action.

Assured of now having our undivided attention, he continued, 'You may think that you are able to escape from here.'

He laughed derisively. 'I don't think so. Your bitch of a mother will be running out of money and she will not be able to claim anything in France.'

Picking up a loose piece of paper which was the French equivalent of the Child Benefit entitlement, he ripped it into shreds before we watched the pieces fall like autumnal leaves to the cold of the floor-tiled earth.

'Soon you will have nothing. You will have to rely on me for your scraps.'

Tom looked truly fearful. Being the eldest, there was no doubt he understood the bile that was spewing from the familiar form of Claude's alter ego. Owen was staring at the twelve-inch knife blade, the indoor lighting reflecting menacingly off its well-honed metal edge. Morgan snuggled closer into my lap, as the sneering voice continued.

'And so you may plan to escape. And what will you use? Ah... The car of course! I can tell you now that you won't get very far. The car will veer off the road into a ditch and you will all be found dead. No one will ask questions. It will just be seen as an unfortunate accident.'

He waited for the impact of his words to settle before performing his final *pièce de résistance*, 'You see, I know a lot about cars and I know exactly what I need to do under the bonnet. You will not know. You will not be aware that there is a fault.'

With an oozing, saccharine smile he departed, whisking the car keys off their hook as he went, before disappearing into the night.

We knew he'd gone, but we didn't know when he'd be coming back. The four of us moved into my bedroom to feel safer and to get away from the place where we'd been trapped for three hours. We sat in a show of solidarity on my bed, like a scene from a macabre version of the *'Sound of Music'*. It wasn't the drama of a ferocious thunderstorm battling outside our windows that brought us together for comfort. This was not the time for singing about *'favourite things'* in order to deflect from the horror of what had taken place. Instead, it was a simple primal fear response – a huddling together of four petrified souls in a bid to increase our chances of survival.

Chapter 39

Can you imagine the guilt and the paranoia?

The guilt for being responsible for putting my children in harm's way in the first place, and laced with a dose of daily fear that something dreadful was going to happen to them. Claude hadn't been back to the house and it was now three days since he'd left. I thought about using the landline and calling Moira in England but fear stopped me. What if he'd bugged the phone? What if he had secretly got monitors installed to track our every conversation and every movement? It was certainly conceivable, after all, given his tech knowhow, he was capable of anything. So, we stayed put and tried our utmost to carry on as normal. Thankfully, there were sufficient supplies in the fridge and freezer to keep us going and I could always buy essentials from the village. Having said that, I didn't want to go out into the world. I wanted to hide.

No one called, no one phoned. We were left alone.

I thought about finding the key for the file box and taking the passports but again, paranoia got in the way. I had visions of Claude putting strands of hair across the box opening, like they do in the spy films, which would show it had been tampered with. I was worried I might not be able to re-arrange everything back into the correct position if I rummaged through likely places to find the keys.

We sat tight and we waited.

On the evening of the third night, Claude returned. He came into the kitchen, and like a devoted father, scooped Morgan up in his arms as he told him that he'd missed him. I noticed that Morgan did not lean into his father's embrace and that nothing could belie the look of wariness in his eyes. He was glad to be planted back on the floor and immediately ran over to me, to cling to my legs.

'I have seen Henri,' announced Claude and I wondered if this great friend of his had mentioned anything about paying me back the money I'd lent him.

'He has a new girlfriend called Martine. They are going to dance classes together and they get on very well. I told Martine that I'd been to Cornwall and she was interested to hear about life in the country over there. I think they're planning to take a trip to England soon.'

This was my window of opportunity. A serendipitous moment which I grabbed with both hands, clinging to it for all I was worth. When you have already lost everything, you have a great deal to gain. Like a ladder of hope tossed into a dark well of despair, I launched myself onto its bottom rung and hung on. This was the first step of my long ascent towards light and freedom; I couldn't afford to let go.

'That sounds great Claude.' I smiled. 'Wouldn't it be marvellous if we could all go together? We could show them our Cornwall perhaps.'

And he bought it. He bought it hook, line and sinker. I'd known it would appeal to his need to feel important and what better way than to make him the expert? He could parade himself around as the Gallic Rooster strutting his knowledge of the local area, displaying his expertise to his dear friends. Let him showcase his superiority. Let him believe he was a leading authority on the topic of my Cornwall. Let him be unwittingly snared in the web I now weaved. I relished the thought of being the one to now trap him for once; to lure him into providing us with an opening to escape back to England. Back to safety. Back to home.

I reflected my sense of elation in the music I chose to put on the CD player whilst I prepared the evening meal. I fished out my Cornish Male Voice Choir album that had been buried under the stack of compilations of French music. Patricia Kaas looked up at me from her monochrome cover and I fleetingly smiled as I thought back to the time I first heard her sing when I met Claude. My life was so very different now. In the whirlwind of falling in love, I'd pitied the woman who sang about a man who played her for a fool, but loved him regardless. Now, I almost envied her and her ability to make light of the way she was treated. I would never be able to do that; the emotions ran too deep. If only life was as simple as black and white instead of the perplexing undertones of grey ambiguity. Maybe we shared the need to be loved and the false hope that it was somehow attainable. And with that, I consciously placed Patricia Kaas' album at the bottom of the pile, where she would stay firmly out of sight.

I heard the spin of the disc and selected the track that felt most symbolic to me. It was one I listened to on many an occasion when Claude was away as it was then that I allowed my yearning for home to surface. This time, however, it would be different. This time I would listen and sing along to it, knowing the title 'Take me Home' was soon to become a desperate long yearned for reality. A sense of quiet elation grew in my stomach as I listened to the Cornish choir, their voices combining to gently build into a powerful crescendo as one verse flowed into the next.

My voice wavered momentarily as I strove to sing these now monumental words. By singing them, I was bringing my reality closer, the reality that we were going to escape, that there really would be an end to it all. I told myself I had to keep singing. Then the chorus began like a triumphant promise of everything which mattered to me; my homeland, and my place of peace.

'Take me home...'

I managed in a voice that sounded so lost, so distant and so very far away, before it fell apart, splintering into jagged, and half choking whispers as I fought to stay with it until the end.

> *'....to my family,*
> *take me home to my friends,*
> *take me home where my heart lies,*
> *and let me, let me sing again.'*

Pulling out the oven rack, blinking repeatedly in order to try and keep my eyes focused, I basted the roast chicken I was cooking. As the fat spat angrily at me, bubbling up like a series of small geysers from the bottom of the pan, I felt someone gently place a hand on my shoulder. I turned around expectantly, but the only presence was the voices of the choir as they launched into a rousing rendition of *'Trelawney'*, but not before the distinct aroma of the long-forgotten Butter Lady filled the air. With the tea towel that I used as oven gloves thrown over my left shoulder, I sank to the floor on my knees, tears rolling unreservedly and silently down my cheeks.

'Please help me, please help me,' I cried inwardly.

I was so alone, so far away from home. There was no one to whom I could turn. No one to rescue me. Isolated and captive on foreign soil, my only solace was to turn to what others would call an 'imaginary friend'. But the derision of others no longer mattered, I might indeed be going mad – I was beyond rationality and caring. All that mattered in that moment was the Butter Lady knew I needed help. Falling into a fortress of warmth I allowed the buttery blanket of comfort to envelop me. As the feeling of complete desolation and despair waned, so it dawned on me that there had to be hope and I'd already planted those seeds earlier in the day.

I would get home to Cornwall.

Unlike the tragedy that befell the Butter Lady, I would write a different ending.

I would see the return of my men folk.

They would go back to their homeland.

Whilst we were all alive, all was not lost.

What had just happened was a sign that I was never truly alone.

I would write my own pages for a happy ending to our story.

I now had something to believe in; a catalyst for renewed hope.

My foot was already firmly planted on the first rung of the ladder that precariously hung in the well. It was time to take the next risky next step up, knowing the window of opportunity would become more tangible with every tread I made.

All I had to do now was to find that inner strength to guide us home to safety.

Chapter 40

December 2002

In early December, Claude confirmed his friend Henri and girlfriend were free to holiday in Cornwall towards the end of the month. Having looked at the costings, Claude announced we'd fly to London Stanstead from Montpellier on 28th December and take a connecting flight the following morning on down to Newquay. That was the only option as it was cheaper to do that than to take the ferry. I was released from my mundane household duties to be tasked with booking and paying for the flights. The passports were duly released from the constraints of the locked file box, as if on home curfew, just for sufficient time to enable me to complete the passenger information on the online booking forms, prior to being locked away again. For the brief time I held the red shiny covers in my hand, I felt as I imagine a prisoner might feel when the jailer dangles the keys through the bars of the cell, teasingly hinting at freedom as the inmate samples the cold of the keys on eager, outstretched fingertips. So near and yet so far. Tantalisingly close.

The sense of excitement generated at the thought of going back to Cornwall far outweighed that of a visit from Santa. Perhaps it was in part because we also recalled our last Christmas in France and it was far from merry. The boys and I made a token gesture to decorate the house, more for Morgan's sake than anyone else's. I was preoccupied in my own thoughts. Excitement for the forthcoming visit was tainted by the fact that because we would not be using the ferry, my dogs, Milly and Shadow would have to remain behind. I dreaded the thought of leaving them. They needed rescuing too and I was hoping that by traveling via by ferry, I'd secure their escape route. It was not to be. So I resigned myself to the fact that I had to prioritise our safety and I couldn't let anything jeopardise our one chance of escape. With great reluctance, a heavy heart and an overwhelming sense of guilt, I arranged for Annie, one of our neighbours to look after them in my absence, knowing she'd bestow ample armfuls of love on them. Annie had an elderly Spaniel herself and I had a feeling she'd be taking my two back with her and allowing them to sleep in their house. Annie was one of the few people I knew I could trust. She would not let me down.

Christmas Day passed like any other day of the year. It felt like *déjà vu*. We'd all been here before. A repeat performance of last years Christmas dinner. Claude, knowing the boys yearned for turkey or chicken, arrived back from his sole supermarket visit, laden with another salmon. None of us had the strength to challenge his choice. I was convinced this was yet another one from Claude's repertoire of tactics, designed to lure us in and take the bait. We made a determined effort not to rise to it. Tom and Owen poked at the fleshy flakes of cooked fish, moving them around the plate, delaying having to eat them. I attempted a diversion tactic by remarking on the delightful buttery flavour of the new potatoes, hoping to prompt the reluctant boys into taking a mouthful. But Claude had noticed and it was already too late. He leapt from his chair, hurling his knife, fork and lighter at the square oak table top. Everyone jumped. Picking up his chair, he threw it against the opposite wall, swore loudly and stormed from the room, slamming the door behind him, leaving us to continue in a hushed and fearful silence, any morsel of appetite, now completely extinguished. Left overs were consigned to the darkness of the pedal bin, as were any other thoughts of rejoicing.

The boys and I spent the remainder of the day in one side of the house, the door firmly closed between us and Claude and sadly, also between their new toys that sat, untouched on the other side of the wall. No one ventured to open the slammed door. It also closed down any conversation for the next couple of days. Claude recommenced conversation with us on the afternoon of the day of our departure. It sickened me to note that this was only due to the imminent arrival of his travelling companions and it disgusted me to hear him later relay to them what a wonderful Christmas he'd spent with his son and family.

Standing on the terrace it was even harder than I imagined it could be. The dogs dogs, sensing something in the air, were waiting expectantly, meandering around the suitcases, sniffing at their bulging forms. They seemed to be on edge, not able to settle and I was sure this was because they remembered of old that they would be included on any outing from home. I swallowed hard and rubbed my beloved Shadow behind her ears in her favourite place and kissed her on the top of her head. Then I gave Milly one of my double handed scratches on her back, just in front of her back legs, making her wriggle her hips from side to side in pleasure.

'See you soon dog-lings.'

And as we trailed out through the side gate, towing

a succession of suitcases, I saw eyes full of questioning, following my receding steps.

'I will be back for you. I am not leaving you. I promise I will come get you,' I silently spoke with my eyes, imploring them to believe me, hoping that they understood and trusting that I would be true to my word.

And with that, I closed the gate and took my first step towards my journey home.

Chapter 41

29th December 2002

I'd been waiting for this moment ever since we boarded the plane from Stansted. It was the sight of my homeland stretching out a limb of greeting as I stared, transfixed out of the window. Tiny clusters forming a myriad of lights, twinkled far below me, shining a welcoming beacon as if in celebration of my return. Darkness was descending but not too fast to allow me to make out the south coast around St Austell, before turning inland and crossing the outlines of the clay tips, whilst glimpsing the granite landmarks of St Agnes Beacon and Carn Brae to the west. Finally I saw the cluster of lights that was Newquay. It was as if they were guiding more than just the plane homeward and my heart rose with joy. Soon our feet would be touching Cornish soil.

Half an hour later we were walking through the tiny homely airport arrivals area, only to be greeted by three very familiar faces, one with eyes smiling through his glasses, another with a glow of red hair and the third and smallest of the welcome party, being restrained from running towards us, by his father's firm hand on his shoulder. It was the Wright family. But where was Moira?

Greetings and introductions made for the benefit of Claude's companions, I looked quizzically at Phil.

'Moira's had to go up north. She's sorry she's missed you,' he said. 'She sends her love to you and the boys though,' he added.

'Oh.' I was lost for words but now wasn't the time for me to start probing into the whys and wherefores. For the moment, it was more than sufficient, more beyond my wildest imaginings just to know we'd made it home.

I busied myself with the task of hiring a rental vehicle which could seat all seven of us. A short while later, we left the airport in convoy, following the tail lights of Phil's car back to his home in Perranporth where we'd staying for the next five days. As we descended the hill from the east side, down into the seaside town, I saw the blaze of Christmas decorations lining the main street. There was a salty tinge to the air and as we took our cases out of the boot to trundle them up to the front door, I could hear the distant breaking of waves carried inland on the late December wind. In unison, Owen and I halted on the doorstep, as with sudden delight, realisation dawned. It was mizzling; true Cornish mizzle. I'd never thought it possible to have missed it so much. Simultaneously, we were laughing delightedly and grinning widely at each other, as if in mutual appreciation of a shared joke. Standing side by side on the doorstep in the darkness we tilted our heads skywards, letting the drops of rain, fine as fairies' tears, tickle our faces as if baptising our homecoming. A shared and truly magical moment.

'I've really missed this,' Owen announced; a statement which sounded like he was genuinely surprised to be making it.

'So have I, Owen. I've really missed it too,' I echoed, realising that it was not only the feel of the fine rain on my skin but also the sound of my child's laughter and it further underlined my determination not to go back to France.

We needed to be here.

We needed to be safe.

We needed to be free to laugh.

We needed to be free to stand like a couple of idiots on the doorstep in the rain if we chose.

We simply needed to be free.

Surely it wasn't too much to ask?

Chapter 42

January 3rd 2003

Time passed far too quickly. I couldn't believe it was our last day and we were due to be catching the flight back to France the following morning. As the time ticked by, it was like a countdown; a countdown to the conversation I knew I had to have with Claude. The conversation which would inform him we wouldn't be returning with him but would remain in England. I wondered if he could sense my unease that was growing with every passing moment. It proved difficult to get an the opportunity to speak with him on his own as he was so wrapped up in showing Henri and Martine all the Cornish sights.

One evening, we'd taken Courtney with us to see the magic of the Christmas lights in the harbour at Mousehole. Having marvelled at the display, we ordered some food in the local pub. Courtney sat, enjoying his fish and chip supper, clad in his aged sou'westers, his trousers tied firmly at the waist with an unruly piece of frayed orange binder twine. I'd made a mental note of the scene in my head, Courtney, the old timer, steaming in front of the roaring fire, a small puddle forming around his feet where he sat, as the rain dripped off his yellow waterproofs. With each sip from his half pint of shandy, his face had become even more ruddy than usual, as the unfamiliar tang of alcohol on his tongue, awakened a new found confidence for conversation.

He'd held court with the bemused huddle of water-logged French visitors. Whether they were in awe of the content of his conversation or struggling to translate his broad Cornish dialect, remained a mystery. I smiled lovingly at him as I watched him dole out a regular supply of chips to an eager little Morgan, who was pulled up firmly alongside him in his pushchair. It was particularly pertinent because I witnessed my youngest son using his fingers to eat. No sign of fear, despite his greasy, squashed potato fists. Morgan had been oblivious to the fact that he was actively defying Claude by breaking one of the major mealtime laws. Seeing this moment of pure uninhibited enjoyment was a memory that'd stay with me, firming my resolve to take the necessary action.

However, I'd still not mustered the courage to speak to Claude. I'd kidded myself into believing there hadn't been an opportune moment. In truth, it'd felt too risky. The consequences of daring to voice my intentions kept me prisoner of my thoughts, leaving time to continue to slip through my fingers. As one day merged with the next, the ticking of the clock in my head, grew faster and louder.

Time passed all too soon. It was now the last day of our visit to Cornwall and I felt sick with fear, in the knowledge that every passing hour was backing me further and further into a corner. Claude had decided we'd all go for a coastal walk. He was eager to show Henri and Martine more of what he referred to as 'mon petit pays', my little country. His words exuded such arrogance and facetiousness, that I seethed every time I heard the phrase.

As we walked across the deserted beach, I was drawn to the unusually vast expanse of sand, exposed by the particularly low tide. It was an uncanny reflection of my own circumstances. When would I ever get the chance to see Cornwall again? Wasn't this a unique window of opportunity waiting to be optimised, enabling my truths which had lain submerged, to finally be uncovered and exposed? Yet tide and time wait for nobody, so unless I acted soon, our chance of freedom would be lost. With this thought in mind, I quickened my pace to catch up with the others who were starting the ascent up a steep path away from the beach.

The old engine houses perched precariously close to the edge of the cliffs their jagged outcrops, subjected to the endless Atlantic swells. Standing on the windswept, desolate piece of coastline, in the distance, St Ives was temporarily obscured by another deep rain cloud sweeping in mercilessly from the southwest. As it dropped its deluge over the sea, a rising sense of panic engulfed me. How long had I got before the tide turned? I was on borrowed time. In an attempt to strengthen my resolve, I focussed on the unyielding terrain, whose rust-coloured fragments of rock, lay in sharpened fragments at my feet.

I vowed silently, *'You have to tell him tonight.'* The voice inside me continued, *'You can't go on endlessly putting it off. You've got to do it when there are other people around so it'll give you the best chance of staying safe.'*

Desperate to reassure myself I resorted to playing a game in my head that had always proved a good omen in the past. I would challenge myself to do or find something within a certain timeframe and if successful it would signify the result I was seeking.

In this instance, I told myself, 'If you find a piece of quartz on the ground within the next ten paces, everything will be OK.'

Ten paces didn't give much leeway. I briefly wondered if I could re-negotiate the goal posts but decided against it in case making last minute changes jinxed the outcome. Ten paces it was. Fleetingly, the thought passed through my head that I might be psychologically deranged. Who in their right mind would believe their future depended on the success of this little game? I exhaled loudly, and started to walk, scanning the ground as I went, sweeping it with my eyes hoping to detect the glint of quartz. The seventh step had just been taken and I realised the odds were stacking up against me. From where I was standing I could already see the remaining three strides were going to be non-productive. I should have changed the search to clinker instead. Clinker was the product of the early smelting of tin and it was far more prolific in this area making it far easier to find than quartz crystals. If only I'd chosen clinker, I'd have massively increased my chances of finding it and guaranteed my own victory. I'd already passed two burnished lumps of it. I'd chosen quartz because I thought it would stand out amongst the clumps of heather and discarded mine waste. Cursing myself for my poor choice, I stepped forward knowing those last three steps would prove me to be a loser.

'Mum! Mum! Look what I've found!' yelled an excited Thomas, as he charged precariously towards me over the uneven surface, his wellington boots making a disgruntled humph-type sound as the distance between us narrowed. He rattled to a halt and extended a tightly clasped hand towards me.

'What have you got there?' I asked him, my own preoccupations immediately forgotten.

'This!' he exclaimed triumphantly, as he uncurled his fist to reveal a small piece of rock, with an array of tiny multi-sized crystals haphazardly glinting in the evening light.

Thomas's excitement attracted everyone's attention, including the French contingent, who now turned away from the historic engine house with its spectacular coastal backdrop, to join us.

'Have you found some treasure Toma?' asked Henri in perfect English, albeit Thomas without the s.

'I think it's really rare,' replied Tom with gleeful conviction, obviously thrilled by his finding.

His victory was, however, short-lived.

'It's just a piece of rock,' sneered Claude dismissively.

Tom's head dropped.

'I think it's a very special piece of rock Tom,' I countered. 'Shall we keep it?'

Tom nodded a yes, gratefully.

'I'll put it in my pocket if you like to carry it back for you. It means you'll have your hands free to look for more treasure!' I smiled and he handed me his prized find.

We walked back towards the car, each of my steps closing the distance between me and the inevitable conversation when we got back to Phil's. With each step, I hoped the fact that Tom was the one to find the quartz, and not me, would still count. I was relying on it being a good omen and my only source of hope, indicating all would be ok when I dared to speak my truth to Claude.

Chapter 43

'Phil – I need to talk to you! I need to talk to you urgently,' I hissed as I passed him the ice cube tray from the freezer in the kitchen in readiness for the glasses of Pernod that he was pouring. We were in the kitchen and on our own. The others were sitting chatting in the lounge.

Phil looked up at me, stopped what he was doing, sensing the urgency in my voice. I now had his undivided attention. I had to be quick because someone could walk into the kitchen at any moment.

'Phil,' I hissed with a repeated sense of urgency. Now that I'd got his complete attention, I glanced rapidly in the direction of the doorway checking that it was all clear, before adding in a stealthy whisper, 'I'm not going back to France. I can't go back there.'

Phil raised his eyebrows before giving an 'I thought as much' smile showing he understood and had half expected to hear this. I frowned at him, momentarily, taken aback.

'Jan. It doesn't surprise me. I can see how he is with you and the boys. Just look at you! You've lost so much weight and I don't think it's due to a healthy life style. You're continually jittery. It's like you're nervous all the time – don't know what to say in case you say or do something to offend him. Moira would say the same if she was here.'

'Is that really how I come across?' I asked, catching myself glancing fearfully yet again, at the open doorway and fiddling mindlessly with a teaspoon on the draining board.

'Yes it is and you need to do something about it!'

'I've already started,' I hissed and then speaking rapidly, divulged, 'I phoned Annie earlier. She's the neighbour looking after the dogs in our absence. She's got a key to the house and I've told her to get the set of papers currently hidden in my bedroom drawer. Legal stuff that I can't allow Claude to find. She's going to post them to me.'

Phil nodded to show he was following my line of thought.

'There's no way that we're going back to France with him. I've got to tell him tonight! God knows what he'll do!'

It was Phil's turn now to check the doorway and I realised we were being too quiet and that the apparent stillness might appear suspicious, so I rattled the half-filled glasses together and said loudly, 'Ice in these Phil?'

He understood and replied, 'Yes, yes just put a couple of cubes in each one Jan and then show me how much water to top them up with.'

I smiled conspiratorially at him and he continued in a hushed tone, 'How many times are you going to get this opportunity? You're all here together. If you go back, he won't let you leave again. You have to make this count. This is your one chance to really escape. I'll back you all the way – you know that.'

'Thanks Phil. I'm so sorry about this.'

'No worries. I need to look out for my Little Sis,' he smiled back.

'Please stay up with me,' I pleaded, 'Don't go to bed.

Don't leave me on my own. I need you to be there when I tell him. I don't think he'll dare do anything if you're present.'

At that moment there was a shout from the lounge, demanding to know what was causing the delay in the preparation of the drinks. Phil nodded to show he was on board and we headed back to join the others as he called, 'On our way.'

Several hours of small talk later, and the whisky bottle was depleting at a rapid rate as Claude stood up to refill his glass for the umpteenth time. It seemed to be having the effect of relaxing him, allowing him to recount lengthy, detailed stories to his audience. Phil stifled a yawn and appeared to sink even further into the cushioned recesses of the sofa. As Claude continued with his latest spiel, Henri finally made his excuses and both he and Martine departed for their beds, on the pretext that they had a long journey ahead of them the following day. As they slinked out of the room, and Henri's hand slipped to cup the pert bottom wrapped in Martine's tweed mini skirt, I rather doubted either of them had sleep on their minds. I felt vaguely reviled by the whole idea. It accentuated my belief that men were self-assured predators. Tonight, everything would change. In a few moments I'd make it clear I'd not fall prey to Claude any longer It was a powerful feeling. It heralded an end to everything that we'd had to endure.

We would be free.

We would be free if I could just stop rehearsing what I was going to say in my head.

We would be free if I could just find my voice but it seemed to be lurking, half hidden and I was struggling to tempt it to come out.

Inwardly, I cursed myself for being a coward. Phil was looking at me as if willing me to speak and I realised the room had fallen silent and that Claude had finally paused for a self-righteous, whisky-embalmed breath.

It was now or never and the latter was not an option. The tide had already turned and was starting to come in. I cast a quick 'don't leave me', glance at Phil, who briefly raised his eyebrows at me, as if to say 'go on' and so as Claude realised his glass was empty once again, and made to get up to refill it, I began.

'Claude. I need to tell you something. I know you won't be expecting this but, I'm not going back to France with you. I am staying here with the boys.'

There – I'd said it. It was out in the open. It couldn't be unsaid. I had fired a direct hit with words which couldn't be misinterpreted.

Silence.

I waited.

Phil waited.

Nothing.

Having launched the missile, I was waiting for the anticipated explosion. Had my words landed wide of the mark?

No reaction at all.

My target remained untouched; no sign of any impact damage. Claude simply got up, made a joke about how he was perhaps enjoying his whisky rather too quickly, and how he planned to visit a Scottish distillery in the near future. Topping up his glass, he smiled fleetingly at Phil and me before proceeding to talk about his favourite blends. It was as if I'd never said a word. Puzzled looks passed fleetingly between Phil and myself, neither of us understanding what had just happened. It was as if I didn't exist, as if life would just continue and the world would continue to revolve. Perhaps he thought so little of me that it didn't merit a response. I tried again.

'Claude – I'm not sure if you've understood what I've

just said,' I started with a view to re-iterating my previous lines, but he cut me short.

'I am not interested,' he replied, waving a dismissive right arm in an upward motion, like swatting away a small cloud of irritating flies and turning his back on me, putting a physical end to the conversation.

There was no point in trying to say anything more because I knew I would be ignored. I also knew I'd said what needed to be said and so he was now fully aware of my plans because I'd been open with him. It'd been up to him to choose how to react to the news and I was quite sure he'd have reacted very differently without Phil as witness. It proved he didn't care whether we were there or not. With this in mind, I dared to tell myself that my decision to remain in England with my sons, might remain unchallenged.

It didn't sit comfortably with me. It had been all too easy. It wasn't in Claude's nature to be amicable. He'd retaliate somehow. Obsessed by his need to control, there was no way, he'd just quietly roll over. It could never be that simple. He'd already be plotting his attack. I needed to be ready. I needed to anticipate his next move so I was armed to defend us. I'd not leave him any room to manipulate me this time. This time I needed to outwit him. He wouldn't manipulate me this time. Rising from my seat, I smiled a mockingly sincere smile in Claude's direction, wished Phil goodnight and I retreated to the bedroom.

Pulling the duvet up over me as it could give me a sense of safety and protection, I lay listening to the gentle sounds of Morgan breathing across the room, waiting for the dreaded door to open, announcing Claude's arrival, filling me with fear.

And the door did open later, the light from the hallway, temporarily casting its light on the suitcases which lay packed in the corner, ready for departure. But there were no words, just silence. It was a silence that dismissed any need for understandings, a silence that ended any hope of communication. It was a silence that put everything that we'd ever had between us, firmly to bed.

Chapter 44

January 4th 2003 – Cornwall

I waited in terrified stillness as the hours passed one by one and daylight finally arrived. Normally, mornings are my favourite part of the day. They brim with new beginnings. This day however, rather than embracing a fresh start, I was terrified at the thought of it.

It was just after 7.30 am and from my bed, I could hear movements and creaks from the floor boards upstairs alerting me to the fact that the lads were awake in the large attic bedroom. Cautiously, I pushed back the covers from my side of the bed, tiptoeing passed a slumbering Morgan and a husband who snored gently. I climbed up the narrow staircase, heading for the attic bedroom and as I opened the door, Tom and Owen immediately sat up, wrapped like little sleepy caterpillars in their navy sleeping bags. Tom's hair was doing its normal tousled blonde curly 'welcoming the morning in any direction' creation, whilst Owen's was the complete opposite – dark and unruffled. Apart from their shared passion for Pokémon cards, the one thing that really united the two boys showing the world they were brothers, was their blue eyes! It was these eyes that pleaded with me before any words were spoken and I knew my plan had to go ahead. I would not let my boys down again. I picked my way carefully across the room, skirting the still sleeping mounds of Chris and Jake, over abandoned clothing and last night's midnight feast wrappers and discarded PlayStation controllers until I could kneel on the floor alongside my sons.

'Listen boys. I have a plan,' I started.

But before I could say more, both boys spoke in unison.

'We don't have to go back to France, do we Mum?'

Then Owen added, 'Please don't let us go back. I want to stay here.'

'Me too,' echoed Tom.

'It's OK. That's why I've come to see you before Claude wakes up. I know you don't want to go back. I don't want to go back either and so this is our one chance to escape. It means we are going to be in a REAL adventure!'

'Are we goodies or baddies?' asked Owen, leaning forward, eager to be getting into character.

'We're the goodies of course! And just remember, it always works out OK for the goodies in the end doesn't it!' I hoped I sounded suitably convincing as I said it. 'Now listen lads. Listen carefully.'

Seeing that I'd got both boys' undivided attention, in hushed tones, I went on to explain, 'I'm going to give you all our passports – that's mine, your two and Morgan's. You have to hide the passports in the front pocket of your hoody Tom. Then I want you and Owen to go with Chris and Jake to the sweet shop. I know I don't normally give you money for sweets, but on this occasion, I'm making an exception. Turning around, two sets of eyes were looking eagerly in my direction, as Chris and Jake joined my attentive audience.

'Hey – someone mention sweets?' said a gruff voice from behind me. Turning around, two sets of eyes were looking eagerly in my direction, as Chris and Jake joined my attentive audience. Jake's ability to act as a radar at the mention of sweets, had stirred him into action!

'I did,' I replied. 'You boys have got to be really clever secret agents in the next hour. We'll need to get some toast or cereal sorted for you for breakfast, just as normal. We don't want Claude to become suspicious. He'd think it strange if any of you gannets suddenly stopped eating! I'll find a way of getting the passports to you – they are in my handbag at the moment. Then the four of you can set off on your special mission. Oh! And something very important that I forgot – we need to agree on a rendezvous! You'll just have to wait for me because I can't give you a definite time. I'll be as quick as possible though. Wait for me over by the boating lake and I'll come and collect you in the hire car. Remember boys, look out for a silver one. Chris and Jake, I'm sorry but you'll have to walk home once I pick the others up. It's not far, as you know, but I can't risk driving you back.'

'No point escaping, only to go back to the place you've just escaped from,' said Jake in his usual to-the-point, matter-of-fact way which was beyond his years as a five-year-old. Jake always had a way of bringing a smile to any moment, however dire it might seem at the time. I was grateful for his voice of reason and more to the point, if a five-year-old could remain calm, then so should I.

'OK boys. Let's go! See you for breakfast once you're all washed and dressed.'

I added the last bit with a hint of drama in my own voice. I needed to convince myself I'd be able to carry this off. I gave the boys what I hoped was a confident, broad 'we can do this' smile and turned to go back downstairs to play my part. As I did so, I heard Owen eagerly asking the others if he should be wearing his combat trousers. I hoped to goodness they could handle what was expected of them. It was vital. Descending the stairs, I was met at the bottom by a little lad in Spiderman pyjamas and red wellies and Doggy tucked firmly under his left arm.

'Hello Mr Morgs! Have you got your special new wellies on?'

My heart melted at the comical sight of him standing proudly in his new footwear. One pyjama leg was caught on his welly top making it appear shorter than the other. He'd put his boots on the wrong feet giving me the impression his legs would take off in opposite directions to each other.

Morgan reached his arms out to me and I scooped him up for one of our special hugs.

'I'm glad you like your new wellies Morgs. You've done really well to get them on all by yourself!'

I couldn't help but admire his determined efforts. I'd bought them for him whilst shopping in Truro but he'd not had the chance to wear them to go puddle sploshing outside. Carrying Morgan into the lounge I popped him on the sofa.

'We don't want to wake Papa as he's still sleeping,' I said. 'You wait here and I'll get your clothes and some socks to go underneath those wellies of yours. Today you can get dressed in here and then Daddy won't be disturbed.'

With that, I tiptoed across the hallway into the guest bedroom and quickly gathered the items of clothing. At the same time, I picked up my handbag, and tucked it under the bundle of clothes, hoping that should Claude awaken, he wouldn't notice that I'd got the bag with me. Returning to the lounge, I rapidly dressed Morgs who quickly became mesmerised by Children's BBC. This was one occasion where I was not going to complain. It allowed me to quickly remove the passports from my handbag and stash them in my dressing gown pocket.

'Morning Jan, exclaimed Phil as he came into the lounge. 'Am just doing some toast for breakfast. Do you fancy any? I've put some on for the boys. They seem to be up unusually early this morning for them and already dressed too! None of this lounging around stuff like they do normally!'

'Oh, I've told them that as it's their last morning together, I'll give them some money to go and get some sweets from the shop,' I replied, and then under my breath, in an urgent whisper I added, I've got a plan Phil. This is part of it. Trust me.'

A couple of minutes later, the four older boys were busy devouring toast and throwing me knowing chocolate spread smiles in anticipation of their secret mission. A wave of relief flushed over me to see Tom wearing his hoodie with the large front pocket, just as I'd asked.

I fished through my purse and sorted the euros from the pounds sterling, giving them each an English pound coin. They eagerly tucked them into their pockets and conversation turned to what the favourite sweets were and how many they could afford – typical banter. As Tom finished his last piece of toast, I reminded him to clean his teeth. It was a mundane chore and it seemed a direct contrast to the wave of growing anxiety that was rising inside me as time advanced. However, it gave me the opportunity needed. It enabled me to follow Tom into the bathroom, pass him our four passports and ensure that he'd stashed them safely away, concealed in the front pouch of his hoody.

Putting a hand on his shoulder I whispered, 'Time for action. Whatever you do, don't lose them! Keep them hidden and don't take them out. Remember, look after your brother and I'll be with you as soon as I possibly can. It's going to be ok Tom. I promise.'

I planted a kiss on the top of his head and hurried off

to get myself dressed as quickly as I could. I'd just pulled my favourite fluffy jumper over my head when I heard the front door close and the sound of footsteps receding down the garden path. The mission was underway.

I turned around with a sense of relief, only to see Claude standing in the hallway. His eyes stared intensely at me with a sense of heightened awareness and I had the uncanny feeling this was how a hawk would focus on its prey. He must have heard the boys' departure.

I tried to break the tension by dutifully asking, *'Tu veux quelque chose à boire? Un café peut être?'* Would you like something to drink? A coffee maybe?

I was doing it again. There I was making the effort to speak in a foreign language. It'd always been one sided. Claude had never tried to master any English.

Claude momentarily relaxed with a, *'Oui bien sûr.'* Yes of course.

But then he added, *'Tu as les passports? Il faut mettre tous les choses dans les valises et dites au revoir à les Cournouilles.'*

He was asking if I had the passports, telling me to pack the cases and say goodbye to Cornwall. He was sneering at me as he said it, knowing the words would inflict as much pain as would his arrogant assumption we were leaving. He was wrong. Enough was enough. I was on home territory now and with it came a resurgence of strength that'd been hidden for too long. I could risk confrontation in the comfort of knowing Phil was in the house.

Valiantly I lifted my head to meet his stare and defiantly responded, 'I have already told you. We are NOT going back to France. We are staying here. I don't know how many times I have to say it but you keep choosing not to hear it. Our marriage is over.'

With that, I turned my back on him and marched out of the hallway into the lounge.

I thought he'd follow me in hot pursuit, but he didn't.

Morgan was bent over a picture book exploring its pages with a plump finger, pointing at the images. A couple of moments later, Phil approached me from the direction of the kitchen.

Frowning and with one eyebrow quizzically raised, he uttered, 'Bloody hell. What's got into old matey this morning? Just came into the kitchen and bold as brass, mixed himself a large Pernod with a drop of water and stormed out again!'

In a hushed tone, I replied, 'I've told him we're not going back to France. I keep telling him but he just won't listen.'

'You can't go on like this,' Phil said but before I could reply, Claude appeared in the doorway, glass in one hand, cigar in the other, exhaling a plume of the putrid smoke into the room. The association I had with that smell would linger with me for many years, refusing to be extinguished.

'Donne moi le passport de Morgan. Tu peux rester ici si tu veux mais je vais partir avec mon fils.'

Not only was he now demanding Morgan's passport but he was telling me I could stay here whilst he departed with his son!

Shooting me a scornful glance he turned his attention to Phil, casting him a look which insinuated that women such as myself needed to be kept in line and that my unacceptable behaviour must be quashed immediately, and treated with the contempt it deserved.

Claude eyed the clock on the mantelpiece and I followed his gaze. We both recognised there was only a matter of a few hours until we needed to be at the airport returning the hire car. This realisation had the effect of launching Claude into action.

'Je vais prendre ma douche.'

Claude left in the direction of the bathroom at the end

of the hallway. This was my window of opportunity. My only chance of escape. With Claude taking a shower, I'd hopefully have just enough enough time to grab Morgan and run. But I had to be certain of Claude's actions. I needed to hear a set series of sounds in the right order before making my move. I couldn't just rely on a bathroom door closing. Claude might open it and catch me mid flight. No, I needed to wait, bide my time and hope to God, I'd got it right. Like starters orders at a race, I was poised for my call to action. As the bathroom door closed, I heard the tell-tale click of the lock being turned. Ready. One step closer, but it wasn't enough. I strained my ears, predicting the next sound I needed to hear. There it was. An echo of water spattering the sides of the shower cubicle. 'Get set' chimed in my ears and with heart thumping, I braced myself for the final call to action. So, so close now, but I had to be sure, had to be sure Claude wasn't just running the water to kid me into a false sense of security. It might be one of his devious ploys. A voice was screaming at me to run and run now, but I knew I had to hold on. Then it happened. I heard the unmistakable dull squeak of Claude's feet as they moved around the bottom of the shower tray.

It was now or never.

Go! Go! Go!

Morgan was busy parading up and down the hallway still sporting his new wellies with Doggy planted firmly under his arm. Grabbing my handbag, I fumbled for the car keys and gripping them tightly, ran to Morgan, swiftly scooping him up.

Trying not to alarm him, I made it sound acceptable by saying, 'Come on Morgs. Let's go find Tom and Owen.'

I struggled with the catch on the front door. Panic was debilitating me and costing me precious time. What was the saying? Was it 'less speed, more haste?' Or was it 'less haste, more speed?' My mind jumbled the sayings, underlining the intensity of my fear. It didn't matter which way around it was, I just needed to get out and get away fast.

Phil rushed to open the door for me, and knowing the urgency of the situation whispered a rapid, 'Good luck, I'll let you know when the coast is clear.'

'Thanks Phil,' I mouthed in reply, half stumbling down the steps, and praying the crunch of the gravel underfoot wouldn't give me away before I had time to scramble inside the hire car.

Please, please, open, I begged as I attempted to beep the remote locking system. It seemed to take an eternity but the doors finally unlocked, allowing me to rapidly put Morgan into his child seat before fumbling with the seat belt restraints. Everything was happening in slow motion – too slow. Each action was laboured in the knowledge I was fighting against the clock, time ticking away, every second bringing the likelihood of being discovered, ominously closer. With an all engulfing sense of dread, in expectation of hearing a harsh shout, barked from the direction of the house – I envisaged the consequence of my action, culminating in a show of violence that was yet to be witnessed in public. I knew my plan placed my family in very real danger. If we were to survive, I had to make this bid for freedom a success, before Claude discovered that we'd gone. I knew only too well what he'd do if he caught me. There was no room for half-hearted attempts at escape; no dress rehearsals. This was my only chance. Fear of failure was too scary to contemplate. I'd watched many a movie where prisoners were re-captured, only to be exposed to unthinkable tortures. My stomach momentarily lurched as I pictured myself and my children at the hands of our captor.

Forcing myself sharply back to the present, I scrambled

into position behind the wheel, throwing my bag onto the passenger seat. Claude had been the last one to drive the vehicle when we'd gone to Mousehole. The driver's seat was set to accommodate his six-foot-plus stature. My five-foot-four-inch frame paled into insignificance compared to his. Fumbling desperately around the base of the seat, I grabbed the lever moving the seat forward so my feet could touch the pedals. I adjusted the rear-view mirror downwards so I could see out of it, checked the gear I was in and taking a deep breath, started the engine. If Claude heard it splutter into life, he'd be down those front steps and after me. It would be game over and certain emotional suicide. Eyes searching manically across the instrument panel, I located the central locking button and pushed it. There was a reassuring chorus as the door locks engaged buying me a bit of extra time if needed and I felt momentarily safer. It meant that Claude would have to break a window to get at me now.

I threw the car into reverse. This car was alien to me in comparison to the one I'd driven in France. I had to consciously remind myself the hand brake was on the left, not the right and I'd have to think quickly, yet carefully about the gear changes. We launched backwards, kangarooing up the unmade track along a steep incline before it met the main road. Involuntary spasms in my left leg made the car reverse backwards in a series of haphazard jerks. Try as I might, it wasn't me, but my fear which controlled the car.

We were now nearing the top of the track. It had never entered my head to put my seatbelt on. It's true that under pressure people behave in very different ways and maybe subconsciously I'd decided wearing a seat belt would jeopardise my safety should I need a quick exit from the car. It crossed my mind that I was in fact backing out onto the busy main road a few metres from a blind bend. However, it was safer to take this risk, rather than waste precious time performing a three point turn. Looking over my shoulder, I glanced quickly, first one way and then the other, up and down the road. All clear. I rapidly reversed onto the main road and rammed the car into first gear. Heart pounding, I sped down the hill towards the town. My brief sense of relief was short-lived. Rounding the bend, I found myself in the path of an oncoming lorry, and swerved violently, pulling the car to the correct side of the road in another adrenalin-fuelled rush. Gripping the wheel, I cursed myself for not thinking straight. This was England; drive on the left!

Seeing the little stone bridge to my right, I signalled and turned to cross it. There was only sufficient space for one vehicle at a time to cross it. Beyond the bridge Tom and Owen would be waiting at the entrance to the boating lake; a local attraction, appearing particularly sad and grey on this desolate January morning. Slowing the car to a crawling pace, I was relieved to see the top of Chris's head; his ginger hair a welcoming beacon in stark contrast to the colourless day. It meant the others would be nearby. The next minute the other three lads appeared from behind the Cornish stone wall at the entrance to the lake.

'Quick! Tom and Owen get in!' I shouted through the closed window, gesticulating furiously to indicate they should leap into the rear of the vehicle. There was no time to lose.

Sensing the urgency, they scrambled through the gap between Morgan's legs and my driving seat and threw themselves onto the remaining rear seats, fumbling to fasten their seat belts.

Leaving Chris and Jake on the pavement, I put the driver's side window down.

'Thank you, boys,' I said.

Chris gave his characteristically toothy grin. 'Mission accomplished! See you soon I hope.'

Then, turning to his younger brother, he advised, 'Just remember Jake, when we get back home, if froggy asks, we don't know anything. We won't have to keep it up for long 'cos he'll be needing to leave to catch his flight.'

He slapped his little brother on the back in comradery style and Jake said, 'See ya Morgs.' and made to grab his doggy comforter, through the open window.

Morgan scowled at Jake, hauling his doggy comforter even tighter to his body and in an unnervingly defiant way for a two-year-old, shouted, *'C'est à moi ça!'*

In response, this caused a chorus from Jake and Chris as well as from the back seat as they all chanted in unison, *'C'est à moi ça! C'est à moi ça!'*

'Don't worry Morgs,' I intervened, 'they know it's yours. They just like winding you up about it! No one's taking doggy from you.'

I looked to the two smirking boys, 'We've got to go.'

There'd been a momentary escape from the urgency of our situation, but now the stark reality returned. No time for loitering. We needed to get away and fast. At any moment, Claude could come pounding into view down the hill. He was capable of anything. I needed to be prepared for the unexpected at all times.

'See you soon I hope.'

With that, I slipped the car into first gear and headed out of town. I knew where I needed to go. It had to be a place of hiding that Claude would never be able to find, somewhere he'd never been; somewhere he didn't know about. I could picture the perfect location. I just hoped the friend who sprung to mind would make an allowance in the circumstances for me not telephoning her beforehand to let her know of our imminent arrival. But then Donna was the kind of person who was sensitive to the needs of others. She also knew how to be strong when it was needed and instinctively, I knew she'd be willing to assist four fugitives, keeping us hidden, until Phil confirmed that Claude was on the plane.

Decision made, I turned the car in an easterly direction and we climbed steadily upwards, rising out of the valley. Within a couple of miles, we turned onto a private lane which meandered into the back of beyond, finally coming to a dead end culminating in an array of farm buildings. All we could do now was wait.

'Oh wow! I hope Carn is in. I haven't seen him for ages!' said Tom.

He was referring to his mate who he'd not seen since we moved to France. It would be lovely to see them all again, not forgetting young Sharnia who was only a day older than Morgan. Donna and I were pregnant at the same time. Our friendship had been firmly cemented as we stood outside the primary school gates. We discussed our expectant trials and tribulations whilst waiting to pick up our sons at the end of the school day. That was already three years ago. Life was so very different then. Tom undid Morgan's seat belt, helping him out of his seat, setting him firmly on the ground. This was the first time his new wellies touched terra firma for real and I hoped it was a good omen.

'Come on Morgs,' said Owen offering an outstretched hand which was quickly taken and the three of them set off in the direction of the house.

The front door was flung open and a radiant Donna exclaimed, 'Well look who's here! What a surprise! Grief you've all grown! Come in! Come in!'

With relief, I picked up my handbag, got out of the car and almost ran towards my friend. It was so wonderful to see her again. As we hugged each other, I couldn't help but raise my eyes skywards in a silent plea, 'Please don't let him find us. Please make him leave and let us be safe.'

I prayed to whomever might be listening. It would have to be a god who believed in justice and doing the right thing, a god who understood we'd no alternative. All I could do now was wait, in the desperate hope of hearing confirmation from Phil that Claude was airborne. Imagine the relief of it all.

We'd no longer have to live in fear.

We'd no longer feel like captives in a foreign country; isolated and alone.

All we needed was the phone call to effectively grant us our freedom.

Was it really too much to ask?

Chapter 45

'Another cuppa?' enquired Donna.

No thanks,' I replied with an edgy smile. There were only so many cups of coffee I could consume to while away the time.

Two hours had passed since our escape and there was still no confirmation from Phil of Claude's departure. I kept going over the events of the morning in my mind, checking I'd not left any clues to give our location away.

Would Chris or Jake say anything?

Had I put them in an impossible position?

How about Phil?

Was Claude at the airport or was he sitting in Phil's lounge at that very moment, drinking Pernod or whisky, refusing to move until I returned?

Each time the door to Donna's large, homely kitchen opened, I jumped backwards as if readying myself for Claude to storm in to tell me it was hopeless to try and escape. It was ingrained in my mind. Claude was so controlling I was now brainwashed into believing that any attempt at escape was futile. I was resigned to the fact he'd get his own way in the end.

But things had changed now – I was no longer in France but in England on my home turf. Would having the home advantage make the difference this time? Would this give me the chance to play the game to my benefit? It dawned on me that there was a faint glimmer of hope on my horizon. Confirmation that Claude had left the country without us would be proof I'd successfully moved the goalposts.

'Can we go and play outside now Mum?' asked Tom.

I'd lost count of how many times I'd struggled to find a suitable excuse in order to keep him inside the house.

'I think it's probably getting a bit late for playing outdoors now Tom. Remember it's winter time and it's nippy and I don't want you catching cold.'

'But I can run around a lot with Carn and we can play soldiers like we used to. I won't get cold – Carn's still got all the army gear,' protested Tom.

'Even the gas mask!' Owen chirped gleefully.

'Tombo, you'll just have to make do with playing indoors today. Hopefully, we can come and see Carn again soon and will plan the visit next time so we'll be better organised.' I offered. This was becoming really difficult. My excuses were wearing thin and inwardly I was screaming, 'I don't want you outside because he might be there! Just stay in the house and stop asking to go out!!'

Morgan seemed completely oblivious to any sense of tension in the air and was happily playing with Sharnia's toys, although he hadn't as yet eaten his half of a banana that the little ones were sharing. It lay untouched on the coffee table whilst Sharnia clung to hers with a chubby fist, getting stickier by the minute.

'It reminds me of old times,' said Donna, nodding her head in their direction. 'Remember when they'd sit in their highchairs together and we'd give them mashed banana? Some things don't change! At least now they can manage the finger foods themselves.'

I shrunk inwardly. I felt ashamed that my son was not

like others his age. He'd been moulded to be different by his bastard of a father. The damage he'd inflicted had consequences in the 'normal' world; a world he'd deprived us of, one in which we no longer knew how to function.

While internally I was imploding, outwardly I wanted to scream, 'My son can't deal with finger food. He's too scared to touch food with his fingers because of the consequences!'

But how could I admit it? How could I tell my friend Morgan was hit for trying to eat with his fingers whilst I watched it happen? A sense of shame enveloped me and I stared through tear-filled eyes at the discarded banana in front of me. None of us were the same people Donna had known. Too much had happened since we'd left Cornwall in search of happiness. Little by little, unwanted changes had snaked their way into my psyche, their poisons seeping under my skin, rendering me helpless, slowly drip-feeding their incessant supply of venomous violations. The stealthy shadow that writhed its coils in the corners of the darkness, hissed almost inaudibly closer, threatening to wrap me in its grip, stifling my ability to breathe.

How had I let it enter my world?

Had it sidled in unnoticed? Was that why, little by little, subtle mind manoeuvres had been played out, executed with guile and manipulation?

Was this why I kept staring powerlessly at Morgan's banana as it lay untouched on the varnished oak coffee table?

Another symbol of an untold story, too raw to verbalise.

Donna broke my ponderings, pulling me back to the present with, 'Nick should be here any time soon to pick Tom and Owen up.'

'I must admit on this occasion I'll be so relieved to see him!' I replied, thinking of the times when it had been very awkward to be in the same room as my ex-husband. Now I was grateful he'd responded unquestioningly to my urgent phone call earlier, asking him to collect the boys from Donna's.

'Credit where credit's due, he's been brilliant. I'm relieved he can come and take his boys for a few days. At least I know that they'll be OK and it'll give me a bit of a break.'

'I remember when you and Nick bought Mithian Farm and you did all that work on it together. Do you remember raising those ceilings in the lounge and finding that enormous fireplace with the clome oven in the dining room?' asked Donna.

'Yes. That takes me back! And dear old Courtney our next-door neighbour! I must go and see him and tell him what's happening. He's so very much a part of our family – like an adopted grandad to all the boys. He's always had my welfare at heart has Courtney. Hey! I'll never forget his face when Morgan was born at home. I remember dear Courtney was completely flabbergasted when he saw Morgan less than an hour after the birth. He came into our bedroom and I passed Morgan to him. He held him and said 'Oooh -ang! He's some small. I'm used to dealing with calves, not a babby small as this!'

'Do you know he still takes his old Massy Ferguson tractor on the main road to collect his agricultural supplies? Gets some angry drivers passing him and giving him all sorts of hand signals! He told me so the other day – said he finally waved somebody past and they tooted and waved their middle finger at him!'

'Oh no! How rude...' I started, only to be interrupted by Donna.

'Wait! That's not the end of it! Courtney said he

thought it was a new type of friendly acknowledgement for other road users and so he's been doing it ever since – putting his middle finger up and waving it at people! Even did it to the old dear who runs the post office. Hope to goodness she is none the wiser.'

I found myself laughing unrestrainedly for the first time in a long time. It was good,as well as refreshing to react spontaneously in the moment, without considering if it was acceptable to anyone else. It was also such a delight to be able to converse in English, reinforcing the joy at being able to communicate and even to joke, in my native tongue.

'Dear Courtney. Perhaps I can get back to doing the Sunday roast dinners for him like I used to. He for one, will be pleased to hear I'm not going back to France! We took him with us to visit the Mousehole lights you know, but now we can meet up whenever we want!'

'He'll be pleased Jan. He must've noticed how you've changed when he saw you though. I know I have. You are so different. I can't believe how much weight you've lost.'

She leant forward towards me from her chair, 'As the boys are off playing and out of earshot, tell me more about what really happened. I know you put your heart and soul into everything and you wouldn't give up on anything unless you had to, so this has to be pretty serious for you to decide that you can't go on living with him anymore.'

'Donna. I'm sorry. I can't tell you anything at the moment. I wouldn't know where to begin. All these thoughts keep tumbling one after the other. There's so much I could tell you but I can't go into it now. It's too much. I can't let go at the moment. I've got to keep going. It just feels such a huge relief to actually be away from him. All of us together back in our home country and most importantly back in Cornwall. Maybe when I know he's really gone I might dare to talk about it. We still haven't heard from Phil and the plane was due to take off twenty mins ago and still no news. Maybe he hasn't gone. Maybe Phil can't get away from him to let me know what's happening!'

'I know. You've been constantly looking at your watch. This is awful – all this waiting. Fingers crossed we hear some news soon.'

'My mum used to say 'no news is good news'. I hope that's right! Just supposing he hasn't gone and he's forced information out of Phil?'

'Phil doesn't know where you are Jan. Stop panicking. There's no way Claude could know you are here.'

At that moment there was a brief knock at the kitchen door and it swung open. I recoiled visibly in my chair and gasped, only to relax when I saw the familiar weather-beaten face of Nick appear.

'Not the easiest place to find, is it? Sorry I wasn't here earlier. Couldn't find the right turning. How are the boys?' and then he paused, 'you ok?'

Nick had always been reliable and honest – perhaps too honest for his own good, but honest nonetheless. I briefly explained I needed him to look after Tom and Owen for at least a couple of days until I'd sorted out some permanent accommodation for us and started the necessary legal proceedings.

'I'm better than I've been in ages Nick. Well, I think I am. It's just such a huge relief to know I'm home and safe, and I've got the boys away from everything that was going on.'

'Look Jan. I know you said in your emails things were difficult. Why didn't you phone me from out there to let me know?' asked Nick.

'I couldn't use the phone. He was there all the time and watching and listening to my every move. If I'd tried to call you and he'd heard the conversation, albeit in English, he'd have punished us by making things very unpleasant. The most important thing is we're back for good, so the worst is over.'

'Where are you going to stay?' asked Nick.

'I'll go to my mum's. It'll be easier for her to cope with just one little one in tow. I really appreciate you having Tom and Owen. I think it'll help them to feel safe and we have to sort out schools and establish a routine now they're back.'

'OK. Keep me up to date and...'

The remainder of his sentence was cut short by the sudden trill of my mobile phone. I looked at the screen. It read 'Phil' and with a large intake of breath, I answered.

'You alright chuck?' said a reassuring voice at the end of the line. Without pausing for any response from me, he continued, 'You're alright. He's gone. I watched him board the plane just to be sure and he's definitely gone.'

'Oh thank God,' feeling the relief flood through me. 'Really, *really* gone!? Are you sure Phil?'

'Yes, I'm sure. Like I told you, I saw him go. I didn't just drop him off at the airport, but waited to be sure he'd left. Nightmare going up there mind – you could've cut the atmosphere with a knife. Kept asking me where you were and I kept playing ignorant, telling him I didn't know and maybe you'd meet him at the airport. Told him I was sure you'd turn up.'

'Oh! Thank you so much Phil. That was so, so good of you. So, he's truly gone?'

It was too difficult to comprehend. Nothing was ever that simple where Claude was concerned. There was always something waiting to catch me out, to trip me up, and to demolish any possibilities of a positive outcome. Both Donna and Nick were looking at me, trying to pick up clues from what they'd heard of the conversation and

I managed a brief smile of confirmation to indicate it was good news.

'Sorry Phil. Can you just go over it again? It's hard to believe that's all. I need to hear it again.'

Phil repeated what he'd just told me and I digested it, allowing the reality to finally sink in.

Then Phil continued, breaking the short silence by adding, 'There's some not so good news though Jan.'

Immediately, my whole being launched into flight mode.

'What is it?'

'Well, he's taken everything with him. When I say everything, I mean *everything*. All your suitcases, your toiletries, the new M&S pyjamas you bought for the boys in the post-Christmas sales – everything! He went around the house picking up everything which belongs to you and the boys and packed every item into a suitcase.'

'What! He's taken all our belongings? So, literally all we have is what we're wearing now?'

'Yup. Maybe he thought you were just trying to play a game with him and that ultimately you'd rock up at the airport last minute.'

'It'd be so nice to think he took the cases because he loved us and didn't want to be without us. But, it's not like that at all. He's taken the cases because he wants to make us suffer. He wants to make it as difficult as possible for us to manage without him – that's what that's about. The bastard!' I spat out. 'OK. Thanks so much Phil. I'll be back later. Nick has just arrived to pick up Tom and Owen, so I'd better go.'

I thanked Donna profusely for everything she'd done. Nick rallied Tom and Owen together who were both full of smiles at seeing their dad.

'Hey boys,' I said. 'Guess what? You get to have an extra holiday with your dad for a few days! Also, best news ever! Claude's gone! He's gone; back to France.'

'Wooooo hooo! Yesssss!' they screamed in unison, before Owen, serious face, asked, 'You mean we can stay here and he's not coming back and we can live here?'

'Too right,' I replied 'we're back in Cornwall boys and as long as we're here and we're together, everything is going to be fine.'

'Does that mean I can go back to Mithian school?' said Tom with a rush of excitement. 'It means I can see all my mates again! Much as I like French schools with staff on roller skates, I'd far rather be here.'

'You've done so well to have managed as you have at French schools – both you and Owen and you'll be able to tell everyone about it, but yes – back to Mithian it is, if I can get you both a place.'

Owen's smile was short-lived.

'What about Millie and Shadow? What's going to happen to them and who's going to look after them?'

Trust Owen. He was always the one who cared more than anyone about our pets. He had a very strong bond with Shadow and Millie whom he'd chosen as a pup. I knew exactly what he was saying because the same fears had already crossed my mind. However, I knew that if a choice had to be made, then my children's safety had to go before everything else, even our beloved pets who were very much a part of the family.

'Don't worry Os. I am sure the neighbours will make sure Claude looks after the dogs until I can find a way of getting them back. I feel awful they're not with us at the moment, but we'll get them back somehow. I promise.'

'I miss them,' said Owen, tears beginning to well up. 'Claude won't let them in the house. We always had them in the house at Mithian and then when we moved, he shut them outside. It's cold 'cos its winter and Shadow might die 'cos she's old.'

It was as if someone had taken a hold of my stomach and twisted it tightly in their hand. Those dear dogs. What could I do? To board a plane to rescue our dogs was simply not an option. With begging eyes, Owen implored me to do something for his precious animals.

'I will get Millie and Shadow back here as soon as I can for you Owen. In the meantime, I'm sure Mills will keep Shadow warm and they'll share the kennel together. Annie and Fernand will look after them until I can bring them home. I've already spoken to Annie. She's going to send me some papers from the house in France and I know she'll make sure the dogs feel much loved.'

'Come on! Time to go boys,' said Nick as he shepherded my two older children towards the door but not before I'd given each a kiss and a hug.

'Have a good time you two and I'll see you very soon,' I said and watched the two little figures head out into the darkened yard, beyond the reaches of the light from the hallway.

Half an hour or so later, I repeated my thanks to Donna and headed off in the direction of my mother's house. I was driving at a much calmer speed than previously and felt generally relaxed. The adrenalin that had kept me in a fight for survival mode, was replaced with a growing sense of relief. I rounded a familiar corner and indicated left to make a sharp turn along the little bumpy lane at the back of the lake front properties. Morgan slept peacefully alongside me, his eyelashes flickering every now and then as if watching his dream. Manoeuvring the hire car onto the uneven parking space, I realised I was physically exhausted, making the simple act of putting one foot in front of the other in order to reach my mother's back door, a seemingly insurmountable task. I gripped the handrail wooden handrail on the steps as a means of support as I willed myself forward, closing the distance between my last footfall and the safe haven that lay over the threshold three feet away. A silhouette of a slight figure, illuminated in the light of the kitchen window, stooped to search for the keys to the back door and in that instant, the effort needed for my final steps was forgotten. Like an infant, I ran to the safety of the person I needed the most in that moment – my Mum.

Chapter 46

There was something very restorative about being in my mother's home once more. It was probably because it felt so familiar and a sanctuary from the outside world.

As I looked around the living room, I could see all sorts of mementoes from the past. There was an old naively sculpted, clay hedgehog I'd made at the age of seven which I'd proudly presented to my mum. For the last 30 years, it remained a fixture on the mantelpiece of every home in which she lived. I noted that it was now joined by a plethora of other bits and pieces – seemingly irrelvant newspaper cuttings, a neat stack of empty yogurt pots and odd bits of toys, including Lego bricks, a tub of playdoh and some odd chess pieces. It saddened me to see my mum unperturbed by this chaos of unaccountable clutter given that she'd always been so immaculate in her housekeeping. One wall was awash with framed photos – a gallery depicting landmarks in the lives of her grandsons, her sense of pride in them emanating from the assortment of frames. As I had no brothers or sisters, my lads took pride of place as there were no other grandchildren to display!

Mum had been absolutely thrilled to see Morgan again and they'd played together on the lounge carpet in front of the fire, stacking plastic cups to see who could make the tallest mountain. Morgan thought it was hilarious to knock the tower down. I think it was probably down to his gran's mock cries of, 'Oh no! Look! It's gone over again!' that caused him to chortle with delight, prior to knocking the edifice to the floor for the umpteenth time.

Now, however, all was peaceful and Morgan was safely tucked up in the travel cot in mum's spare room. There'd a lot of excitement for young Morgs but he was now sound asleep, doggy tucked firmly under one arm. Not once had he asked 'where's papa?' It was such a relief not to have to provide him with any explanations.

Mum and I sat chatting together. I gave her a brief overview of why I'd decided to stay in England and not return to France. As usual Mum was one hundred percent behind me in my decision. She understood my reasons and never once doubted me. I was so lucky that not only was she my mother, but also my very best friend. I felt blessed that she'd chosen me. As far as I was concerned, I had the best adoptive mother in the whole world.

I checked my watch. Nearly 10.30 pm. I'd have to head to bed soon as there was a lot to do the following day. It was agreed we could stay at Mum's until things got sorted out. I needed to buy a set of bunk beds for the spare room as well as some other furniture too – drawers to put clothes in. Funny really – I'd need to get my priorities right and buy the clothes first, before thinking about buying drawers to put them in!! It'd mean kitting them all out from scratch and would prove an expensive undertaking, bearing in mind the cost of school uniforms. I'd use some of the money that I had transferred into my English bank account. I'd opened a second personal account in France, one to which Claude had no access, therefore making him completely ignorant of when I made an international transfer. It seemed incredible now, sitting in the peace of my mother's home that I'd allowed Claude to have rights over my first French bank account. He'd told me it would be prudent for him to have access to the account so he could keep an eye on it, given it would take me time to adjust to the ways of managing my finances abroad. Initially, I believed he had my best interests at heart.

However, with suspicions mounting, I'd written to our bank manager in Paris six months earlier to request Claude's rights be removed from my account. Then I transferred the majority of my funds to a local branch of *Crédit Agricole Midi* in the south of France. The details of this second account were one of the pieces of paperwork I'd left hidden under a bundle of clothes in my chest of drawers in France. It was in the file along with other secret details, such as the address and contact number of a French Avocat/Lawyer who specialised in divorce proceedings, as well as the boys' original birth certificates. It was this file that Annie promised to post to me at my mother's address. I hoped to goodness she'd found the file and successfully removed it from the property before Claude returned. Annie had been such a dear friend during my time in France. I smiled, thinking about her because she understood. Towards the end of one phone call with her, she stressed that she didn't want Claude to know she'd been involved in helping me. She was scared of what he might do to her. I assured her I'd say nothing and she touchingly replied, *'tous les meilleurs s'en vont'* – all the best people have gone. I was touched to hear she thought of me in this way and I hoped sincerely that she'd managed to retrieve the documents whilst Claude remained none the wiser.

From the peace of my mother's home, the life that I'd fled, seemed to belong to someone else. It wasn't mine.

Yet my thoughts drew me back to it – as if doing a post mortem would somehow help me make sense of it all.

How had I let it happen?

Had I been so blinkered that I couldn't sense what was around the corner?

I thought moving to France two years ago would give me the dream of a happy-ever-after. It hadn't. I now held myself culpable; guilty for being responsible for what my boys had been put through.

Sitting quietly in one of my mother's homely armchairs, I was reassuringly comforted by its familiar shape. I recognised it of old. The same contoured form to it, just a different cover. I wondered how many layers I would find underneath its current large, floral pattern. It was this very seat cushion I'd clung to as a toddler, as I took my first wobbling steps. It helped me keep my balance when I was wavering and afraid of falling. I was afraid of falling now. Alone with my thoughts, I barked questions into the silence of the listening darkness.

What had I done wrong?

Was there any going back?

That last question was the only one I could answer. Going back could never be an option. We were home and that was how it needed to stay. A wave of relief flooded over me in the knowledge that I could, at last, allow myself to relax. I realised I was completely exhausted, both physically and mentally drained. Tomorrow was another day and I would face it with renewed energy but right now I needed to sleep. I smiled as I bent to pick up the two empty teacups from the coffee table, recalling the number of times my mother and I had put the world right over endless brews. I tiptoed towards the lounge door mindful of my mother who was sleeping in the bedroom just off the hallway.

Reaching to switch off the lights, from within the

room, the telephone suddenly shrilled. I jerked violently, rattling the teacups. Who'd be phoning at this time of night? It couldn't be anyone who knew my mother because they'd have realised it was too late to be calling. With a growing sense of unease, I walked slowly towards the phone. Its ring tone became more dominant, more demanding, more aggressive in its bid for my attention. With a large intake of breath, I lifted the receiver and said 'hello'.

Silence.

I repeated myself.

No silence this time.

Instead, it was replaced with slow, calculated breathing, the breathing of someone watching and waiting, invading the room with an ominous presence, menacing in the darkness and biding its time. In a blind panic, I dropped the receiver back onto its cradle and ran from the room. Heart pounding, I anticipated seeing a malevolent figure, manifesting from the shadowy darkness. Taking two stairs at a time in a rush to reach the refuge of my attic bedroom, I knew it would take more than physical distance alone to keep me safe. Claude would stop at nothing. Without pausing to change into my nightwear, I scrabbled into bed, pulling the covers over my head, in a desperate need to hide from anything which might threaten to destroy my very being.

Chapter 47

I awoke to watery winter sunlight filtering through the windows, the type of sunlight that told me the sky would be patterned with striations of high cloud, symbolising the approach of another weather front, striding in from the Atlantic Sea. I looked at my watch and saw it was almost 7 am telling me I'd had at least slept for a couple of hours, my last clock watch being just after 5 am.

Levering myself out of bed, I decided to take a shower in the quiet of the morning, hoping to feel suitably invigorated as a result. There was a lot to sort out in terms of practicalities and I needed to make the most of it before Tom and Owen arrived later in the afternoon. Clutching a towel under my arm I was just passing the door of my mother's bedroom when the doorbell rang. My first thought was that the boys were returning early for some unexpected reason and so frowning, I turned on my heels and went to answer the door. Through the glass screen, I could see two uniformed policemen standing side-by-side. Had there been some sort of terrible accident? Were they here to break the news to me of the tragic death of my sons? Policemen didn't just turn up on the doorstep for no good reason at that hour of the morning. Panicking, I fumbled with the key and turned the lock to open the door.

'Are you Mrs Jeanette Mary Campait,' asked one of the officers in a serious tone?

I could feel a sudden constraint in my throat as I forced myself to confirm my identity to them.

In response, the officer continued, 'May we come inside?'

I nodded, stepping back to make way for them to follow me over the threshold. We'd no sooner got into the hallway when the officer told me the reason for their visit.

'Mrs Jeanette Mary Campait,' he said, 'can you confirm you are the mother of Morgan Campait?'

'I am,' I replied, the two words being forced in a hoarse whisper from the tightness of my throat.

The policeman continued, 'we have been sent by Interpol as you are charged with child abduction. This is a very serious matter.'

That was just not possible. It could not be happening! Child abduction – I was being charged with abducting my own son?

'How can I abduct my own son?' I ventured, in disbelief.

Did they not realise I was the one who'd taken a monumental risk and we'd fled because we were in fear of our lives? I had not abducted him; I was protecting him.

'You have effectively kidnapped your son Morgan. His father does not know his whereabouts and you have deliberately refused to return him to France. As I have already said, this is a very serious matter and I must caution you to remain at this residence until the High Court Hearing. In the meantime, in order that you do not attempt to leave this country, I must ask you to hand over your passports.'

It was getting worse by the minute! So much for the saying that 'justice will prevail'! No one had heard my version of events and here I was being branded a criminal! We'd only just got to a place of safety and now these men had the nerve to insinuate I might try and escape! Didn't they realise we'd only just done that?

'Leave the country? Why would I want to leave the country? You don't realise what it's taken in order for us to get BACK here! The last thing I want to do is to LEAVE!'

The words were out. I was incredulous. I was so taken aback in that moment, I couldn't give a shit about how I was speaking to the law. I didn't care whether I was being respectful or not. I was just reacting. This wasn't how it was supposed to be. I'd always been told that when in trouble, find a policeman and he'll know what to do. Know what to do? My arse! It was laughable. I opened my mouth to protest, only to be stopped by the echoed stomp of toddler feet approaching at a pace. Morgan appeared, pushing his way between the two police officers, as if he were an explorer on a mission, forging through a dense undergrowth of legs as he went.

'Mummy,' he said, wrapping his chunky arms around my left leg and looking up at me. I scooped him up onto my hip and held him close, feeling the reassuring warmth emanating from his little body. This was my little man and come hell or high water, Claude would not take him away from me. I'd do whatever it took, however it took it to do it, to make sure that we'd never be parted.

I looked directly at one of the uniformed officers, defying him to dare to make any further ridiculous accusations. My response was voiced with utter contempt as I spoke my words with a sarcastically and deliberate slowness in order it might aid understanding.

'Wait there. I'll go and get the passports but I can assure you, we are going *nowhere*!'

Chapter 48

I needed a break. I needed a change of scene - a diversion, some sort of escape, a means of temporarily stopping the non-stop chattering images that were flying around my head. In the last couple of days it had been increasingly difficult to remain positive and energised with the boys. Some time out was needed and so I jumped at the chance of a couple of hours at the local pub with Phil, whilst Gran entertained her grandsons.

I was warmed by the welcoming golden glow that spilled out of the ancient sash windows of The Driftwood Spars. It was steeped in history, its walls bearing witness to times gone by. The 'Spars' in its name, was a reference to the enormous beams and spars, salvaged from shipwrecks along the coast which were then used in the construction of the building in the 1650s. Over the years the building had lent itself to a variety of purposes which included a tin mining warehouse, chandlery, sail making loft and fish cellar. Somehow, I felt comforted knowing it had stood the test of time, now a thriving pub for the community of St Agnes to meet, its whitewashed exterior, set into the cliff on the final descent to the beach. As I passed by each window, I caught glimpses of gatherings of people, still in festive spirit. Placed to the left of the main entrance door,

I smiled at seeing an upturned motorcycle helmet secured to the ground, the words 'Mutts not butts' painted on its side. A kindly offering, catering for the thirsts of our four-legged companions.

Crossing the threshold, I was greeted by the sight of the large fishing nets of yesteryear, now draped with an array of fairy lights, and tinsel hanging between old oak beams. To my right, an enormous granite fireplace danced with flames, the sound of the intermittent crackle and spit of burning logs refusing to disturb the slumbers of the dog who lay outstretched on the hearth. Jostling our way to the crowded bar, Phil ordered the drinks whilst I delighted in the knowledge that everyone around me was actually speaking my native language. It was such a treat to hear English being spoken, snippets of conversation, whose content I understood. For the first time in a long time, I was no longer an outsider, but someone who belonged.

'Hey! It's nice to see you smiling,' said Phil.

'In the past I'd have taken all this for granted Phil,' I replied 'It's only when you don't have something you realise just how much you miss it, how much it means to you. So when you have the chance to experience it again, you really appreciate it!'

Phil looked perplexed; he'd obviously not understood so I clarified it for him.

'Hearing English being spoken! Bet you thought I was referring to the beer! Well, I'm not, although a proper Cornish pint is something I've missed. No, you have no idea how special it feels to hear words around me and to understand each one of them. I was so isolated in France – I'd understand more words than I was able to speak, so I spent most of my time listening, rather than actually participating in conversations. I could never joke in French with a play on words. I've missed having humour in my life!'

'Well you can be sure of getting some here,' laughed Phil, 'especially as I've seen some of my old mates at the bar. Actually I think you might see a few familiar faces. Let's go and join them. They've already told me today is the day Gill the landlady does her annual Lucky dip.'

'Lucky dip? Have they renamed the Christmas swim? Good God – you'd have to do more than that to get me in the sea without a wetsuit at this time of year!'

'No, that's been and gone! You dodged that one successfully Jan! This particular lucky dip is when Gill takes all the surplus stuff from the pub promotions that've happened throughout the year, wraps them up and then people can buy them at a pound a go. She gives the money raised to charity. You never know what you're going to get for your pound, but it's all for a good cause!'

I smiled. It felt good to be in an environment where everyone was enjoying themselves and, in the mood to put their hands in their pockets, not just for their own benefit.

'Let's go and join the others then,' I grinned and we meandered over to jostle for position with Phil's friends at the bar.

A couple of hours later and I was heading homewards, juggling a pile of assorted items on my lap in the passenger seat, steadying the swaying bundle with every tight left or right-hand bend in the road.

'Whoa! Take it easy Phil! This lot's going to fall if you don't slow down for the next bend!' I laughed.

'Bet you're glad you went!' replied Phil, taking his eyes off the road for a second to glance at the small mountain of goods on my knee.

I smiled graciously at the myriad of gifts I'd received, still completely overwhelmed by people's response. How could I ever show how grateful I was to everyone, many of them complete strangers, who upon hearing I'd lost everything, had without pause for thought, dug deep into their Cornish pockets and donated their Lucky Dip pickings to me? It was thanks to them I now had several oversized Coca Cola t-shirts which would make perfect nighties, pens for the boys to use, a couple of sweat shirts, a Chinese wall calendar and an alarm clock advertising the local takeaway. Unwittingly, these kindly souls had not only blessed me with their Cornish generosity, but also given me a glimmer of hope for a different future. It proved there were stillgood people in the world.

Still smiling, I said goodbye to Phil and went into my mother's home carrying my precious gifts of kindness. I'd just put everything away when my mobile phone rang. Thinking perhaps I'd left something in Phil's car and he was calling to let me know, I answered it without looking at the number. It came as a surprise to hear the voice of an old school friend, Vicky on the other end of the line.

'Jan! Are you alright? What's happened?' she said, her words gushing down the phone.

'There's been a lot happening Vicky, I can't even start to tell you about it. I don't know where to begin,' I replied. 'I suppose...'

She cut me off short.

'Jan, look I don't know what's going on but I thought I must contact you. I've had an email from Claude. He says he's looking for his son Morgan and you've disappeared with him! There's a photo of Morgan in his pushchair, fast asleep. Looks like a recent photo. He's desperate to find him and get him back!'

Her words tumbled out one on top of the other and she paused briefly for breath, before adding, 'I didn't know what to do. I knew something terrible must've happened! You wouldn't just disappear! Does he really not know where you are?'

So, he was at it again. He was trying a different tack this time. Always having to twist things, to regain control, and worst of all, to make people feel sorry for him. How dare he make out that he was the victim in all this?

'Vicky. He knows exactly where I am. I told him a couple of days ago that I was staying in England with the boys and that I was not returning to France. Yes, I disappeared with them because he wasn't listening to me. I had to get away from him. I couldn't go back there after everything he's done to us. I'm convinced it was him who called me here at my mum's, the other night!'

'Why? What did he say?' asked Vicky.

'He didn't say anything, it was just the sound of someone breathing – slow deliberate breaths. It was so scary. I know it was him. It's just the sort of thing he'd do in an effort to get at me, even though he isn't here.'

I was now questioning the sanity of what I had just said to Vicky. Was I being irrational? Maybe I was beginning to go mad. After all, I had nothing to prove it was him. Who would believe me? Yet, despite what anyone else thought, I just knew in my gut it was him who'd called. Only I knew the monster I was dealing with. It was essential to remain hypervigilant at all costs, no matter how ridiculous it might seem to others.

'Oh God, this sounds terrible,' said Vicky 'I know things were a bit tricky but I didn't think that it would go this far.'

'Vicky, look I'm away from it all now, although can you believe the police have been, on behalf of bloody Interpol, and taken mine and Morgan's passports in case we try to leave the country! Claude's accused me of kidnapping my own son! Clever though, isn't it when you think about it? He had to give them an address where they could find me and they did, so how come he's making out I've disappeared and he doesn't know how to find Morgan?'

'Sounds devious Jan. Look, I just wanted to get in touch to let you know and to see what on earth had happened. Perhaps you need to be thinking about all the other friends he might be contacting? I bet I'm not the only one to get an email.'

She was right. I'd considered that.

'Ok. Thanks Vicky. Look I'd better see if I can go to a mate's house tomorrow morning and use their computer to access my email. That way I will be able to alert people.'

Vicky asked to be kept in the loop and we said goodbye. How could this be happening? I sat heavily back onto the settee, the weight of everything too oppressive and exhausting to contemplate. Claude had obviously hacked into my email account in order to get the names and addresses of my friends. I felt violated, exposed, raw and helpless. He was one step ahead, deviously plotting from across the Channel. Lost in a turmoil of fear whilst attempting to devise a practical plan, I was oblivious to the initial shrill of the landline. As it loomed into my consciousness, I realised yet again, it was ringing out, late into the night. I had to answer its call.

'Hello,' I said, prepared now for what was to come next, accepting it, as if I'd no choice but to resign myself to it. But this time there was no sound of breathing. He'd upped the ante, no longer shrouded in the anonymity of the previous call. Words spoken in a native tongue unleashed themselves, calculated to cut and wound.

'Oh! The bitch answers! What a mistake you have made! You think you can run away? You cannot run!' There was the predictable sneering laugh. 'By your actions, I shall prove that you are an unfit mother who is psychologically deranged and Morgan will come to me!'

Momentarily, held hostage by his words, I fought to free myself, no longer willing to be subservient to his threats. This was not just a fight for my freedom, but for my son and with that realisation, there arose in me a force which transcended all others. With a surge of strength from the depths of my most maternal instinct as protector of my child, I unleashed my response, screaming my words like a woman possessed.

'You will never take my son! You will have to kill me first you bastard!'

I slammed the phone down. Conversation over, my terms, my decision. Shaking with rage, the emergence of a different self, began to make its presence known. This new acquaintance was a warrior, equipped with a formidable inner strength and she'd show me how to use every single last bit of it. Together, we'd do whatever it took by whatever means necessary.

Let the battle begin.

Chapter 49

A month later and that phone call's content still echoed in my ears. The more I heard it replaying in my head, the more it acted to strengthen my resolve that I would not be beaten.

Whilst Tom and Owen were happily re-instated at their old Primary School, I made the most of my spare time between school runs. I attended meetings with the family solicitor and filled in paperwork in readiness for the forthcoming High Court Hearing, the date of which had still to be set. It had been shocking to see the Summons with its official stamp and print, already portraying me the perpetrator of a heinous crime. How could I possibly be labelled in this way? All I could do was to hope I'd be in a position for the court to hear my side of the story. Once they knew what we'd been through, they'd see who the real criminal was in all this. Justice would prevail and they'd understand the reason why we had fled France.

I'd already noticed a visible difference in Tom's and Owen's demeanour – they weren't being quite so hyper-vigilant. Some of the fear had vanished from their eyes. This didn't mean they were unscathed, they still held a haunted look in their eyes. Recovery would be slow and healing take a long time. Tom had had a series of nightmares, his latest one documented in an exercise book he'd brought home from school. Spelling mistakes and punctuation aside, it was the content that mattered.

"Last night I drempt about Claude but is was not a dream it was a nightmare. HE banged on the front window. Gran did not know who he was but she let him in because she recognised him. I hid to hide behind a chair but he saw me. He said 'What is it?' I said 'Leave me alone' and I ran in to the dining room and Courtney a friend of mine, about 80 years old, drove from a sky light in a silver sports car and I whispered to Courtney 'Claude is here!' By this time Claude was pulling Morgan out the house. Me, Gran, Owen and Courtney we took Morgan and pushed Claude out the door to the out doors. He was pushing to get in and I jerked awake. This is a reall nightmare I promise on my heart"

Underneath the writing, Tom had drawn a picture showing a tug of war scene depicting his little brother being pulled, as the warring parties fought to take possession of him. I imagined Tom's subject matter being a stark contrast to those of his peers. I doubted that any of his classmates had ever been exposed to the trauma my Tom had suffered. His writing served as a horrific reminder of how my children had been traumatised by their ordeal and how I'd allowed it to happen. It took away their childhood innocence, their time for age appropriate experiences, only to replace them with dark, forbidding, fearful memories. Although I was powerless to undo all the horrific things that had happened, I knew

I had to do absolutely everything in my power to ensure their futures would be better and they'd never have to go through anything like this again. With this figuring so strongly in my mind, I set about leaving no stone unturned in terms of building a case to stand up in court, without any shadow of a doubt, and consequently, allow us to remain in Cornwall where we belonged.

In the weeks that followed, I contacted a series of professionals. I met with counsellors, teachers, doctors, and applied for specialist intervention from children's services in the form of therapeutic help, although this never materialised. We were not deemed to be a priority as the children were no longer at risk. Due to the nature of the charge against me, whereby Claude had instructed a lawyer who was well versed in the enforcement of provisions under the Hague Convention which I had allegedly contravened, my solicitor arranged for me to meet with a barrister in Exeter. I had no idea what the term meant and what the implications were and so I was grateful for meeting with Christopher Naish, who specialised in family law in relation to the European Court. My stomach lurched and I felt my mind depart from my body to float near the ceiling of the oak panelled office as Mr Naish explained the gravity of the situation. In simple terms, he advised me that I had indeed broken the law by retaining Morgan in England, although as his mother I did have custody rights. My only hope of being able to stay in the country was to prove it would put Morgan in great danger if he was to return to France and into the care of his father. He asked me to give as many examples as possible of the psychological and physical trauma to which the boys had been exposed. He asked me to gather statements from others who had witnessed this first-hand. These would be submitted as evidence to build a case against having to return Morgan to his father. He told me it was going to be a hard battle to win but this would be the only option. Based on what I told him, he said he'd write a statement in my defence opposing the return of Morgan to France on the grounds it would present a grave risk, exposing him to physical or psychological harm.

I was convinced that given everything we'd been through, the court would find in our favour but just to give us the best possible chance, I gathered statements from all those I felt could have a valid input. At the same time, across the waters, Claude was obviously building his own case and it was not long before a pile of statements from the French contingent arrived through the letterbox, forwarded from my solicitor. Matters were complicated because being written in French, I needed to translate them accurately before my solicitor could work on them. I prepared myself for being annihilated by Claude's family so the contents of their rantings were not unexpected.

However, what surprised me the most, was the lack of any statement from JC. It it was conspicuous by its absence. It proved to me JC had been ill at ease from the outset and was now purposefully excluding himself from any further involvement. I found myself smiling, although thinly. Boisterous and full on though he may have been, I secretly felt JC was not an enemy and the lack of any condemning statement on his part, was proof enough.

Manu, Claude's eldest son wrote a statement with a glowing reference to his father. But where were the statements from Claude's other children? I'd formed a close bond with them when they'd made regular visits to our home. Gael in particular had been a brick, often defying his father in a bid to protect my boys. He was well aware of what we were being subjected to made regular visits whilst posted at the naval base in Toulon.

The more I thought about it, the more it played on my

mind. What was their reason for not getting involved? Did they know something I didn't and if so, could I use it to my advantage? I decided to make contact with Gael whose contact details were still safely stored in my pocket address book. It was a long shot, but anything was worth a try. The gloves were off and I'd nothing to lose and maybe something to gain. I emailed him telling him we'd escaped to England and I was now being charged with abducting Morgan. I ended with "Please help if you can".

Nothing could have prepared me for the reply that I received within six hours.

Chapter 50

Gael wrote:

Dear Jan

I am sorry to hear about what has happened but you have made the right decision for both yourself and your boys to return to England. My mother suffered at the hands of my father and she escaped on a train back up to Paris with us with only what we were wearing. While awaiting the date of the custody hearing, my father managed to get Manu and that is when my mother lost him. He took him from his school and that is the last she saw of him. When he went to court, he had Manu alongside him and so the court ruled he could keep him. It broke my mother's heart. It is because of him that I did not speak for over 2 years and had to have a school psychologist help me to overcome this. I know this experience has had a profound effect on my sister Rapha and it has altered the way in which she looks at men. She does not trust them and prefers women and I blame my father for that. I have spoken with Rapha and she has agreed we will help you as much as we can. She is going to contact our mother and ask her if she would

be willing to speak with you so that you have the best
possible chance of keeping Morgan.
A+ Bisous
Gael

Those poor defenceless children!

Suddenly I was not the first victim but realised that his ex-wife must have been through a terrible ordeal herself. Only in critical situations do we do desperate things. She had fled to Paris for safety. And yet Claude had played the part of the victim in it all. He'd never told me any details, just that he'd been left to bring up his eldest son on his own when his wife left, and that she'd re married and his other two children sadly, resided with her.

This in itself was an eye opener, but most concerning was the news Claude had abducted his son from school – a place his mother must have considered safe. Where did this leave Morgan? Could Claude sneak back into the country and take him too? He had just started mornings at pre-school. I needed to alert them. I was not being paranoid. There was no telling what this man was capable of doing. I couldn't take any chances. I needed to speak to Gael and Raphaelle's mother as soon as possible.

I replied to Gael, thanking him profusely for his email and appreciating that this put him potentially in an awkward situation. I asked him if I could have a contact number for his mother at his earliest convenience and waited yet again for a response.

It came but this time it was not from Gael but from Isabelle, Claude's ex-wife.

Dear Jan

It is necessary for you to ask your lawyer for a psychological assessment on the boys as well as for yourself and for Claude. I believe that this is the best chance you will have of keeping the boys with you. It will be necessary to state how it was before, during and after you knew Claude.

Above all, be very careful prior to the court hearing that your little boy is always with you. He needs supervising whilst in and out of school and must never be left alone. It was thanks to Claude that he was able to abduct my son from school the day before the hearing and in doing so, he knew he had the best possible chance of keeping him. I've been there, I know what I am talking about!

Above all, do not frighten him, but just tell him to be careful, that's all. The general rule in France is that a judge will not separate the children.

Do not trust any of his family. At one point, Josie and I were like sisters but she turned against me to help her brother, without even knowing what happened and why it got to that stage!

I am here to listen and to help you in any way I am able. I wish you luck because I know it will not be easy.

Love Isabelle

I could feel the bile rising in my throat. I felt sick. It confirmed everything Gael had told me and more. That cute, sweet little sister of his should never have been trusted either! Why had she introduced me to her quiet, charming brother in the first place? What was her motive? What could have happened to Isabelle to make her take her children and run? I needed to find out. The more dirt I could dig up, the better my chances. I'd need to be careful, but terrier instinct had already taken hold and I was not going to let go until I knew the truth. I searched the email again, looking for clues but found none, all except for a PS which I had overlooked as it was several return spaces below the rest of the text. The PS gave me Isabelle's mobile telephone number and without any hesitation, I dialled it.

Chapter 51

I needed a drink to settle my nerves. I was still reeling from the disclosure. Try as I might, I couldn't stop shaking. Seated at Phil's PC, my back to the lounge bay window, the winter sunshine flooded through the small gap between the navy curtains that hadn't been drawn fully back to embrace the day. I wouldn't be the one to pull the curtains back. It would be too risky. The rest of the day needed to be safely contained at a distance from me. I couldn't cope with allowing any more of it to infiltrate my space. My phone call to Isabelle was already too much to deal with. So I sat, motionless, facing the wall, trying to absorb what I'd heard and the gravity of it all. The biro was still clenched in my hand, with the piece of paper on which I'd quickly scribbled a name, lying haphazardly in front of me on the desk, alongside the keyboard.

I'd completely forgotten Phil's presence until I heard a groan from a disgruntled sofa spring as Phil leaned forward and asked, 'Well, what happened? I'm here waiting with baited breath. I couldn't understand a word of what was going on. What did she say? Was it useful?' and then a pause and he tried again, 'Jan?'

I swivelled around in the desk chair to face him and the words tumbled out of my mouth.

'My God Phil. This is awful! Isabelle just told me Claude came after her and he pulled a gun on her! A gun! Can you believe it? From what I understand, it happened prior to their court hearing when Claude appeared out of the blue. She was outside on the terrace. He demanded she hand over the children and when she didn't, he pulled a gun out that'd been tucked into the belt of his trousers. She was so shocked she couldn't move. She didn't say anything. And then when she realised the seriousness of her situation, for some reason which she doesn't understand to this day, she started to laugh!'

'Bloody hell,' spluttered Phil.

'Yeah, a gun pointed at her and she laughed! Anyway, she said she reckoned her reaction wasn't the one he was expecting and so that it threw him completely. He stared at her with a surprised look on his face, before lowering the barrel of the gun and storming off.'

Phil responded with a long drawn-out, *'Fuuuck!'*

'I asked her if the police were involved. She told me she did report it and there was issued with a log number but of course it was so many years ago now. Still, there must be a record of it somewhere. If I can get it, at least it'll show what the monster is capable of!'

'Why don't you get her to write a statement? That would be really good in terms of evidence.'

'Hmmm. I already tried that option. She's not willing to be named in the proceedings. Feels it is too risky and of course, she's got her children to think about. I suppose she wants to protect them too, especially as they still have to put up with him in their lives for weddings, funerals and the like.'

'Can't it be anonymous or something Jan?'

'No. It wouldn't carry much clout if it was, would it? The problem is that a witness in France has to identify themselves by their *'Carte d'identité'*, like we would use a passport for verification purposes over here. She doesn't want to do that because it would be all to obvious who'd supplied me with the information.'

'There must be something you can do!'

'Well, Isabelle's given me the name of the lawyer she used at the time – a Maître Humbert Guy de Paris. Goodness knows if he still exists or if he'd be willing to disclose any historical information on a case that's – what – at least 15 years old now.'

I took the slip of paper with the lawyer's name on it and added it to the list of things 'to do' in my A4 exercise book where I stored every detail I considered important in fighting my case. Looking down at the list, I realised I'd an appointment to see Matthew Taylor, my local MP in the afternoon.

'Phil, I've got to go. I need to be in Truro by 2.00 pm. Look, whilst I'm out can you run a search on that French lawyer, see if you can find him listed in the Paris region? That's going to be the most likely – that's if he's still practising. I'll catch up with you later. Fingers crossed you find him!'

Phil gave a willing nod and so I passed him the piece of paper with the name on it.

'Thanks Phil. You're a star!'

And with that I set off for Truro, armed with all my legal paperwork to date. I wanted to see the MP as I'd been advised he could have some useful contacts with Members of the European Parliament and might be able to give me an insight into how best to avoid being charged with international child abduction.

I marched purposefully to the side street, housing the yellow front door of the MP's drop-in office. I arrived five minutes early for my appointment and was greeted by a lady who introduced herself as Matthew's secretary. Explaining that I had an appointment with him at 2 pm, she looked somewhat puzzled, so I repeated the information to her.

'I'm sorry dear but I've no record of it in his diary and I'm afraid he has gone out for the afternoon and won't be back in the office until later in the week,' she informed me.

'He's not here? Well, I spoke to a lady on the phone a few days ago and she booked me in to see him today,' I tried, as if this would make any difference, but already knew the outcome.

'I'm sorry. You'll need to make another appointment I'm afraid,' she responded, starting to thumb through the pages of the enormous leather-bound desk diary in front of her.

'No. I'll leave it. Don't worry,' I snapped back, turning on my heels and storming out of the office, closing the door abruptly behind me.

I was so angry. Why were all these people in authority just not listening to me? The very people I'd thought would be offering me support and standing up for my rights as a British Citizen, were either legally biased or physically absent!

The more my experience to date underlined my viewpoint. Already criminalised by the police, shrugged off by social services whose intervention proved non existent left a sour taste of invalidation in my mouth. In terms of legal advice, it was a battle to find anyone who knew anything remotely relating to European Law and how its dynamics might affect me. And to top it off, the bloody MP had done a runner! It compounded my feelings of helplessness and worthlessness. My heart was racing and I was almost shaking with rage. At any moment I could lose the plot completely. It could only go one of two ways. Either I'd hit something or I'd cry but the tears were pushed so far down, feeling pain was more readily accessible.

Still smarting from the feeling of injustice, my bundle of legal papers, weighing heavily in my shoulder bag, I spotted a sign outside the entrance to a small alleyway. The sign read *'piercings'*. Without hesitation, I entered the little mews of shops, nestling together fronting the cobbled alleyway that ran between them. After a few paces, I saw the same advertising logo, in the third shop window and took a side entrance through a paint peeling door, only to to be guided by a set of neon arrows up a musty, carpeted staircase at the top of which was a glass-panelled door. I opened the door and went in. Twenty minutes later, I walked out again, no longer a virgin to body piercing, but now sporting a stud in my belly button. I've absolutely no idea what possessed me to do it as I'd never even considered it until that moment. In retrospect, I believe I wanted to externalise some of the pain I was feeling on the inside. If no one else could be bothered, I'd validate my own suffering.

The pain of the piercing gave me a short-lived sense of relief and in that moment, I vowed I'd no longer conform by bowing down to rules and regulations that served absolutely no useful purpose whatsoever. I'd lookd for alternatives. If I couldn't find justice via the normal route and no one was going to listen to me when I was in the right, then maybe it was time to bend the rules a little. Perhaps, I should start to play dirty. I'd spent all my life doing everything by the book and where had it got me? It certainly wasn't serving any useful purpose when I needed it most. I'd change my way of thinking. From now on, I'd be open to any type of plan, lawful or unlawful in my fight for justice.

Chapter 52

Phil's thorough internet search revealed nothing in terms of a lawyer bearing the name Monsieur Humbert Guy, not just in the Paris region, but throughout France itself. Whilst Isabelle remained unwilling to write a statement, this was another avenue we couldn't pursue any further. I passed the information on to my solicitor in a vain hope he might have some way of tracking the person down, but it was a long shot – this was France after all.

The inevitable official paperwork for the hearing arrived from the Supreme Court of Justice. Hands trembling at the enormity of the situation, I scanned the correspondence to locate the forthcoming date. 15th April 2003. Only three weeks away. Try as I might, it was impossible to keep the impending hearing away from Tom and Owen who seemed watchful of my every move and general demeanour. I promised them all would be well and no one was going to be sending us back to France. It was just not plausible. I assured them the powers that be would realise the atrocities to which we'd been subjected if anything, Claude would be the one to be brought to justice.

The days crept by, the clocks ticking down the hours until the day of reckoning. With each passing day, I realised that Claude could be getting more and more desperate in his bid to snatch Morgan prior to the hearing. With this in mind, I reminded the playgroup to be particularly vigilant. Any foreign registration on a car caused a sharp intake of breath, combined with the sudden panic that Claude could be driving it and had returned to take my son. I was hypervigilant by habit now. It was a learnt behaviour. One slip, one moment of not watching Morgan and our future as a family, could be thrown into jeopardy forever. I did not want my family to be torn apart, as had happened to Isabelle. Her words kept echoing in my head as a continual warning, repeating over and over.

On the morning of the day, I was to set off on the drive to London, I embraced all three boys fiercely as if for the last time. They were heading off to school and it was important to try and keep some air of normality about it all. I could not voice my deepest fears to them.

'When will you be back Mum?' asked Thomas.

'Tomorrow evening Tom,' I replied.

'Good luck,' said Owen, clutching his school reading bag in his hand and his packed lunch box in the other.

'Whatever happens Mum, don't let us have to go back to France,' said Tom, looking momentarily fearful as he realised the implications of his words.

'No, don't let us go back there!' chimed Owen, ringing alarm bells for all of us as he spoke.

'Don't worry. I promise you won't be going back to France boys. You're here and I will make sure you never have to go back; I promise you.'

I reassured them – a lot of promises that as their protector I was determined to keep. I would not fail my boys. The only outcome I'd consider was the one which ruled we were free to stay in our home country. If was up to me to make sure I'd be telling my boys the good news within 48 hours.

With this thought in mind, I got in the car, started the engine and set off, waving back to the frantic, exaggerated goodbye gestures from the hands of two small figures that stood huddled on the pavement, their size diminishing as the distance between us increased. And then, they were gone.

Chapter 53

Nothing could have prepared me for how overwhelmed I felt as I stood on the pavement opposite the vast, architecturally ornate, structure towering in front of me. It stood as if its whole being was a force to be reckoned with from the exterior alone. Behind its neo gothic façade, its physical presence seemed to echo the magnitude of the cases it dealt with. I could not avoid the watchful eyes of sculpted statues; stone sentinels secretly scrutinising me as I stood, scared and silently stilled by the immensity of it all. I could appreciate how this building would have been chosen as the location of The Supreme Court. Given its status as the final court of appeal in the UK for civil cases, and for criminal cases from England, Wales and Northern Ireland, it was here that cases of the greatest public or constitutional importance affecting the whole population were heard. Mine was one such case.

'Ah! You're here Jan. That's good.'

I turned to see my barrister in a navy suit and red tie, handkerchief tufting out of the breast pocket of his jacket.

'Yes,' I almost whispered in shaky tones, 'Phil came up with me last night and we stayed at some friends of his before catching the train into the centre of London first thing this morning.'

'That's good. I'm glad to hear you have someone with you. I take it you're going home immediately after the hearing?'

'Yes. I just want to get back to the boys as soon as possible so I'm driving straight back.'

He glanced at his watch.

'Think we ought to be going in now. We will need to go through security and the up to the office and see if the other side are here yet,' he said and started to cross the road to the grand entrance steps.

I took a deep breath and followed him.

Having cleared security, I found myself in an ornate entrance hall that was more akin to a grand stately home, although it was filled with the echoing footfalls and subdued voices of legal professionals. We were directed up a wide, sweeping staircase to a vast, galleried landing which we crossed before locating a small door on the right. On entering, we found a room which was in direct contrast to the enormity of all that we'd encountered so far. A clerk was standing behind a desk and there were four chairs, backed against the walls of the miniscule office space. My solicitor told me to take a seat and he proceeded to talk to the lady behind the desk. I was very aware that at any moment, Claude could walk in and it felt suddenly claustrophobic. I tried to brace myself for how I'd cope with being so close to him in such a confined space and I struggled for breath, gasping for air in short intakes. At that moment, I became aware of a tweed pattern skirt of a gowned woman appearing through the small entrance door. Striding a few paces to reach the enquiry desk, she introduced herself. Claude's barrister. I stopped breathing completely as she informed the clerk she was representing the Plaintiff, who would not be attending in person. My barrister raised his eyebrows at her statement and then ushered me outside to sit at what could only be described as something akin to a refectory table. He advised me to wait whilst he went to speak with her in private and to locate the barrister who'd be defending my case. I nodded my understanding and agreement. Hands cold and clammy I fished in my handbag for my mobile phone to text Phil and update him.

'He's NOT here,' was all that I had time to text, pressing the 'send' button as my solicitor returned with a flustered gesture to indicate that I should follow him immediately.

'We're going in now,' he said. 'Just remember if the judge does ask you anything, which is unlikely, just make sure you tell him exactly what you've already told me.'

I nodded and followed him along the landing. This was the moment of truth and I had to muster every ounce of strength to maintain a calm façade and to face whatever the future held.

I could not fail. The future safety of my boys was reliant on what happened in the courtroom.

Chapter 54

It was all too much.

I didn't want to live anymore.

I didn't want to think about the consequences of the hearing.

I couldn't cope.

It had taken so much strength until this time and now all the fight had gone out of me.

There was no justice.

There was nothing left, just the stillness of the panelled Jacobean-styled interior which made a mockery of the whole legal system. With its polished veneered glaze, it echoed with a contemptuous façade, masking my reality with pomp and ceremony, covering its timeless cracks, an edifice of crumbling legal failures. I sat shrouded by its historic dust, just another victim; just another nobody.

I'd listened in wide-eyed horror at similar cases to mine, cases whereby women had escaped from other countries, believing that they were saving their children from further despicable atrocities, only to be told they were to be sent back to the country from which they'd fled. I could associate with every single individual – the strength it had taken to make the decision to escape in the first place, the haunting fear which permeated every part of your very being until the overwhelming sense of relief felt on successfully fleeing the abuser, only to be told you have to go back. Not just return to the country and the situation from which you'd fled but to be threatened with extradition if you failed to return within the time scale scheduled. There were simply no words, no comfort, and no consolations.

According to the law relating to child abduction cases, any child who has been kidnapped from a member state, has to be returned to the country in which they are deemed to be 'habitually resident'. Morgan would have to return to France with or without me. Once returned, court custody hearings would be dealt with over there. There was absolutely no way I would be sending Morgan back into his abusers arms on his own. I'd made it very clear I would not be separated from him. But where did that decision leave Tom and Owen? How could I leave them behind? Yet how could I possibly put them through even more trauma, should I decide we should all return? We were going to be thrown like lambs to the slaughter. Tears of helplessness spilled unabated down my cheeks as I hung my head from the world; not through shame, but through complete brokenness. An outstretched hand offered a large white handkerchief, which I took to try and still the sobs that wracked my being. Looking up, I saw the compassion in the tear-filled eyes of Mike Willson, my solicitor.

'I'm so sorry Jan,' he said and I could see the dreadful outcome had moved him too. In this moment, he was no longer my legal representative, but a friend who felt my pain.

Tapping my arm in a consoling fashion, he ventured, 'I know this isn't the outcome you were hoping for but we have at least got things in place in order to help keep you safe. The French court will have to bear that in mind when it comes to the custody hearing.'

I glanced up at him expectantly and he continued, 'The custody hearing is set for 21st May and they have been lenient by allowing you to stay in England for nearly two weeks from now. You don't have to go until the deadline of 28th April. Sometimes they have a much shorter time frame of just a few days! The judge has acknowledged there is a risk to yourself and your children and that's why she's inserted the section stating *'in order to avoid a possible Article 13.b case'*. She realises there is potential for physical and psychological harm and, as a result, she has put a non-molestation order in place. It means Claude cannot come near you at the property when you return there. He cannot harass or pester you and he cannot threaten or use violence.'

I looked up at him as he pointed to the relevant section of the draft Court Order. Did he really believe this ruling in England would be enough? These were just words. They did not equate to Claude's compliance.

'So,' he continued, 'Claude has been asked to pay for your return fare on the ferry and I will return your passports to you the day before you need to travel. I will be in touch with you in the next couple of days but for now there's nothing more I can do. You'll get a formal copy of today's ruling and a set of papers to take with you to hand in to the French police, so they're aware that you are in need of protection.'

I nodded my understanding; we stood up and he shook my hand. Time to leave, time to contemplate how I'd ever find an acceptable means to pass this outcome onto the eager, waiting ears of my children. Mine was the figure of the forlorn; the ghost of hope extinguished and whose footsteps joined those of others who remained invisible. Invisible to a system echoing with the weight of the downtrodden as they thronged with those who'd gone before. I descended the austere staircase whose pretentiousness now reviled me even more, each tread aligning with every unjust ruling, each step symbolising my deepening descent into the abyss of the unknown. Finally exiting the building to witness a day of glorious Spring sunshine added to the agonising truth that the world went on regardless, no one cared, no one gave a damn.

I was physically and mentally exhausted and Phil drove, as I stared silently out of the window as we sped westwards.

'You ought to try to eat something,' Phil ventured as we had passed yet another motorway service station and once again, I refused the need to stop.

'I can't eat. I'm not hungry,' I replied emptily.

Although his well intentioned words endeavoured to break the silence, I was in no mood for talking. There was nothing more to be said. Any consolatory words would be futile. Sincerity in silence was the preferred option. He understood it was pointless to fob me off with worthless assurances. I had lost all concept of time. It was all just merging together into a blur, into a timeless entity to which I could see no end. It was the start of a nothingness into which I wanted to disappear as if I'd never existed.

When we finally arrived back in familiar surroundings, the clock had just turned 10.30 pm and Phil slowed the car in preparation to turn into my mother's road.

'No Phil!' I implored, the enormity of what I was going to have to do, too big to deal with, 'Keep going. I need a drink. Can we go to the pub first?'

And with that, the little car picked up speed once more and we accelerated up the hill and out of the village. I just couldn't cope with the thought of having to face my boys. How could I ever tell them I'd failed? I hadn't done enough to protect the little beings that I loved more than life itself. I couldn't face myself, let alone them.

Within a couple of miles, the illuminated pub sign came into view and we pulled into the car park which at this late hour was deserted. It was mid-week and most people were home in their beds with the prospect of another couple of working days until the weekend, when late social nights were more acceptable to the locals.

I remember someone telling me brandy was good for dealing with shock, so I chose it. I downed it quickly, the amber liquid hot in my throat, coupled with a warm afterglow which hinted at its ability to regenerate the rest of my numbed being. I hoped it would act as a restorative wake-up call, giving me the resolve needed to be able to face my children.

However, as Phil drove me homeward, disorientating dizziness engulfed me. Desperately trying to focus on the invisible horizon through the darkness, I swallowed hard. Rounding a tight left hand bend, the wave of nausea hit and I'd just enough time to yell for Phil to stop, before throwing my door open and being violently sick on the verge.

Chapter 55

When is it ever the right time for a mother to tell her children, 'I'm sorry. I've failed. I can't keep you safe'.

The previous day's legal ruling made me the abuser, forcing me to inflict further injury on my children. Although Morgan was too young to understand the devastating implications, I'd no choice, but to tell Tom and Owen the horrendous outcome and in doing so, I'd be guilty of meting out the next devastating blow. I played out all sorts of scenarios, searching for the right words. How could this type of news ever be sugar-coated enough to make it remotely palatable? It was impossible. The more I thought about it, the more I realised that I needed to document their reaction. The best way to do this would be to get a professional to witness it. It could then be submitted as another piece of evidence in my fight to keep Morgan. It was apparent Claude wasn't just intent of getting us back to France, but was actively seeking custody of our son.

When Tom and Owen questioned me about the events of yesterday, they'd already drawn their own conclusions. The edge of excitement in their voices indicated they already assumed I'd been victorious. And why wouldn't they? After all, they'd watched enough Disney films to know there was always a happy ending. Dismissively, I fobbed them off with, 'I'm going to talk to you about it later.'

Having hurried them off to school, I returned home to make the doctors appointment.

We sat side by side in the waiting room, anticipating the sound of the buzzer, summoning us to our appointment with Dr Fussell. The icy coldness of my hands acted like an emotional barometer, a direct indicator of the level of my fear. Restless with waiting, the boys got up to rummage through the assortment of well-thumbed children's books to find a story we could share.

'The Animals of Farthing Wood!' exclaimed Tom as he brandished his discovery aloft.

'Yes!' shouted a triumphant Owen as he punched the air and both boys scurried back to their seats handing me their prize possession in readiness of sharing a well-loved story.

'It's Fox,' said Tom, 'he was my favourite.'

'I liked Toady the best,' said Owen eagerly, 'he was funny.'

'But it was fox that led all the animals to safety when they had to leave where they lived and find somewhere new that was safe,' said Tom, his tone deliberately slow, emphasising its content as he stated this simple matter of fact.

'White Deer Park,' shrieked Owen, as if it was a competition to be the first to recall the detail.

I opened the book at the first page, realising the irony in what was happening, drawing parallels between the children's book and our own real-life story.

'They had so many adventures along the way, didn't they?' I ventured, 'But it was worth it in the end. They found a much better place, made lots of new friends and

I'm glad they got to White Deer Park.'

I hoped those words echoed somewhere in their minds because having just offered a beacon of hope, the buzzer sounded and the book was rapidly returned to its place. Like the small group of assorted animals in the story, our own little tribe made its way up the corridor, knocking on the door out of politeness, to hear a voice on the other side call out to us to enter. There were only two seats for patients and so Tom took one and Owen climbed to sit on my lap. I braced myself for what was about to happen.

'So Jan, what can I help you with today?' asked the doctor, swivelling in his office chair to face us, giving us his undivided attention.

The boys looked at me expectantly because they'd both queried our need to see the doctor, given that we all appeared perfectly healthy.

My words tumbled out.

'This is very difficult for me. I don't know what to do. I've thought about it but I still don't know if I'm doing the right thing... I think I am... I hope I am.'

The doctor nodded, realising that once I'd started, I shouldn't be interrupted because in doing so, I might not be able to bring myself to continue.

'I've got some news to tell the boys and I wanted to tell them in front of someone who's a professional,' I rasped.

My throat was closing up and I had to force the final words out. All eyes were on me now, watching and waiting. I took a deep breath and my lips moved as if blowing on an invisible balloon as I exhaled.

'I'm so sorry boys. I don't know how to say this, but we have to go back to France. The judge says we have to leave in a couple of weeks' time.'

Thomas hung his head and I watched the large tear

drops running down his face, dripping to splatter on to his school sweatshirt, leaving little dark marks like ink spots. I reached out putting my hand on his and to gripping it tightly, aware of how my little man was struggling, unable to combat the flow of tears despite being in the presence of a stranger. Then Owen spoke. No visible tears, but grief etched on his face by the haunted look now returning to his eyes. Old fears, rekindled in his consciousnessreturned as old fears rekindled into his consciousness.

'But Mummy, I'm afraid! I'm scared of Claude and what he'll do!'

'Gouge out my eyes! Saw my fingers off one by one! Give me the pain and the agony! Torture me! Make me suffer, but leave my boys alone,' I screamed internally, knowing it would fall on deaf ears and in my mind's eye I pictured the face of Claude, smirking knowingly at the pain he was inflicting.

Struggling to emotionally bring myself back into the room, I replied, 'It's Ok Owen. Claude is not allowed to be there. He won't be anywhere near us. It'll be OK.'

Owen looked back at me, his beautiful round eyes a startling shade of blue, his lips pursed in a tight smile of acknowledgement.

'I can see you're all upset and it must be a very difficult time for you,' Dr Fussell intervened, the latter part of his response aimed directly at me and I vowed to make another appointment to see him to ask for some tablets to help me to cope. I couldn't carry on holding it all together, this endless anxiety was too much.

'We'll be all right won't we boys?' I rallied, 'Thank you for seeing us today,' I added as I rose to stand. There was nothing more to say.

In the next couple of days I'd request a transcript of our visit today and add it to the growing number of statements to support our battle. In the meantime, I had to find a way of making sure I was true to my word, that we would be all right and that no harm would come to us. The boys had no option but to put their trust in me. I knew in my heart if I took them back to France, I couldn't be sure of keeping them safe. There had to be an alternative, regardless of what the court had ruled. It was becoming a game of cat and mouse and I was not going to knowingly walk into a trap to be a sitting target. To all intents and purposes, if we allowed ourselves to be lured back to the house in France, we'd be just that. It was all too easy for Claude and the risk was too high for us. I needed to think beyond the obvious – forget playing it by the book because it was proving futile. I needed to consider the psyche of my opponent in all this and how his devious, warped mind operated. Somehow I needed to find a way to be one step ahead of him. If, by being sent back to France, I was effectively being made to walk into his lair, I'd do it in the least suspecting way and with pre-determined escape routes already mapped out. Time to think outside the box. I'd resort to playing a different game. The more I thought about it, the strands of a plan began weaving themselves together in my head.

Under normal circumstances, I'd have welcomed some input from Moira. I knew she'd be willing to help me devise a suitable plan. However, she was currently up north, nursing her mother who was terminally ill. My heart went out to her. There are no words to offer which can possibly console the aching void of an inevitable loss. It threw a different light on my situation, providing respite from my own troubles and replacing them with those of my dearest friend. Each of us carried our individual pain. I didn't want to detract from the magnitude of what she was going through but Moira saw through my seemingly transparent attempts at assuring her I was OK. Her terrier instinct kept digging until she uncovered the truth of my situation. Devastated by the news and wishing she could be with me to offer support, she agreed to the plan I was proposing to carry out. What were the words she'd used? Something about *'if you always do, what you always do, you'll always get what you always get'* – it was time for me to do it differently, something radical. There might be rules to follow, but it'd be down to me how I chose to follow them. I'd learnt to expect the unexpected. This time the shoe would be on the other foot. I'd make a stand.

It was time to get my power back.

Chapter 56

'A camper van,' I announced triumphantly, realising I'd got everyone's attention.

'That's a good shout Jan. He won't be expecting that! Like you said mate, there's no way that you should return to your gaff in France and just wait. The English reg on your car will stand out like a fucking nun in a brothel! You need to keep a low profile,' replied Sweeny, his cockney accent deep and growling as he drew on another Golden Virginia roll-up, blowing the smoke into the air in a prolonged stream of thoughtful contemplation. He was holding counsel from his customary place in the corner of the bar, a seat which only an unsuspecting tourist would dare to unwittingly settle on, but that the locals respected was reserved for the 'big man' himself.

'Sounds like a plan,' nodded the man adjacent to Sweeny. He had a shock of unruly white hair which he intermittently swept back from his eyes in a theatrical flourish with hands like enormous shovels tightly gripping his pint. Word was that he had, on occasion, covered the relief shifts of the local grave digger – at least that is the story he spun to unsuspecting visitors. A tale of a hard day's graft, so the grieving family of 'old Mrs Trenerry' or whoever it was that sprung to his mind at the time, could finally get the burial they deserved and the closure they needed, had proven a very lucrative means of earning a free pint.

'Who's going with you though gal?' asked Josh, the tallest of the five. A good six feet tall and almost as broad he was sporting his red faded by age lifeguard shorts in the depths of winter, together with a pair of well-worn flipflops, thankfully minus the socks. Being a retired lifeguard, he had treated my boys' feet for weaver fish stings on many an occasion in the past, when they'd inadvertently trodden on the spines of the fish at low tide. Josh was very adept with an old ice cream tub and water as hot as could be tolerated. He'd come to our rescue in the past and now it seemed he wanted to come to our aid once more. I felt hugely grateful to this assortment of men around me.

'Little Jimmy's your man. Hey! Little Jimmy! You'll go with Jan, won't you? You've got sod all else to do anyway now that you're retired!' Sweeny mocked, raising his head to look directly at Josh's small friend. Unlike Josh and Sweeny who'd left the same council estate in the big smoke, some thirty years ago, to make a new life in Cornwall, Jim was the outsider of the group. Hailing from Hull originally, he'd come to Cornwall where he'd worked in the construction trade, and it was here that he'd formed lasting friendships with those that stood around him now. It amused me to discover he'd also paced the sands of Perranporth beach, providing donkey rides for the visitors of yesteryear. It reassured me to meet someone who'd a long-standing connection with a place I held dear. I got the feeling there was probably an awful lot I didn't yet know about this man with the wry smile and quick-witted humour. Little Jimmy was swamped in stature in comparison to Josh. A wiry little figure of a man, in his conformist style, twill checked shirt and jeans, he certainly didn't stand out from the crowd, but was the type who'd easily blend in and go unnoticed. He sported a greying handlebar moustache, the downward corners of which, he'd habitually twist methodically between thumb and forefinger. Little Jimmy although probably now in his mid-sixties, had a litheness about him and whilst his posture intimated at him being a relaxed person, his eyes darted continually, vigilant and alert, never missing a trick. Now his eyes glinted as he looked knowingly back at Sweeny, as if he knew what was expected of him.

'All right son. I'll go. I'll sort the froggy bastards out,' he nodded, smiling and jutting his chin in the air defiantly.

'Any problems when you're on the ground over there and you make the call,' Sweeny replied. 'Remember what we said. We've got people on stand-by if needed.' The power of his directness was so strong, it was uncomfortable and I had to look away, but not before I saw Little Jimmy acknowledge the gravity of it. To establish the subject of conversation was now firmly closed, Sweeny lent forward across the bar in an exaggerated gesture of looking at one of the many shelves.

'Terrence, I think it's time to sell some more of our wares,' he grinned with a brief raising of eyebrows as he indicated some potential buyers had just walked into the characterful bar with its low beamed ceilings. Terry flicked back the locks of hair that had flopped once more over his face. Leaning purposefully across the bar, he made his trademark flamboyant gyrating gesture with his wrist towards a couple honey pots on the shelf behind the bar.

Exclaiming loudly solely for the benefit of the ears of the new arrivals he announced, 'I see we only have two jars of honey left!'

The eyes of the unsuspecting incomers were

successfully lured to the pots of honey, each sporting a suitably rustic label which read Barkla Bees Honey. Terry launched into an avid blow by blow account of how he looked after the swarm. His persuasive narrative included the many mishpas he'd endured in the collection of the honey and how its unique floral fragrance was exclusive to the area surrounding the hives. Ten minutes later, the visitors purchased the last two remaining pots of this rare honey, its individuality reflected in the somewhat extortionate price.

A series of large grins were knowingly passed around our little gathering at one end of the bar and I was wondered what had prompted Terry to take up the art of bee keeping. It seemed an unusual pastime.

Before I could ask, the answer came, when Sweeny muttered to the others under his breath, 'Guess that means another trip to the cash and carry gentlemen. Took bloody ages to soak the labels off that last batch! Here's to the Barkla Bees!' and he raised his glass to toast the labours of the imaginary insects.

'To the Barkla Bees,' we buzzed back at him.

Chapter 57

Although reluctant to adhere to the procedures of the high court ruling, I'd no choice but to collect our passports from the solicitors office, the day before our departure. It sickened me to think all my efforts to escape had been in vain and that for all intents and purposes, Claude remained the puppeteer; no doubt delighting in pulling the strings, steering my every movement.

Seated opposite Mike Willson in his somewhat pokey office, he informed me that whilst Claude had adhered to the ruling in terms of paying for our return travel costs, he'd played it to his financial advantage. I waited for him to elaborate further.

'We've not actually received a ticket for you to travel. All we have is a quote forwarded from Claude's solicitors on his behalf, detailing what appears to be the cheapest ferry crossing. It's a reservation that's on hold for a one way ticket from Plymouth to Roscoff in Brittany.'

Typical. He'd taken great pleasure in reserving a crossing which would leave us facing the longest drive of all through France. How did he expect a toddler and his two brothers to cope with such a tedious road journey, trapped in a vehicle for twelve hours on end? He was trying to make it as difficult for me, given that as far as he was concerned, I'd be undertaking the journey single-handed.

'Well, that's ridiculous,' I replied 'I'm not going to take my children on that route. What about the fuel and motorway expenses that he's also supposed to be covering? Has he sent any money for those?'

Mike pushed a cheque across the desk towards me. £30. An absolute pittance. Claude was really showing his true colours to my solicitor now. The real nature of the beast! Maybe Mike would get some sense of what this vile excuse for a man was about.

My solicitor squirmed uncomfortably in his seat. Smiling sympathetically towards him I said, 'Mike, it doesn't surprise me. It wounds Claude to part with money. He's limiting the extent of his self-inflicted injury! How the hell he truly thinks that £30 will cover all the diesel to travel 800 plus miles, I don't know! No – actually I do! He's well aware it won't cover the costs. He's being deliberately difficult and paying the most minimal amount that he can get away with!'

Mike continued shifting his weight on his chair and his eyes averted my gaze. There was a pause and with a long exhalation as if gearing himself up to throw something else into the mix, he raised his head and with a pained expression said, 'Jan, the £30 is to cover all your costs. It includes the ferry as well.'

The poor man looked ashamed to have been the one to impart this information. It was ironic that his sense of disbelief appeared greater that mine. Crazy to think a legal professional could have the wool pulled over his eyes! Did he really believe Claude would play fair? He's obviously not spent enough time studying the mind of the manipulator. I sympathised with the fact that he'd been duped. Claude was a law unto himself so this latest antic came as little surprise to me. I'd expected foul play on his part but I couldn't imagine him being prepared for what I'd got in store for him. Time to employ the first tactic. With the full backing of my solicitor, I changed the destination of our sailing, taking us to Santander in Northern Spain instead. It meant less time to be cooped up in a vehicle and halved the driving distance required at the other side.

I drove back from the solicitor's in the knowledge this was to be my last night on Cornish soil. With no idea when I'd be back in Cornwall again, needed to strengthen my resolve. Claude's efforts to locate us would be focused upon a small hatchback with an English plate. A vehicle that would be travelling south from the northern tip of France, a woman on her own with three children in tow. Little did he know, plans had changed. Instead there would be a large camper, crossing the border into France from northern Spain with a very different passenger list. We were going in under the radar.

All relative paperwork appertaining to my case had been forwarded to my legal representative in France, a lawyer by the name of Mme Caparros who spoke no English whatsoever. We'd had a demanding time communicating effectively with one another on the phone. I wasn't familiar with the legal terms she used. However, we'd agreed to meet in person, as soon as possible, prior to the non-conciliation hearing at the Tribunal of Grande Instance, Montpellier, sheduled for 21st May. I hoped I'd be able to make myself understood and that my lawyer was suitably equipped with a means of translating the preparatory paperwork which had already been emailed to her.

Word had spread about the local woman who'd been accused of abducting her son and I'd been approached by the local press wanting to cover the story. The more exposure our circumstance got the better because maybe someone would read about it and offer their help, someone who carried enough clout to put an end to it all. So, when the local reporter arrived on the doorstep a couple of hours before we were due to leave, he asked to take a photograph of the four of us. I'd deliberately given the boys England football team backpacks which Tom and Owen filled with items of their choice. I wanted to make an unspoken statement that we should matter because we were English. We were British citizens and yet what did it count for? Nothing to date. Over the last few months, I'd been acutely aware of news stories illustrating how our nation continued to support refugees from all corners of the world by allowing them sanctuary in the UK. Whilst this was honourable, I bitterly resented being denied a basic human right. The British legal system had belittled our plight and failed in its duty of care at a time when we needed it most. When the local reporter departed, armed with everything needed to compile his headline article, there wasn't the slightest prick of conscience on my part. I'd willingly supplied him with as much information as possible to guarantee he'd be in a position to expose all the injustices of the legal system. Maybe, just maybe, there'd be someone out there who'd read about our plight, someone with enough power to poke a large stick in the spokes of the wheel of so called justice, killing its momentum and bringing it to a timely halt. But until then, I'd no one but myself to rely on. Forget the imposter's who feigned having the best interests of my children at heart. They were nothing but fakes. I was the only one being real, the only adult with the lived experience who'd witnessed the hellacious truth. Consequently this made me the expert in comparison to all the judicial ignorant, incompetent idiots who'd backed me into this corner. Armed with my existing insight, I'd deploy it to my advantage and play it for all it was worth to protect my boys.

Under the Hague Convention I'd be facing a prison sentence if I didn't return Morgan to France, so I knew I'd been left with no alternative but to take him back. Believe it or not, I was in an enviable position because there were no restrictions on my travel. I'd heard of cases where visa implications prevent mothers from accompanying their child. At least I didn't have to face the unthinkable notion of Morgan being taken from me and sent back alone into the hands of his father. The court knew I'd be accompanying him and made the assumption we'd all be returning as a family. Claude would be on the lookout for a family of four. He'd probably find a means of tracking our progress. More worrying was my suspicion he'd give a detailed description to the authorities, ordering them to take Morgan from me once we were in France. Isabelle's words of warning echoed in my head.

Mind made up, I called out, 'Tom! Owen! Come over here a moment. Bring your backpacks with you,' I called.

They scurried over, hearing the urgency in my voice.

'You'll be pleased to know you two are staying here. I'm not taking you back to France with me. Apart from anything else, it'd mean you missing school and I know you'll be perfectly fine here staying with Gran, until I get back with Morgs.'

'But you can't go back there on your own mum!' Tom repsonded, looking horrified at the thought.

'Of course I can Tom. It's the only way. Anyway, I'm not going to be by myself. Morgs will be with me and a friend of mine has very kindly offered to come too. He's an old friend of Sam Sweeny's dad and Josh the lifeguard.'

'Sam's in the year above me at school,' said Tom.

'I know Sam too,' said Owen indignantly, as if it was suddenly a competition between the two of them and he wasn't willing to lose out.

Then he added mischievously, 'Tom only knows Josh cos he's always the one to be stung by a weaver fish! Ouch! Ouch! Oh Mum! My foot, my foot!'

And he proceeded to hop theatrically around the hallway, mimicking his brother. A couple of moments later Gran's hallway was full of hopping boys with a rather bewildered Morgan joining in as best he could with a wobbling hop and a high pitched 'Ouch!' as his cries of delighted excitement joined those of his older brothers.

'Okay, okay! Enough is enough you lot!' I tried, my voice reaching a crescendo in order to be heard above the rally of rioting hoppers at my feet. 'STOP!'

'Gosh! What's all this noise about?' said Gran, emerging from the dining room, 'I thought I'd a house full of raucous rabbits for a moment!'

'We're going to stay with you Gran!' exclaimed Tom.

'Yes! Bouncy bouncy, boing boing!' squealed Owen, exaggerating his delight by a series of frenzied leaps.

'Oh! Well, you know I only have well behaved boys in my house don't you?' said my mum, smiling dotingly at her grandsons.

'We'll be good, we'll be good,' replied Owen between bounces

'Just make sure you are. And make sure you listen to what Gran tells you. You've all got to look after each other until we get back,' I added. 'Come on Morgs! You and I are going on an adventure! We've got a date with a pirate! His name's Captain Jim.'

Soon everything was stowed away in the spacious camper that was to be our home for the next three weeks and Morgan was buckled in to his seat. I clambered up into the cabin to sit in an elevated position, ready for departure. Little Jimmy arrived on foot, carry a well-worn kit bag and he stowed it neatly away in one of the lockers. I made the introductions and Morgan immediately warmed to his new ally who was showing an avid shared interest in the newly purchased pirate play figures

'Ah-haa!' exclaimed Captain Jim, head titled slightly to one side in a gesture that accentuated his keen discovery of the assortment of miniature pirate crew that lying on the table in front of an equally fascinated Morgan.

'If I'm not mistaken,' he continued with an emphatic west country drawl befitting a pirate captain, 'You must be young Morgan and you've brought the rest of the crew with you.'

Picking up one of the rubberised figures in its nautical blue and white striped shirt, he added, 'Oy think we 'ave Blackbeard aboard – see that Morgan, see that beard of 'is?'

Morgan responded with an eager but serious nod indicating he'd understood the unspoken significance of the Captain's words. Smiling at the smallest crew member, Captain Jim took the helm, knowing that his introductions had cemented an initial bond between the two of them thus limiting the risks of future mutinies.

'Time to set sail! Let's go find that ship! I feel an adventure coming on! I can feel it in me bones.'

Giving me a nautical wink, he flamboyantly twisted the ends of his handlebar moustache before taking his place on the seat alongside me. In that moment, I felt everything would be alright. It was the right decision to have Little Jim on board. He instilled a sense of hope. Between us, we could and we would rise to any challenges which lay ahead. The play pirate figures had proved successful and I hoped my secret stash of other toys would keep my three year old occupied throughout the long journey that lay ahead.

Time to make tracks. Key in the ignition, I started the

engine which rumbled throatily into life, signalling that from now on, we'd be heading bow first, into uncharted waters.

Three pairs of concerned eyes watched me through the glass of the driver's window, intent on finding clues to my mood. Knowing they sought reassurance, I wound the window down to muster an upbeat farewell to the fragmented members of my loved ones lining the pavement.

'Remember I love you lots and I'll see you soon,' I tried, my voice wavering despite my efforts to conceal the emotions threatening to erupt at any moment. Not wanting them to witness my tears, I put the van into first and it started to creep forward.

'Wait!' yelled Tom and he turned to dash back up the front path to his gran's house. I paused, wondering what was going on and why he'd taken off so suddenly and purposefully. Moments later, he rushed back down the path, taking two steps at a time to arrive in a breathless halt. With clenched fist waving above his head, he extended his arm to a full stretch as he strove to pass me whatever he was holding.

'What is it Tom?' I asked, lowering my hand to meet his over the side door of the cab.

'It's my special stone,' he replied. 'It's for good luck. It's the one I found on the day when we were out walking. Do you remember? Claude said it was just a piece of rock but you said it wasn't. You said it was a very a special one, so I've kept it ever since. Here, take it Mum.'

He dropped it into my palm and I carefully drew it towards me through the open window. 'Thanks Tombo, I'll keep it with me.'

Tom grinned up at me, a look of accomplishment on his face. Then, suddenly as if in afterthought, he cupped his right hand to the side of his mouth, in a gesture indicating he was about to pass on some vital secret information.

'The Butter Lady told me to give it to you,' he whispered, eyeing me as if it was a coded message that only I would understand.

I frowned at him, not comprehending. When had he been communicating with the Butter Lady? What on earth could she have to do with any of this?

Seeing my puzzled expression, he added some clarification for my benefit.

'She was in my dream last night. She's still watching. It's OK. She just wants you to take the special stone with you. It'll help you Mum.'

'That's lovely,' were the only faltered words I could muster.

To try to say more, would result in an outpouring of tears and I couldn't allow my vulnerability to surface. It was down to me to show the boys I was going into battle with confidence, let them see I already knew I'd be victorious. Clutching the stone like an amulet, as if our future lay in its hands, I realised the futility in relying on the blessing of a rock and a kindly spirit to keep us safe. How could it possibly be enough? And yet, it was all I had to hold onto. The worldly legal system on the physical plane was proving useless. How ironic to be in the position of having to turn to the spiritual realms for protection. Who knew what influences might be at work? My only certainty was the fact that the symbolism of Tom's words were held in the unknown of our tomorrows, and only then might we unravel their meaning.

Chapter 58

The ferry crossing was relatively relaxed and Morgan enjoyed being entertained by the infamous 'Captain Jim'. With his cries of 'me hearties', 'shiver me timbers' and impressions of Long John Silver, Jim wooed Morgan over as a veritable crew member aboard the enormous pirate ship on which we found ourselves.

Just over 24 hours later, Morgan dozed as we progressed along the meandering motorway that wove its way through mountainous passes into Catalan territory, and ever closer to the border between Spain and France. Little Jimmy was proving to be an ideal travelling companion. He was a diamond map reader, ensuring we stuck to the route. His humorous quips were a welcome antedote to the tedium of covering the many miles of arid terrain through which we travelled. Thankfully he also knew when to remain silent when we negotiated the complexities of passing through busy urbanisations. In these instances, it was reassuring to know there were two pairs of eyes on the alert. I was thankful that I enjoyed driving and wondered how someone who wasn't a natural behind the wheel would fare driving on the other side of the road to which they were accustomed in a right-hand drive vehicle. However, I enjoyed the challenge and felt familiar with the dimensions of the vehicle, having taken it on a few dry runs around the Cornish lanes.

We crossed the border into France mid-afternoon, taking the autoroute keeping the mountains of the Pyrenees to our right as we followed their peaked ridges southbound. Although we were making good time, on the advice of Little Jim we left the motorway, entering a vast agricultural region, where undulating fields of grapevines stretched as far as the eye could see. There wasn't a single dwelling in sight, making it the ideal environment in which to remain inconspicuous. We pulled into a field gateway at the side of a tiny lane, the ridge of long grasses which splayed from its centre, indicating it was rarely used for access. It was the perfect stopping place for the night. Not only did it give us chance to recuperate, but played to our advantage because it meant we'd arrive at my property in *Vic La Gardiole* in daylight. I didn't argue with him. In fact, I was relieved. The more I could delay the inevitable, the better. So, we set up camp for the night and feasted on some tinned supplies from the store cupboard. No doubt the French would've been suitably horrified at our cuisine, but it was a means to an end and served its purpose.

Even after the cicadas ceased their squeaky, lengthy and leggy conversations, Jimmy and I continued planning in our makeshift 'ops room' set up between the side of the camper van and the sea of vineyards stretching into the silent distance. We sat conspiratorially perched uneasily on fold-up deckchairs, hunched in conversation, two solitary silhouettes, under the glimmer of the hurricane lantern. Jimmy was covering all bases and leaving nothing to chance. He explained the strategy for tomorrow in the hope there'd be no loose ends. He was now fully conversant with the internal layout of the property, both its entrance and exit points and access from the road. The entrance to the residence was gated and relied upon the mechanics of a remote-controlled beeper in order to get in or out of the enclosed area. He'd immediately dismissed this as a suitable option for us. Instead, we'd approach the property from the road so we could get away at speed if the need arose. Via in-depth questioning, Jimmy extracted detailed descriptions of all those people who posed a potential threat to Morgan's safety. He was also aware of where these people were located in relation to the target area and how long it'd take them to arrive at the property from their normal location.

Satisfied we'd explored every avenue, I finally climbed up the ladder into the overhead sleeping cab to lie beside my little lad, arm tucked firmly around his doggy comforter, thumb resting on the bottom lip of his open, sleep filled mouth. We'd done all we could to prepare ourselves.

There was nothing more to do but wait for dawn, an invisible, unstoppable force, hurtling its way towards us, and now only three hours distant before it rose to shed its light on the day.

Chapter 59

Not a single cloud dotted the sky, leaving the warmth of the spring morning touching our surroundings in a golden light. Under normal circumstances, I'd have relished the prospect of such a wonderful day. However as each mile closed the gap between us and our destination, my sense of unease was growing larger by the minute.

Just as Little Jimmy planned, by early afternoon we neared the familiar landmarks of the hilly *Mont St Clair*, marking the old town of *Sete*, known as the *Venice of the Languedoc* on account of the myriad of its canal waterways. We skirted the vast expanse of the *Etang du Thau*, the first of the salt lakes to flank the shores of the Mediterranean. As we continued driving, taking a short cut, off the main A-road to travel along the side of *l'étang de Vic*, the familar sight of the pink flamingoes still held a mesmerising effect on me I remembered why I loved the area in terms of its geographical location. The golden glow from the sandstone terrain, combined with the sun to wrap the visitor in a sense of gentle warmth. A clump of pine trees marked the landscape on the far side of a small bridge. Their scent, caught on the breeze, filled the coloured sails of windsurfers, sending them scudding through the saline shallows. We'd cycled this route on many an occasion and

I knew it was only a five minute cycle ride away, through the local vineyard, from where we lived.

'We're nearly there Jimmy,' I said. Easing my foot off the accelerator the implcation hit me. 'I'm scared.'

'How much longer?' asked Jimmy sharply, all signs of his relaxed demeanour vanishing on hearing these words.

'Less than five minutes if I take the back lanes. It's a short cut not used by many people. It'll bring us up right outside the property on the road side.'

'OK. Approach slowly from that side. Keep driving. Slow and steady.'

'What happens if he's there?'

Real panic was setting in.

The fearful reality of it was getting terrifyingly closer, making my senses go into a state of heightened alert. Stumpy, serried lines of the field of vines, the sound of our wheels as they rumbled over the rounded cobbles crossing through a farmyard. A right hand bend lay immediately ahead, marking the last obstruction between us and a clear view of the road where I'd lived.

I didn't want to round that bend.

I didn't want to face what lay around the corner. But we were still moving forward, passing the neighbouring field with its assortment of patchwork patterned ponies and the odd white goat, their intermittent bleats a siren of warning.

And still we kept going.

Rounding the final corner, I took a spontaneous, intake of breath, as if preparing to dive into the a flooded cave, never knowing if I'd find my way out from its stranglehold of subterranean passageways

'I can't see his car,' I voiced hoarsely, 'but he could have parked it around the back, through the securely gated entrance.'

'No, I can't see a blue Scenic,' confirmed Jimmy. 'I

want you to pull over and park up behind this vehicle coming up on the right. We're already drawing attention to ourselves with this bloody great bus and English plate! That pair of lads we passed, just clocked us.'

I pulled in as he ordered, clipping the front tyre against the pavement as I did so. We were now directly opposite the little walkway which crossed the *fossé*, the narrow ditch often overflowing with water during heavy rainfall. The boys and I used to joke about the little plank that we used to bridge the gap between the pavement, the *fossé* and the high garden gate at the road entrance to our property. We named it the Billy Goats Gruff Bridge and would call out "Who's that trip trapping over MY bridge?" each time we used it. This time the troll lurking beneath was beyond my worst imaginings.

I startled as Jimmy said, 'Right. You have to go and get the keys from Freddy or whatever he's called, don't you?'

'You mean Fernand,' I corrected him. 'Yes. Fernand and Annie. Annie's the one who sent me my secret paperwork back when I left Claude and we stayed in England. I think, well I hope I can trust her. Fernand is in charge of the maintenance at the residence. He knows what happened to Owen. He's the one who saw the finger mark bruising around Owen's neck but wouldn't say anything – didn't want to get involved. Said Claude could make him lose his job. So, I don't trust him so much but I think Annie's OK.'

'OK. Yes, I remember. I'll stay here with the van and with Morgan. If he wakes up, I'll keep him occupied but I don't want him getting out of the van. Be as quick as you can.'

With that, I hurried off in search of the little house within the complex, through its winding pathways and with the high privacy hedges, praying that no one would be lurking around each and every twisting corner. Just as I approached the entrance to Annie and Fernand's place, so Fernand appeared in the pathway ahead of me. He was brandishing a small bunch of keys holding them aloft, as if enticing me to make the effort to reach upward for them. He smiled but behind the effort of a smile, his face looked troubled. Fernand spoke no English, but I was sure by the look in his eye, that he had been he'd been sworn to secrecy. Fernand would no doubt be on standby to alert Claude of my arrival and all it would take, was one phone call. Who knew how near he was already? I needed to act quickly. Time was of the essence. Feigning delight at seeing him I made a sweeping gesture of greeting him as an old friend.

'Fernand! How wonderful to see you! It's been such a long time! I trust both yourself and Annie are well?'

I spoke in fluent French and I kissed him without sincerity, my three customary kisses barely brushing his alternating cheeks.

'Good to see you my dear,' he replied, 'although the circumstances sadden me.'

I sensed his eyes shift from side to side as if something or someone were missing.

He ventured, 'And where's young Morgan? I thought he'd be with you.'

He uttered the latter part with such undeniable curiosity and sense of needing an urgent answer, I felt the hairs on my arms stand up.

Alarm bells were sounding loudly, pealing in my head; resonating like an unstoppable death knell.

'It's just me that's come to collect the keys Fernand,' I replied, knowing he couldn't challenge the fact. It was self-evident. 'Talking of which, thank you for acting as a collection point! I'll take them now.'

I stepped towards him, removing the keys firmly from his hand, adamant they'd not be used as a delaying tactic on his part. For all I knew, Annie could be inside right this minute, making the phone call to Claude.

Isabelle's warning began chiming in my ears. So far, I'd managed to keep Morgan safe, but now we were here, it'd be so much easier for Claude to grab him. This was a trap. I was convinced. My gut instinct was screaming at me – "Get out! Get away!"

I needed to get back to Jimmy as fast as possible. I turned on my heels, retracing my steps, trying to keep my sense of composure as I felt Fernand's eyes burning into my retreating form. "Slowly, steadily", I ordered myself, "don't let him sense you suspect anything. Keep walking, stay relaxed. Don't let him see the panic". Pacing myself, I waited for the cover of the last bend, knowing it would obscure me from Fernands eagle eyes. Only then did I break into a run.

'I've got the keys!' I panted, hands momentarily on my knees as I bent to regain my breath. Adrenalin coursing through me in a fear-filled energy rush, filled Jimmy in on the details of my meeting with Fernand. He looked solemn and as he listened to me, his ferret like eyes darted over my shoulder, scanning for any sign of movement behind me.

'We haven't got long,' he said. 'The net is closing in. You've got fifteen minutes Jan, no more, to take whatever you need from the house. It's a quick in and out. It's not safe here.'

'I can't go in on my own!' I completely understood the importance of his words. This threat was very real and growing more and more tangible with each second that passed.

'No. It's OK. I'm coming with you. Morgan will have to come too. I'm not going to risk leaving him in the van on his own. I'll take care of Morgan.'

He disappeared into the van and I heard the rustling of him rifling through his kit bag, shortly followed by gentle tones of reassurance as he lifted the still dozing young Morgan into his arms.

Exiting the van he stressed, 'Just grab the things you want. Only take what's practical. Remember fifteen minutes, no more. Let's go!'

With that we hurried across the little bridge and threw open the high wooden privacy gate which opened onto the small, terraced garden of the property. Out of nowhere, a familiar sound exploded into the air, splintering the uncanny silence. Desperate to meet the maker of the noise, I turned in its direction, just in time to catch the glimpse of a large shape hurtling towards me at an unstoppable pace.

Chapter 60

I fell to my knees, arms open wide, tears of sheer joy at seeing my beloved Labrador, Milly. She came bounding towards me, hips rocking from side to side, panting and launching into me at full force. She greeted me with slobbering kisses for a reunion that was long overdue.

I wrapped my arms around her, hugging her tight, voice breaking with the words, 'Milly, my Milly.'

She pushed me backwards, knocking me, as Sweeny would have put it, onto my 'arris', still eagerly licking my face, her breath hot with excitement. I regathered my composure, patting her reassuringly and scrabbling to my feet. A movement caught the corner of my eye and yet, because Jimmy hadn't said a word, I sensed it wasn't something to be feared. Tucked around the corner of the house, half hidden from view by a dilapidated kennel, I saw the black and white markings of my dear Shadow. As I moved towards her, I heard the trail of a chain dragging on the ground. At the end of its meagre six foot length, Shadow was shackled, her freedom limited to the extent of its range. Forlorn and beyond the reach of a water bowl; a cruel mirage through which a filthy oasis paraded itself as a potential lifesaver, its poisonous contents shimmering seductively in the thirst making heat. The sight of red fungus flourishing on the inner wall of the ceramic bowl disgusted me, as did the revolting bulbous yellow mound that bobbed like a capsule of puss on the surface of the stagnant water. How long had the bowl been there, purposefully placed for optimum cruelty, teasingly mocking her endless struggles to reach it?

Had the passage of time shrouded Shadow's ability to recall the happy chapters of her life? Or, had she packed all the good memories away because the pain of abandonment had proved too much to bear? Maybe she'd discarded them in the same way she must believe I'd discarded her. An object once precious, now of little importance. My Shadow, my rescue, my first family before my children were born. The emotional ache of letting her down was unbearable. I fell to the ground, simultaneously overwhelmed with a grief and self-loathing, sobbing deeply, guilty of deserting her, a traitor to her undying loyalty. And yet, here she was, watching me with her soulful brown eyes, eyes whose gaze was now hazy, as if glazed into vague recollections of having once been loved. She stood before me stiff limbed wary of putting one leg in front of the other in case she was unable to support herself. My heart broke into a thousand pieces, to scatter around her broken form, chained like a convict to both undeniable cruelty and cataracts. She took two stiffened steps towards me. Her long fox-like tail brushed the ground as it swept from side to side in the realisation I'd come back for her. She opened her mouth to bark but all I heard was a simple desperate hoarse type rasp. The familiar bark I'd known for fourteen years had vanished. The little soul who stood before me was no longer the aptly named shadow who'd followed me everywhere even when the sun wasn't shining. My beautiful girl was now a 'shadow' of her former self. Rushing towards her, my grief poured in unrelenting sobs, wetting her dusty coat as I nestled my face into the white fur of her neck.

'Shadow – my Shadow. I'm so sorry. I'm so, so sorry. Please forgive me.'

I swaddled her in my arms, holding her close and tenderly rubbing her behind the ears. It was an old habit I knew she relished. Fervently, I wished with all my heart to bestow upon her a sense of love, warmth and healing through my hands. I could feel their growing heat and I knew I was channelling unconditional love into her frail body. Tenderly, she nuzzled into my neck.

'You're safe now girl. I've missed you so, so much. It's OK. I'm getting you out of here. I'll never leave you again. I promise. Oh Shadow, I'm so, so sorry.'

'Ooh! Stop it now! You're making me cry!' said a companionable voice over my right shoulder and I turned to see Jim, wiping an eye with the stub of his finger, genuinely moved by what he'd just witnessed.

Morgan reached out, leaning his body weight away from Captain Jim and towards Milly, who was waddling up and down gleefully on the terrace, tail wagging and muzzle exposing the tips of her teeth, in what I knew to be a wide grin.

'Milly,' said Morgan, opening and closing his palm of the outstretched hand.

'Milly.'

It was obvious he wanted be released from Jim's arms and reunited with his real life doggy. Jimmy placed him on the terrace and he ran towards her, only to be smothered in doggy kisses on a head that was only just higher than her own.

'You get on with things from the house, whilst I watch this lot,' said Jimmy.

Opening the shutters, I unlocked the front door and walked in. It all looked very much as I remembered it. It was strange to see my paintings of local Cornish scenes hadn't been removed, but were in their usual place above the dining table. I crossed the room, heading for Morgan's bedroom and opened the door. It was empty. There was no indication it'd ever been inhabited by him. Even the wall mural I'd painted for him was gone. No toys, no bed, no books. Nothing. I ran up the stairs to the boys' bedroom. It lay untouched and I quickly grabbed items that I thought would be of importance to them, including Pokémon cards, the PlayStation, some games, as well as their most loved cuddly toys.

Back down the stairs again and I dived into the kitchen drawers to grab my favourite vegetable knife and the olive wood cheese board that'd been a rare find at one of the local markets. Moving at a pace, I went into the lounge, the large sofa still in situ and I briefly recollected the trauma of being thrown onto it, the threat of being punched in the face and the desperate need to fight Claude away by tucking my legs up as high as I could muster to push him away. The snap shot disappeared and my gaze turned to the shelf with ornaments on it. I grabbed a couple of them from their dusty resting place and quickly placed then on the dining room table, to add to my growing collection of items that I'd be taking with me. I decided it would be worth scanning the spare bedroom but wasn't expecting to find anything of any importance within its walls.

It was only when I opened the door, I discovered the room had been shockingly transformed. It was a bedroom for Morgan What on earth was it doing on this side of the house? Everything had been relocated lock stock and barrel where it lay positioned with an uncanny sense of ordered neatness; soft toys placed against the back of the bed in regimented ranks, books carefully stacked in order of size, not in order of 'most used favourites'. The pictorial rug with its road system layout, positioned equidistantly between the wooden legs of the bed. Something was missing though. Where were the toy cars Morgan loved to play with? Suddenly it dawned on me his toy box was missing. It was a really useful piece of furniture I'd personalised for him and which kept everything tidily out of sight. Surely this would appeal to Claude's nature, so why wasn't there? Perhaps his need to erase any remnant of my existence surpassed his need for tidiness.

I looked up, intent on not allowing myself to be sidetracked, only to spot some sort of note, stuck to the bedroom wall with blue tac. It was in a prominent position ensuring whoever opened the door, wouldn't fail to spot it. Obviously, it was meant for me to read. Handwritten in French, at first, its lines resembled the form of a poem. Had Claude written it especially for Morgan, in an attempt to welcome him? With furrowed brow, I began to translate the scant lines.

An overbearing, stifling claustrophobic all engulfing dread began flooding through my body. The undisguised threat becoming ever more palpable with the knowledge of it being Claude's hand which had guided the ink across the page as he penned each letter.

Deliberately personal.

Handwriting far more deadly than the anonymity of computer print, I felt I'd entered a scene from a psychological horror movie.

It read:

"Winter has passed and Spring is here.
It won't be long until I have you back with me again."

'Jim!' I yelled urgently as I struggled to force the sound of my cry into the air, striving to force a noise loud enough to carry beyond the constraints of my fear filled throat.

'Come quick!'

He arrived skidding to a halt at the door, Morgan tucked up on his hip once more. He was obviously taking no chances. I translated the words into English for him and explained how Morgan's room had been moved to this side of the house.

'We need to leave now,' he responded.

I nodded. 'But why's he moved the bedroom?' I asked, throwing a glance towards Morgan which intimated to Jimmy to be mindful of his response.

'Think about it Jan. Think about the layout of the place. How much more accessible is this side of the property? He's relocated his room so it's right next to the exit gate and the alley way. He was too tucked away over the other side of the house. Too remote. Much easier to nab him from here and be gone. That 'quick in an out' I told you to use could just as easily apply to Claude. The neighbours on this side will turn a blind eye 'cos the bastards have sided with Claude. I tell you! This is all set up with a view to getting young Morgs. Just take what you came for Jan and let's get out of here. I don't want to be in this bloody trap one moment longer than necessary. Come on.'

He turned away passing back through the kitchen before disappearing onto the terrace with Morgan and the four-legged followers. One last glance at this 'trap' of a bedroom and I turned briskly on my heels, to follow. It was suddenly too stifling in there, too oppressive. I was beginning to struggle for breath as I briefly paused by the table to stuff my little assortment of belongings into a bag. I needed to get out. Making a quick exit, I left the trap which lurked within the walls of the house to mutter its discontent to the unheeding ears of its empty rooms. It would not be getting us this time.

Jimmy was leading the way, just a few steps ahead of me, when I suddenly remembered an important item I'd left behind.

'Hang on! Wait! I haven't got any dog leads!' I shouted, turning rapidly on my heels. 'I'm going to check the shed for some rope.'

I ran to the storage shed, heaving it open on its rusting hinges. For a moment it struck me how ironic it was that this outside area was lacking upkeep. The quiet tucked away place, the least accessible, the furthest away from the main thoroughfare, the place where the one window of Morgan's original bedroom was situated. No wonder Claude had contrived to swap the rooms. A quick scan of the interior of the shed confirmed there was no rope or anything else that might be suitable to use as makeshift leads. However, a couple of my fishing rods, complete with tackle, were there for the taking. Knowing they'd prove useful, I swiftly hoisted them out of their overhanging perch in the rafters, before launching a hefty kick at the door to close it.

Jimmy, surprised by my show of force, cast an expectant look in my direction. Calling across the terrace to him I urged 'Open the gate. There's nothing we can use as leads. We'll just have to time it right – make sure there's no vehicles around before we let the dogs across the road.'

He did as instructed and gave me the all clear.

'Come on dogs! Let's go! Milly, Shadow, this way!' I clicked my fingers as a sign of needing their immediate attention and launched into a run.

We'd no sooner got the dogs on board along with an increasingly irate Morgan who was protesting vocally at being put back in his child seat, when the figure of someone approaching caught Jimmy's eye.

'Looks like we've got company,' he said to me out of the corner of his mouth. 'Carry on as you were – go round to the driver's side and get in.'

I started around the front of the camper van only to

see Fernand closing the gap between us, at a surprising speed, given his years.

As if in fear of my imminent departure, he called, 'Jan! Jan!'

I faltered as Jimmy climbed up into the passenger seat, slamming the door behind him, putting a barrier in place to shut Fernand out. Winding down his window, he eyeballed the rapidly advancing figure until he came to a halt in front of the bonnet.

'Fernand!' I exclaimed, as if surprised to see him, 'hello again!'

I could see he was busily absorbing the new intel and digesting the fact I was manning a large camper, as opposed to the small hatchback he'd no doubt been alerted to look out for.

He seemed equally bemused to discover I wasn't travelling alone, but had a male companion with me. Stating the obvious he said, 'You are not on your own Jan. I see you have someone with you.'

His eyes glanced uneasily past me, over the bonnet of the camper, where Jimmy eyeballed him from his elevated position in the cab, causing Fernand to avert his gaze in obvious discomfort.

'Oh no Fernand. I'm not on my own,' I replied, smiling like a cat with the cream, 'I really don't think it would've been very wise of me to come all this way on my own, do you?'

'But, you are going already?' Fernand asked, and I sensed an element of ill-disguised panic in his tone.

'Ooh yes! I'm going to show my friend the area – show him some of the local sights and give the dogs a good long walk,' I replied with a stare which indicated there was nothing further to be said.

With that, I turned my back on him, in a gesture which showed he was beneath my contempt. It felt good. It felt even better to climb aboard, roar the engine into life, the end to any further communication. Putting the van into first gear, Fernand was forced to step out of my path.

My closing view of him through my large left, wing mirror, was of his small figure standing in the middle of the road, a pair of arms thrown to the heavens, waving exasperatedly as if trying to swat an annoying wasp.

Chapter 61

It was only after we'd cleared the confines of the village and were moving along a small minor road passing a field of ostriches on our left my tension began to ease.

'That was a close call back there,' remarked Jimmy. 'I knew the net was closing in, I could sense it. If we'd left it any later, I think it'd be a different story.'

'I'm sure Fernand was up to something. I'll bet he'd already alerted Claude when I went to pick up the keys and was playing for time when he rocked up in front of the bonnet! And to think those flaming court papers ordered Morgs and I to stay at the property! They're having a laugh! And as for the bedroom? I couldn't believe it! Yeuk, so sinister.' I shuddered at the thought of it. 'You're right Jimmy. All a calculated set-up to abduct Morgs.'

'We've got to be careful. I'm sure Fernand has enough French wits about him to make a mental note of our registration plate! Let's face it, this English blunder bus stands out a mile!'

He was spot on. The sooner we got to the police station, the better. I squeezed down on the accelerator pedal, willing our travelling time to be as quick as possible.

'It's only a couple of miles now until we get to the village where I'll hand my papers over to the police.

They'll be able to advise me and once we know we're protected, we'll be able to relax a little.'

Jimmy responded with an unconvincing, 'Maybe.'

Thankfully the parking fairy was on my side, allowing me to glide the large hulk of the campervan into an available space, without drawing any undue attention to us. Little Jimmy passed me the paperwork from the glove compartment and armed with the knowledge that this document would guarantee our safety, I walked confidently through the door of the gendarmerie. An armed officer stood behind a desk, surveying my entrance with suspicion. Without further ado, I passed him the papers and underlined their importance, stressing they were protective measures issued by the High Court in England, under the jurisdiction of the European Court, stating we needed police protection.

The officer turned his back on me to speak to another colleague in a rapid spiel that was too quick for me to understand. Straining to listen, I had the impression they were talking deliberately fast as means of ensuring I wouldn't be able to follow their line of conversation.

The discussion came to an abrupt end and the officer turned back towards me, waving the papers I'd given him in a sweeping arc above his head.

'These papers were issued in England, not France.'

I agreed. However, I couldn't see how this made any difference. It hadn't made a difference to the court who'd issued them had it? Once more, I reiterated I'd been told to bring the papers to them so they'd give us the help we needed in order to be safe. No response was forthcoming. I tried again.

'We are in need of police protection. I have the legal reassurance of the High Court that you'll make sure we are protected.'

It was like speaking to a brick wall. My words bounced

off its surface, unheard. Instead, the officer muttered something to his colleague which I'm convinced was derogatory, had I been able to translate it.

'Madame, they were issued in England, not France.'

'But it's all part of the Hague Convention and France is a member state, so you *have* to abide by its laws. Anyway, we're all members of Europe,' I objected, exasperatedly.

'We cannot protect you.' He paused. Shocked into silence, aghast at the implications of his words, I stood transfixed, before he continued 'but your husband is dangerous. He has already been here demanding we take your son. You are not safe. You must not go back to your property at *Vic La Gardiole*. You need to get out of the country.'

How could this be real? How could this actually be happening? Was it some form of sick joke; some sort of wind-up? If so, it was in disgustingly bad taste. Was this officer only maintaining his serious composure to mask the fact he'd been pulling my leg all along? I knew the French were lacking in a sense of humour but this was bloody ridiculous. He'd long outplayed his dead pan expression. Time to pack it in. It was becoming tedious. Time for the game to be up, time for him to break into a smile, assure me that of course they'd follow protocol and protect us. Searching for the smile to break through his unyielding expression, all I saw was a face laden with the gravitiy of the situation. The smile never came. Instead, he thrust the papers back at me with a speed suggesting he wanted to rid himself of any possible contamination, were he to keep the corrupt material in his possession any longer. Game over. He was firmly passing all responsibility in my direction.

Returning the papers to their official envelope, I turned away from the law as a whole. The system was pointless. An absolute farce. It's not clear whether it was fear or rage which shook my every step as I returned to the campervan.

Clambering unsteadily inside, unable to comprehend the enormity of it all, I slumped in my seat, speechless at the implications of what had just happened.

'Well?' asked Jimmy, prompting me into some sort of verbal repsonse.

'Jimmy!' I replied in an incredulous tone, echoing my complete and utter disbelief of what I'd just experienced. 'They won't do a thing! They won't honour the papers because they were issued in England! I told the officer the papers were issued by the High Court and that France is a member of the Convention but it made absolutely no difference! The officer just kept repeating that because the papers were issued in England, he wouldn't do anything! It's absolutely ridiculous! I just can't believe it!'

Jimmy frowned at me as if questioning the truth of what I'd just told him. I think he thought I'd got it wrong.

Unstoppable, I gushed, 'So what's the point of being accountable to this law when France decides to take absolutely no notice of it? There's no point in having these fucking laws in the first place, if they're not adhered to! Easy enough for a judge to make a ruling in some pompous legal palace, but it's worth sod all if no one abides by it. Just make up your own bloody rules why don't you?' I yelled, now out of control, my rage soaring ever higher at the injustice of it all.

I could see Jimmy was just as taken aback as I was. His mouth was agape and his eyes visibly widening as he digested my words.

There was more he needed to know, so spitting with outrage, I carried on, 'Ha! As if that isn't enough, I haven't even finished yet! It just gets worse and worse! That officer has just told me Claude is a dangerous man! He says it's not safe to stay at Vic and Claude's already been to see them, demanding Morgan is seized and... wait for it... that we've got to get out of the country!'

Jimmy let out an elongated '*C h r i s t!*' Then he added, 'You couldn't write this stuff! No one would believe you!'

'Well it's real and it's happening!' I yelled feeling a sense of hysteria rising in me. 'So what the hell do we do now? What the hell do we do Jimmy?'

'We get away to somewhere quiet, somewhere we can't be seen or found and you need to call your French lawyer pronto.'

'Sorry. It's all too much. I just can't think straight at the moment.' Tears of desperation now welling up as I spoke.

'You've got to stay calm Jan. This is exactly what Claude wants. Don't go playing into his hands. Number one priority now is to find somewhere nearby where you can gather your thoughts and make the call. Your lawyer might want to see you, so we can't be too far away. We've got to be able to get to her office if necessary. Is there anywhere suitable to hide?'

A brief moment of contemplation and the perfect, away from it all location, edged slowly into my mind – a place already visited, a place of sanctuary, a place for fugitives such as us. Without further ado, we were on the move once more.

Chapter 62

In some small way, the beauty of our surroundings quelled my fury at finding Madame Caparros was out of her office for the day, attending court. This meant I couldn't have my much-needed conversation with her until the following morning. I endeavoured to explain the urgency of the situation to her secretary, but her lack of comprehension culminated in a repeat of what she'd already told me. Was she being deliberately evasive? So many of the French population seemed unreasonably hostile once they realised they were dealing with an English person. I'd already experienced this on numerous occasions whilst resident in the area. Everything was further complicated due to my lack of understanding regarding how French systems operated and how to access appropriate advice. Add hostile attitudes to the mix and it exacerbated my feeling of helplessness.

There was nothing to do but wait. So, I drove us to an idyllic location I'd discovered on one of my walks when I lived in the area. The campervan bumped and bounced along the unused track jostling all its occupants. The end of the winding trail opened onto an expanse of coarse stubby grass which touched the shores of a very small lake, another offshoot of the larger *Etang de Vic*.

I'd escaped to the shores of this very place on previous occasions, taking the boys fishing for *les dorades* – sea bream. Claude never discovered where we went and I vowed never to tell him. We'd whiled away many an hour in this secret place of peaceful seclusion, so perhaps that's why it felt so reassuringly safe to be here again.

I was physically too exhausted to think about driving anywhere else just on a whim we might discover a suitable place to hide for the night, so we agreed to stay put. The dogs delighted in being able to stretch their legs and discovered their new-found freedom in an assortment of smells and paw paddling ventures in the shallows of the lake. Young Morgan busied himself exploring his immediate surroundings and trying to catch tiny fish with one of the plastic cereal bowls I'd given him. Having dined on an assortment of olives, saucisson and chunks of bread from a somewhat stale baguette, Little Jimmy armed himself with one of the fishing rods. Casting his line out across the reaches of the water, he was on a mission to catch supper, whilst he kept his yet unopened bottle of French lager bobbing merrily in the shallows to keep it cool.

In those beautiful, peaceful surroundings, with the Mediterranean sun still pouring its warmth from the Spring skies overhead, it was so easy to remember why I'd initially been drawn to this area of Southern France. I thought about the throngs of holiday makers who descended there, not only from the UK but also from northern France, to bask in endless days of sunshine, glorious beaches and of course, the lure of French cuisine. A dream lifestyle.

But not mine anymore. I sneered inwardly. My reality was a lifetime away from this depiction of paradise. It was all hollow, a successful cover up, a façade to conceal the atrocities which my memory would never be able to erase. My recollection of the *Languedoc Roussillon* would be linked for eternity to a shroud of darkness, a burial site for the souls, lost amongst the boulders of unmarked graves, scattered across this arid, unyielding landscape. A place I never wanted to revisit either physically or mentally. And yet there we were, having been forced to return; forced to face our fears. Déjà vu in limbo land. Trapped geographically by a failed legal system; unable to stay in England, unable to stay in France.

What options did we have left?

Chapter 63

'So what did Madame *'What's-her-socks'* say?' asked little Jimmy as he poked his head out from the camper door, patting his face dry with a towel from his morning shave.

'Believe it or not she didn't sound overly surprised when I told her what the police had said. Just as they'd told us yesterday, she said we should heed their advice, stay away from the house at *Vic* and get out of France.'

'So you mean we've got to go and hide somewhere until the date of the court hearing? Three weeks is a hell of a long time to hide!' Little Jim guffawed sarcastically.

'I said much the same thing to her but it was strange. I asked her about High Court hearing in Montpellier on 21st May. Her response was weird. She told me to leave it with her, she'd make some enquiries and asked me to call her back in three days' time.'

'What? She didn't give you any information about what to expect on the day of the hearing and how to prepare for it beforehand?' Jim responded quizzically.

'No, it didn't feel like it was a priority as far as she was concerned. She seemed very laid back about it all, given that we haven't got a whole lot of time, in the grand scheme of things to prepare for it. I thought she'd want a face-to-face meeting at her office as soon as possible.

The only thing she was passionate about, was stressing the importance of getting out of the country at the moment!'

Jimmy's frown signalled he was equally as perplexed about it as I was. None of it made sense.

'In that case we'd better take note of what she says. It's only a couple of hours drive from here and we can be across the border and into Spain. I think that's our best bet in the circumstances. So, how about you get young Morgs showered, the dogs fed and watered, and let's pack up and get out of here?'

'I don't think we've got any other options. Spain's our closest country and with a bit of luck we can lie low there until I get an update from Madame Caparros in three days' time.'

Two hours later we were on the road again, motoring along the A9 autoroute, heading back in a westerly direction towards the distant outline of the jagged summits of the Pyrenees mountains. I was aware from my artistic perspective how the lighting seemed to change as we left, as we left the region of Herault and entered the neighbouring county of *Les Pyrenees Orientales*. The lighting in Herault yielded a warm, golden ochre hue, a vast contrast to the region we were now entering where a colder light accentuated the greens and greys of the landscape. Wondering if this was caused by the influence of the mountain air, I noticed the highest peaks of the Pyrenees were still clad in their winter shawls of snow. Formidable in their jagged topography, they loomed up ahead of me as a physical barrier, stretching all the way from the Bay of Biscay on the Atlantic Ocean, to here on the shores of the Mediterranean Sea. Beyond this ridge of mountains lay the Iberian Peninsula and as every kilometre drew us nearer to them, the fear of being stopped on the border grew. For all I knew, Claude may have already reported us missing. He'd know with the dogs gone, we'd weighed anchor and wouldn't be returning. We'd succeeded in outwitting him on this occasion, but this would only act to fuel his fury even more as he'd fight to regain control. It meant our opponent was potentially more dangerous than ever. He'd be hell bent on seizing his son by whatever means it would take.

This realisation, combined with the knowledge we were not protected in any way by the authorities, left us vulnerable and wide open to attack. Jimmy was thinking along similar lines. Keen to pinpoint our current location, he grabbed the road map, and proceeded to unfurl it with an overzealous haste. The fully opened map spilled across the cab, a wave of paper, touching the shore of the passenger window on one side, whilst its back wash dragged over the central gear knob. Momentarily taking my eyes off the road, I glanced to see little Jimmy as he battled to extract himself from this drowning sea of paper. I giggled as a furious rustling ensued as Jim made a grab for the extremities of the map, bringing them together like someone striving to still flapping wings of a uncooperative goose.

Moments later cursing under his breath, he muttered, 'Why is it that every bloody place you look for is always on the fold of these damn things?'

Still miffed by the unaccommodating map, he added 'I'm just checking to see if there's an alternative route into Spain, other than this blue A9 auto route.' He prodded it accusingly with his finger to illustrate what he meant.

'I was wondering the same thing. You mean so we can go in under the radar? Take a minor road to sneak in over the border just in case Claude's alerted the police that we might be fleeing?'

'Might be the best bet,' he replied. 'Look, there's one

here. It's a winding coastal road. It'll add some miles to the trip, not to mention fuel, but it could be the better option.'

'I'll take your word for it. I daren't look now.'

I gripped the wheel readying myself for the next heavily laden lorry to pound past me, it's speed of passage, threatening to throw me off course.

'There's too many lorries all storming down to the border and it's difficult to hold the van steady. These flaming cross winds aren't helping. Just let me know when we need to start looking for the exit sign and tell me the name of the place I should be looking out for,' I replied, as I counter steered once more in an attempt to compensate for the funnelling crosswind threatening to shunt us into the adjacent lane of the motorway.

'There's a place called *Argeles sur Mer*. I reckon we'll take the exit for that and go from there.'

'That's a resort on the coast, isn't it?'

'Yes – looks like it according to the map.'

Eyes peeled for road signs and other landmarks that would give us a clue to our current location, we continued to clock up the miles. Before long, we saw an exit sign to take the next slip road off the motorway. Although this was going to be a tedious journey for young Morgan who, to date, had been a superb passenger, I was relieved to think we'd be leaving the most obvious route into Spain. Changing progressively down through the gears, we began our descent towards a roundabout that lay ahead. There was an unusually large amount of congestion, which was puzzling considering the peak commuter period had already passed. Advancing slowly, we eventually joined the roundabout where, stuck in the unprecedented traffic jam, we queued nose to tail.

Twenty minutes later, we'd inched far enough forward for Jimmy to say, 'Get ready to take the next exit after this one.'

'Aye, aye, Captain,' I replied, mocking a left-handed salute.

'Aye, aye, Captain Jim,' shouted a little voice from behind me.

We edged forward into the space left by the vehicle in front of us. It wasn't a great distance, but it was distance enough to reveal the reason for the delay. A road block straddled the exit we were planning to take. Our secret route into Spain was not only barricaded, but guarded by swathes of armed police out in force, stopping vehicles and asking for I.D.

'Oh God!' I exclaimed. 'It's Claude! He knows we're coming this way! They're looking for us!'

As we drew closer, so the traffic flow eased and I cursed the sudden lack of congestion because it would only be a matter of seconds before we were channelled directly into the hands of the armed officers. No excuse to escape. It was too late. We were snared like rabbits in a trap.

'They've got guns,' I hissed through clenched teeth.

Jimmy said nothing but just watched through the panoramic windscreen as the vehicle in front of us was flagged over to the side of the road, stopping just yards from the barricade of police cars and vans. There was nothing I could do.

'We're English tourists that's all,' said Jimmy, his tone akin to an undercover agent, his expectation of how I should therefore be presenting myself, crystal clear. 'No drama. Nothing to hide. Just follow what they tell us to do.'

All I could focus on were the guns and batons attached tthe black belts of the military uniforms, as each officer paraded an officious black peak cap, banded with gold at the top. Despite Jimmy's expectations of me, I couldn't overcome the pounding in my rib cage as my heart threatened to explode out of it. My mouth was dry and as one of the officers stepped forward, raising his hand, signalling for us to stop.

In fear I disassociated. Unable to cope, I felt myself float upwards out of my body to watch the proceedings from the safety of the ceiling of the cab. A voyeur. I saw the part of me I'd left behind wind down the driver's window before smiling expectantly at the officer whose eyes scanned both occupants and vehicle. A brief exchange of words ensued, too muted for me to hear and then the officer was waving us forward in a repeated gesture to continue our journey.

Clear of suspicion, I sensed I was dropping back into my place behind the wheel and once within my physical being, began steering us away from trouble once more.

'What the hell was all that about?' I managed to utter, my confidence returning. 'Where do we go now?'

Jimmy laughed. His sense of relief both palpable and infectious, making me relax as he offered, 'Let's just say we took a bit of a detour. Might as well join the motorway again! Find us the way out of here Jan. Let's just get to bloody Spain. I'm feeling rather parched! I need a sangria.'

Thankfully, the remainder of the journey proved uneventful. Relaxing into tourist mode, we allowed the awe of the spectacular scenery to enliven our spirits as we wove our way across the high mountain pass, before crossing the unmanned border control taking us into Spain.

That night, we camped in the mountains. The unmistakable scent of wild thyme wafted through the open windows of the camper filling it with its unique fragrance. An evening lullaby was being performed by an orchestra of Spanish cicadas. They were music to my ears.

As I drifted peacefully off to sleep, the weight of my worries lifted, knowing tonight we'd successfully crossed another border.

Chapter 64

By late morning the following day, we were faced with a dilemma. Two important onboard storage containers needed urgent attention. Our fresh water tank was almost empty and needed refilling. Conversely, the toilet waste recepticle risked overflowing and needed emptying. We resolved to find a proper campsite. Although I felt uneasy at the prospect of coming out of hiding, a formal campsite would give us the facilities we needed.

Slowly descending the hairpin track down the mountain, we joined the main road following signposts towards *Figueres* where we hung a left in search of the coast. My shoulders began to relax as obsessive thoughts of being on the run were dissipated by the warmth of the sun and a growing sense of curiosity for our new surroundings. It began to feel as if I was on holiday. Just after 10.00 am it was already 18° Celsius with the blue sky promise of a glorious day. Suddenly, I felt I was in an enviable position. Back in the UK, folk would be clad in socks and sweaters and yet here I was in flip flops and shorts, basking in the promise of a blue sky and heading to the beach! With the option of making the most of a bad situation, the present moment didn't seem so terrible after all.

Catching my first glimpse of the Gulf of Roses shimmering in the distance, I felt refreshed and invigorated. Squeezing the accelerator pedal, the van responded and minutes later we were skirting the edge of a vast crop of sunflowers. A field of floral compasses, their flower heads facing directly south. In French they are known as *'les tournesols'*. I've always liked this name because it means *'turn to the sun'*. I smiled. Nature provides so much uplifting positivity. Coming to a sharp right-hand bend, I spotted a large heavily grained wooden sign, strategically placed to catch the eye on the side of the road. It read *'Camping'* in bold white paint. Underneath the word, a large red painted arrow, faded by the heat of time, indicated the direction we should follow.

We spent the next ten minutes following tracking a trail of erratically placed arrows which had a habit of shooting into view at the last minute. Their appearance seemed planned to coincide with particularly tight bends or last minute well concealed turnings. Some arrows were plastered slap dash on discarded wooden pallets in lay-bys, whilst others appeared on ramshackle farm buildings or any available structure that abutted the road. In the absence of a suitable surface being available, a series of arrow bearing boulders had been dropped strategically along our route to keep us on course. Soon the three of us were fixated with our *'Who can spy an arrow?'* game. As Morgan's enthusiasm grew, so too did his ad lib excited screams of *'arrow!'* However, this wasn't because he'd actually spotted an arrow, but because he found my urgent shriek of *'where?'* to be particularly amusing. Apart from an unplanned detour to the municipal swimming pool in the quaint village of St Père Pescador, the directions for which had adopted a strikingly similar set of 'look alike' red arrows, to those we were tracking, we arrived unscathed at our destination. As the terrain flattened out, the shimmer of the sea acted as a backdrop to the gently undulating sand dunes which stretched as far as the eye could see. It looked perfect. The campsite entrance lay directly ahead. A sign of civilisation. Individual camping pitches were large and at this time of year, the site was was barely occupied. It looked promising given the sparse scattering of fellow campers. The less human contact we had, the better. Most importantly, there was a low rise building which I assumed housed the essential facilities we were after. We drove in.

Planning to stay for just the one night in order do the necessary with our storage tanks, we proceeded to meet the site owner. It was a welcome relief to find he spoke good English and an added bonus to discover we shared a mutual love of dogs. We pitched the van on a level site, within walking distance of the toilet block, children's play area and strolling distance of the bar-restaurant.

It was such a lovely location that either the two-legged, nor four-legged campers relished the thought of being on the move again and so after the first night we booked ourselves in for another couple of days. Whilst revelling in the sense of genuine relaxation, we waited for the time to pass until I could contact Madame Caparros for an update.

In the meantime we became tourists enjoying a welcome escape to the sun. The adjacent unpopulated beach stretched as far as the eye could see into the heat shimmering distance. A bronzed Morgan and his favourite pirate captain searched for treasure along its length and a growing assortment of findings placed carefully on the picnic blanket at the side of the camper van. Amongst their riches was a length of rope which Captain Jim cut deftly in half with his pocket penknife to make two leads for the dogs. To avoid bringing copious amounts of sand into the van, he'd solved the problem by slotting the shower head through the window of the toilet compartment. Standing in our swimwear to wash in the great outdoors, with the mountains a magnificent back drop, was good for the soul – so much more exhilarating than using the confines of the on-site shower block. It felt liberating.

I hugely appreciated Jimmy's gentlemanly behaviour throughout our trip. Given that I'd not known him very long prior to leaving the UK, I'd been particularly anxious at the prospect of sharing the forced intimacy of living in a van with him. However, I needn't have worried. He always tactfully took himself off for a walk, or to check on something outside of the van, each time I needed to change clothes and I'd done likewise with him. With a mutual respect for each other's privacy it had become more like a dance routine in which we anticipated each other's need for having the dance floor to themselves.

Morgan's collection of treasures continued to grow. The latest additions included an assortment of little toys he'd discovered with great delight when Captain Jim treated him to an ice cream from the on-site shop. We all marvelled at the surprise treat which lay hidden under the foil wrapper at the base of the individual ice cream container, as an excited Morgan cheered exuberantly. His latest trophies included a blue bubble car, a miniature yellow yo-yo and a princess with pink plaits and tiara. Given half a chance, his staple diet would comprise a continuous flow of these ice creams for breakfast, lunch and tea.

By the second day of our stay, Morgan was responsible for unwittingly playing his part in securing postive Anglo-German relations with our neighbours. Free from the confines of the camper and preoccupied with thoughts of Spanish ice creams, he took off at surprising speed for a toddler, making a beeline for the freezer section of the shop. Choosing the most direct route, he ploughed his way purposefully across neighbouring pitches whose occupants sat in deckchairs, reading their morning newspapers. Spotting the rapidly departing figure of young Morgan, Captain Jim gave chase to the mutinous toddler, repeatedly calling out his name as he went after him. As if by coincidence, the timings of his increasingly exasperated calls of 'Morgan' were uttered as he passed our seated neighbours. Looking up amicably from their papers, they called 'Morgan' to the departing figure of an increasingly perplexed pirate.

I recounted the tale to Tom and Owen when I called them in the evening. It was good to give share something we could all laugh about. When they asked as they always did, when I'd be home, I replied, *"as soon as possible. I promise."*

Heavy hearted, I said a final goodbye, as the reality of not knowing when I'd see them again, or if I'd be returning with Morgan, descended like a ton of bricks.

The following day I'd make the phone call to my lawyer and hopefully get an answer.

Chapter 65

'There are no words, Jim! It's just got worse!' I exclaimed, still holding my mobile phone at a distance from my ear, reeling in shock.

Before he could respond, I went on, 'There is NO court date in May! NO date set in May!'

'What do you mean no court date?'

'Just that! No court date! It hasn't even been set yet!'

Extremes of disbelief, astonishment, a sense of being duped and the beginnings of an anger that I wasn't sure I'd be able to control, even if I wanted to, raged within me.

'Madame Caparros has just confirmed Claude got us here under false pretences! You know what that means? Not only has he lied to us, but he's lied to the High Court!'

I was shaking with a wrath, the extremes of which I'd never experienced. It was surging destructively, capable of engulfing and destroying everything in its path, gaining unstoppable momentum. I was losing control. I looked around for something to kick or to lash out at. I wanted to thump something so hard with my fist that my knuckles would bleed and maybe I'd break some bones. Beyond caring. I needed to externalise the pain, a pain that couldn't remain invisible. It was welling up and it was about to spill out, unleashed and raging.

Turning abruptly to search for anything I could quickly bring to hand, to hurt myself with, I tripped over Shadow who was standing directly in my path. She stood unyielding, making a stance, a heart-breaking loyalty reflected in her eyes. A look telling me she understood and despite everything, she'd not falter from my side.

It brought me up short. Intense anger swapped places with an overwhelming sadness. There was no saviour of fragility for the already broken. I'd no fight left in me. Nothing more to give. I couldn't physically go on anymore. I was dangling too close to the edge of precipice to which I'd clung for so long. My weakness as a mother, helpless, unable to protect my children effectively, someone unworthy of owning two beautiful dogs and who now questioned her own sanity.

Shadow sat patiently at my side, licking away each salty tear as I hung my head in shame. Sniffing loudly, struggling to stop my nose running, I wiped it with the back of my hand. I couldn't care less what anyone thought. The whole world could go to hell. Let them judge me, let them walk in my shoes. So what if I was wallowing in self-pity? What did it matter? Nothing mattered anymore.

'Mummy,' said a tentative voice.

I looked up to seeing Morgan holding out a long length of toilet paper, gently undulating in the breeze like the tail of a kite. My precious child in his nautical striped t-shirt, red shorts and stubby little legs, a look of anguished concern on his caring face.

Seeing him changed everything.

Of course, I'd go on.

Of course, I'd never give up.

Whilst there was breath in my body, for every moment my children were in this world, I would always be there for them, doing whatever it took, whenever they needed me.

Reaching for the proffered ribbon of toilet paper I sniffed, nose still blocked from crying, before responding in a nasal tone, 'Thank you Morgs. You're an absolute star.'

I drew him close to hug him on my lap. Cuddling into me, he looked up, a concerned look on his little face.

'You were crying Mummy,' he said, his chubby little hand gently stroking and patting my arm in a bid to comfort me.

'I know Morgs, everyone cries sometimes you know. Not all the time, but sometimes it's a good thing to cry. It gets it out of your system and makes you feel better. I'm feeling better now and thank you so much for just being here making everything all right.'

With that we had one of our special Morgs and mum hugs and all was well with the world once more. Suitably reassured, Morgan got to his feet and walked back to Jimmy who was waiting awkwardly several feet away.

'My Mummy was sad,' he said matter of factly, 'but she's all better now.'

Case closed, he picked up the pink princess from the picnic blanket and went to dabble her meaningfully in the dogs' water bowl.

Chapter 66

There seemed to be no escape from my surroundings. Even when I closed my eyes, an image of the Pyrenees appeared before me. It became a constant feature of the landscape, a striking backdrop, a scene setter in which I found myself taking centre stage to play the performance of my life. A mountainous setting, bearing witness to every event as it unfolded. Integral to my story, these stoic spectators would always symbolise a foreboding time associated with a place I was desperate to leave behind. Something had to change.

Trying to establish the date of the genuine court hearing, was like asking *'how long is a piece of string?'* No one could give me an answer. What was I supposed to do? Did they expect me to bum around endlessly in the camper as a long-term fugitive? It was ridiculous. Little Jim and I sat down to discuss our options.

On the basis that all French parties were advising us to leave the country, we concluded I was perfectly within my rights to return to England for the time being. Should anyone challenge my return, I could legitimately inform them I was acting on the advice of the French authorities. In addition, money was running short and this provided another valid reason for going home. But above all, I wanted to see Tom and Owen. I was sick of all our lives being put on hold. Being forced to go over to France had proved to be a dangerous waste of time; a time which would've been far better spent looking after the needs of my sons. I held the pathetic excuse for a legal system accountable. Failing abysmally to protect us, its ruling leaving me no option but to fragment our family. In addition, the trauma of the past eighteen months had been swept under the carpet, left unvalidated and with no consequence to the perpetrator. And yet, this was a system that appertains to have the interests of a child at its heart, allegedly pivotal to the policies and procedures to which it adheres. I knew I could achieve more single-handedly, than this bunch of legal hypocrites put together. To hell with the consequences. Our little family needed each other and I wasn't prepared to spend any longer in the hands of these incompetent legal professionals, played a pawn, catering for on their every whim, in their fight for superiority. My little brood needed to be reunited, given the time to heal, time for nurturing to take priority, a time to be gently caressed, held safe, as we reclaimed a sense of normality in our lives. My mind was made up. Tomorrow I was going home.

I couldn't stop myself from casting regular glances in the side mirrors of the camper, proving to myself the peaks of the Pyrenees were well and truly retreating into the distance. The further away they became, the more I dared to believe my ordeal might be reaching an end and the more my emotions began to surface. Was I finally letting go, finally feeling I could begin to relax? I'm sure it had a part to play, but the peak of my emotion lay in the overwhelming certainty of knowing with each mile, I was closing the distance between myself and home. Cornwall was beckoning for the first time in what felt like a life time. As its glorious image of it filled my head, a voice, hauntingly mellow, rich as the softest butter, began to sing, *"take me home to my family, take me home to my friends, take me home where my heart lies"*. And knowing I wasn't alone, but being guided back to the place of my belonging, my heart soared as I joined in the last line of the familiar chorus, *"let me sing again"*.

Time to look forward, letting the memories of the past fall away behind me. With a new sense of purpose, we continued our journey north. Knowing we faced the threat of Claude facilitating the blocking of western ports, we headed up the east side of this vast country, intent on crossing the Channel through the Eurotunnel. Tickets were booked for all travellers, both two-legged and four-legged. Milly and Shadow seemed particularly cheerful. I wondered if they sensed the excitement building in the air as we notched up the kilometres, or if they were just grateful to be included. A niggling worry at the back of my mind began to emerge, shouting louder as we slowly closed the distance between us and the channel. Neither Shadow nor Milly had pet passports, nor were they vaccinated against rabies prior to leaving Cornwall. It hadn't been a concern of mine when we moved to France because we weren't going to live in a rabies zone. However, bringing the dogs back into the UK, was a different kettle of fish. Fingers crossed my previous conversation with a veterinary nurse was accurate when she assured me that because the dogs hadn't lived in a rabies region, it wouldn't be a problem bringing them home. I hoped the custom officials shared her viewpoint. There was absolutely no way I was going to leave my dogs behind. Not again.

After a tedious fifteen hour journey, we were entering the last leg of our route. Nearing the coast of northern France, the road signs were increasingly highlighting routes to both Calais and Dunkirk. Although difficult to adequately express in words, I found it particularly poignant which both destinations held significance for people intent on leaving France, whether in the present day, or historically. If only the sons of the Butter Lady had survived the first World War, perhaps they'd have fought for their country for a second time. Imagine if they'd been rescued from the beaches of Dunkirk 63 years ago to this day, by a small Cornish fishing vessel. My heart went out to the Butter Lady. I was the lucky one. My sons were still alive. The port of Calais was much larger than I'd imagined, a broad sweep of numerous lanes to choose from, depending upon the vehicle you were driving. Finding the relevant queue, we assembled our passports, in readiness for passing through the control point. I couldn't help but smile as I thought about the characters who lay behind the mug shots of our motley crew; an ageing crook turned part-time pirate with a heart of gold, a gloriously innocent young child whose future was on hold, and a woman on the run, with surprising resilience, who'd stop at nothing to earn her title of being a mother. I giggled to myself picturing the possibility of the Butter Lady sitting alongside Morgan. Another member of our team, a nomadic Cornish spirit of yesteryear, unpredictable, yet who'd be relied upon to show up when needed. A lovable ghost, beyond the realms of needing a passport!

With every rotation of the wheel, my fear increased as we inched forward. Was there a port alert? Would our route to freedom be blocked? So near and yet so far. The next hour would be pivotal. I glanced at Tom's lucky rock in its place on the dashboard.

Could it bring good fortune once more?

Could I rely on it to help me again?

Why was the legal system so futile I was pinning all my hopes for fairness and protection on a piece of rock?

It was wrong. So, so wrong.

Having cleared passport control, successfully leaving our first obstacle behind us, we were directed onto one of the bright, air-conditioned carriages to take us through the tunnel. Was this truly the last part of our ordeal? It was difficult to believe. An unexpected wave of excitement rippled through me. Only one last hurdle. We were close to seeing light at the end of the tunnel in more ways than one. And not just any light, but English daylight. Who would've thought it could mean so much? I knew I'd still have to wait for the date of the official court hearing, before going back to France, but for now, I'd push the thought to the back of my mind. More vital than anything else was knowing how close I was to bringing Morgan and my dogs home, back to the land they should never have left.

The train started to move and I gauged its speed by watching the walls of the tunnel as they sped past the window. We were on our way, our fate in the hands of the subterranean train, which my over active imagination depicted as part of the modern day French Underground network, secretly helping its allies to escape to safety across the channel – the only remaining obstacle between us and England. The steadily increasing darkness of the tunnel wall indicated we were moving ever closer towards English soil. However, it wasn't time to celebrate yet. Flickers of excitement were heavily punctuated by a growing sense of unease which continued to heighten as the minutes ticked by. This was too simple. Experience taught me not to trust anything appearing to be easy. After what we'd been through, I was automatically suspicious. Having learnt to expect the unexpected, I now sought ways to limit potential risks, swerve setbacks and pre-empt situations before they happened. I stood up.

'I'm going to hide the dogs,' I told Jimmy as I scrambled

quickly and purposefully into the rear of the camper.

Time was of the essence.

Shadow was resting peacefully. I gently woke her before struggling to carry her precariously up the ladder onto the overhead bunk. She'd be well hidden there and, unlike Milly with her youthful energy, I could rely on her to stay put. Covering her with the duvet, I quickly descended the ladder, only to be greeted by a flamboyant Milly, eagerly wagging her tail and keen to take part in whatever game I'd obviously got planned for her.

'Milly! Here!' I ordered and she came to me, hips swinging playfully side to side.

I led her into the shower compartment.

'Milly. Stay. Be a good girl and stay there. I'll be back soon.' I commanded, hoping she'd comply with my urgent request on this occasion.

Closing the door quickly behind me, I returned to my driver's seat, just as glimpses of daylight started to flash past the carriage windows. It signalled we'd soon be entering the port of Folkestone on the far southeast coast of England – the opposite side of the country, some 350 miles from home, but one step closer nonetheless.

'God Jimmy. I hope we can do this. I'm not taking any chances. I just hope we'll get through without a hitch and don't get pulled over by customs.'

We spent the following minutes in an oppressive silence, each of us consumed by our thoughts. As if sensing tension in the air, Morgan stopped chattering. Disembarking from the large carriage, to follow the snail-like procession of other vehicles, I wanted to scream with joy because our wheels were touching English tarmac and we were near to crossing the finish line. However, the flickering light of victory was quickly extinguished as a formidable customs official, stepped out directly in front of the van. Blocking our path, she raised an arm, signalling for us to pull over into a side bay, where two of her armed colleagues were waiting.

Obeying her orders, I drew up in the allocated area, wound down my window and awaited further instructions.

'Turn your engine off and step down from the vehicle,' she barked. Dutifully, we complied with her directive.

'We need to search the vehicle,' announced a mini-Hitler, full of her own importance. Behind my appearance of non-plussed demeanour, I eyed her scathingly, realising just how much I despised authority.

'Do you have anything to declare?' she demanded, head pitched upward looking down her nose at me, her eye brows arching in anticipation of a suitably subservient response.

Should I slap her with the truth?

Maybe turn the tables on her?

Make her the one to feel uncomfortable and wrong footed.

Maybe I could load my reply in such a way that it'd give me enough ammunition to put the fear of God into her, instead of me, for a change?

Maybe I could push *her* to teeter on the edge of the precipice so she'd experience first hand the feeling, the the exhaustion of living in perpetual fear of falling?

Maybe I could let her give her a sense of walking in my shoes? Ironically footwear never designed for my feet in the first place. Too tight fitting, wrong size, completely out of character and style for me, but shoes I'd been forced to wear nonetheless. Not anymore. Oh no! Content in my own skin, without any regrets for my actions, I'd embrace my power by walking barefoot from now on. My feet planted firmly on the ground, I'd throw every ounce of my anger, resentment and distrust of authority at her. Holding my head high and proud before imparting the following credentials and say, "Yes.

I've been charged with child abduction. I'm a criminal ordered to return my son to France or face a prison sentence. But guess what? The French authorities told us to leave their country, cos it was too dangerous to remain there. We've been on the run for nearly three weeks now, even roughed it in Spain for a bit, but you know what? Enough is enough. I'm not playing your games anymore. I'm coming home. Must say, I was hoping to sneak back here without being caught. But hey! As we heathens say in Cornwall 'Madder do it?' Oh! And by the way, I've just smuggled two dogs and a ghost into the country. And what the fuck are you going to do about it?"

This of course was my internalised rant and sadly my manic moment of anger-fuelled flippancy passed as 'fear', my devout friend returned, rendering me verbally inept. A solitary 'No' was the only response to leave my lips.

Fear continued to hug me, wrapping me fastidiously in its blanket of nausea. Gripping Morgan's hand, I watched mini-Hitler violate my temporary home, breaching my place of safety as she strode into the van. All the while, her little army of colleagues stood poised, ready to erupt into action on a single command. Captain Jim was wandering aimlessly about on the dusty tarmac, seemingly trying out his land legs. Turning his attention to Morgan, he came to stand alongside us, adopting the perfect grandad persona by pointing excitedly to the trucks growling past us in their low, throaty gears. Why was he playing it so cool? How could he be so bloody relaxed? Didn't he realise what was at stake here?

I peered to catch glimpses of the customs officer, as she continued her search, hearing an intermittent clicking sound as she pulled on the catches to expose the contents of the cupboards and drawers. As she systematically made her way around our kitchen she she was moving progressively closer to the closed door of the toilet cubicle. Milly hadn't uttered a single sound from beyond the thinly panelled walls. Surely, it was only a matter of time before she'd be discovered.

Moments later, mini-Hitler threw open the bathroom door, emitting a sudden scream as Milly launched out to greet her from the confines of her hiding place. Instant back up arrived as the other two officer leapt into the interior of the van, brandishing their fire arms. Eyes transfixed on the scene, I held my breath as I pictured the absolute magnitude and subsequent consequences of their discovery

A silent pause was followed by an undeniable tone of relief in the woman's voice.

'It's all right. Stand down. It's only a dog,'

"Only a dog," I repeated silently in my head, "Only a dog," were the cue I needed to finally allow myself to exhale, in the relief of knowing we'd earned a temporary reprieve.

The rest of the search culminated in the discovery of a sleeping Shadow on the top bunk. Unaffected by all the commotion, she continued to slumber peacefully, posing no further threat to the now somewhat embarrassed customs officers. With no further untoward discoveries made, we were granted permission to continue on our journey.

Once clear of the port and following road signs for the M20, I allowed myself to relax.

Tentatively I ventured, 'Jimmy, I think we've done it!'

The enormity of knowing we were free to go home seemed unreal.

Recalling our lucky escape, I continued, 'That was so close back there! I was terrified they were going to take the dogs!'

Jimmy laughed a hollow laugh 'You were terrified. You weren't the only one!'

Something in the tone of his voice, warned me there was more at stake here than just the discovery of the dogs.

I glanced at him, frowning and quizzical.

'I was more worried they'd find my bloody gun,' he replied.

'Gun! *What gun?*' I shrieked, staring at him in utter disbelief, before having to swerve violently in a last-minute bid to stop us from piling into the verge.

'A Browning.' Came the casual reply.

'A Browning?' I questioned, brow furrowing, not having any idea what it might look like. 'Why didn't you tell me?' I choked.

Jimmy gave a short dismissive laugh, 'Look at how you were behaving knowing you were smuggling dogs back into the country. You were all over the place! How do you think you'd have reacted if you'd known there was a gun on board?'

He had a point. I got where he was coming from.

All I could muster was a long drawn out, '*Bloody Hell* Jimmy!'

I needed time to digest it all.

A gun!

We'd been travelling with a gun on board?

A real gun?

Where'd he hidden it?

Inconceivable. It wasn't so much the horror of being party to concealing a weapon which hit me, but the realisation Morgs and I had been deemed to be in sufficient danger to merit the need of a gun at the outset!

'So, you've had this gun stashed on the van all the time?'

I needed confirmation and justification for bringing the weapon.

'Yup. I shit myself when we got stopped boarding the

ferry in Plymouth. Thought I might've been rumbled then!'

Jimmy laughed briefly before continuing, 'I didn't know what we were going to be up against and I wasn't taking any risks, so purely as a precautionary measure, thought it best to be prepared.'

A slight pause and then smiling conspiratorially, he added, 'I can tell you this now – we had people on standby in Marseilles. They were just waiting for me to give the go ahead.'

'People in Marseilles?' I echoed.

'Yeah, in case it all kicked off. Thought I was going to have to make the call when we were in Vic and that weirdo moved Morgs' bedroom around. I tell you, it was a lucky escape that one.'

The enormity of his words took a while for me to grasp. I'd known we'd been sent into a threatening and dangerous situation, but hearing Jimmy put a voice to it, served to underline and amplify the horror of the ordeal we'd faced. We'd been put in a situation forcing us to take the law into our own hands in order to protect ourselves. I could understand why, as a result of being pushed to their very limit, someone might rebel. After all if a legal system turns its back on those who need it the most, what can they expect? Respect the individual and maybe the individual will respect the system. Had I acted illegally, when I failed to follow the court rulings, or was I just a mother doing what any other mother would do in the same circumstances? What I'd done might be *'illegal'*, but in my mind, on thing was sure, I was not the one who was *'ill'*, that prefix deserved to remain firmly attached to the current system. Maybe one day, the system will recover its health, allowing it to function better. Until then, desperate times call for desperate measures. I was living proof of that.

The consequence of one such desperate measure, arrived no more than two weeks later.

A well-meaning Cornish soul reported me to DEFRA, under the illusion I'd illegally smuggled two rabid animals into the country. Our dogs were taken into quarantine up country for six months. Being separated once more, took its toll on Shadow and I was left to burden the guilt of believing she died with a broken heart.

Chapter 67

A pile of Christmas cards sat in their addressed, yet-to-be-sealed envelopes, because I didn't know how to write the mass bulletin, documenting the events of the year. How could I even begin to express what we'd lived through?

Would anyone believe me?

The memories were so deeply carved in my mind, I could instantly press the *'play'* button and the entire story would begin to unravel on cue. Once started, I couldn't press pause, I couldn't make the reel stop with its technicolour images, sounds and smells. Scenes would replay relentlessly over and over and I couldn't edit them from my mind.

I was still coming to terms with the bizarreness of the custody hearing and its outcome in relation to Morgan.

Rather than being tricked into travelling to France again by Claude, I'd waited for the court order with the official date to attend the hearing at the beginning of September. Choosing to treat my previous trip like a dress rehearsal gave me the advantage of how to play it a second time around. Bearing in mind I knew I was dealing with people who completely disregarded the protective measures put in place under the Hague Convention, I happily dismissed the notion of taking Morgan with me.

Two could play at that game!

During the late morning on 3rd September, I drove to the rendezvous point to meet my French lawyer, Madame Caparros. Given that the centre of Montpellier was a rabbit warren of one-way systems, she'd kindly offered to drive me there. From her front passenger seat, I gazed out of the open window, numbed by nerves, unable to take in the surroundings. Knowing the importance of making the right impression on the judge, I'd chosen a below-the-knee, pale blue dress. It was quietly understated but sufficiently formal to show indicate my respect for the occasion.

Within a matter of miles I began to sense a feeling of dampness, emanating from the seat on which I perched. Perplexed, I waited to see if this was a figment of my imagination. It wasn't. I squirmed uncomfortably on the seat knowing I had to say something.

'Madame, my seat feels wet.'

My lawyer eyed me quizzically before her gaze went to the open passenger window.

'Shit!' she hissed, 'I went through the car wash before picking you up and must have forgotten to close the window!'

She pulled up at the kerbside, telling me we'd leave the car here and walk the short remaining distance. Dutifully, I disembarked, unnerved by the sensation of my dress clinging unusually to my backside. Turning my body awkwardly, I angled myself in order to obtain the optimum view of my bottom by using the pristine wing mirror of the now gleaming vehicle. To my absolute horror, a large wet patch was spread across the back of my dress!

'I can't go into court like this!' I shrieked.

Madame Caparros rounded the front of her car, bending to peer at my bottom as she assessed the damage.

'Ah,' she said. 'This is not good. It is very wet.'

How could she have been so careless? If this was the shape of things to come, it didn't bode well! At any other time, I'd have seen the funny side, but not now. Not when I was going to face the magnitude of a hearing in which a French judge would be deciding who would be granted parental custody of my son. Scowling at my lawyer, I told her to wait whilst I dug about in the bag I'd brought with me, in search of a change of outfit. There was nothing appropriate. My only option was a set of comfortable jogging bottoms and a rather crinkled t-shirt. They'd have to do. If this was a reflection of things to come, I dreaded what might happen. I fought to pull the joggers up under my dress, prior to removing it over my head. Pushed beyond my comfort zone, I stood rawly exposed and vulnerable on the *Montpellier* pavement in my bra for all to see. Stripped of all dignity I hurriedly shimmied into my t-shirt.

Satisfied I was ready, Madame Caparros retrieved a pile of lever arch files from the back seat of her car and ushered me along the busy pavement. Scurrying along in her wake, I silently sent up a little prayer of thanks that she'd remembered to shut her back window! Imagine rocking up to the high court in gym kit and court shoes, accompanied by a legal rep whose bundle of waterlogged papers left a trail of soapy bubbles in their wake.

All high courts in my experience oozed superiority and this one was no different. If I wasn't so preoccupied with what was going to happen inside the building, I might have appreciated its architecture. Entering the marbled foyer, Madame Caparros proceeded to the main reception desk to ascertain which courtroom the hearing would be held in. My eyes swept the space, knowing Claude would also be within the confines of the building. I dreaded the thought of seeing him. Would he be wearing his leather trousers I wondered? Would he be clean-shaven for once, determined to show himself in the best possible light? How would I compare to him as a parent, given my current ludicrous attire? Looking like a complete misfit, without even having the chance to open my mouth, I was already on the back foot.

'Jan,' said a male voice behind me.

I pivoted awkwardly on my heels to see the kindly face of Jacques. It was so long since I'd seen him – a lifetime away.

'I said I would be here for you,' he continued, smiling warmly at me.

He looked completely at ease, but then again, given that he'd been a chief police commissioner, I suppose he was used to making court appearances. I grinned at him and he reached his arms out to me, taking me in a brief embrace to exchange the familiar three-kiss greeting.

'Thank you so much for coming Jacques,' I replied, genuinely touched he cared enough to come and see me after all this time.

'I told you I would be here. I will stay here until you leave as well,' he replied in faltering English.

'Thank you, Jacques,' I said, nodding in gratitude.

As I did so, Madame Caparros swept back across the floor towards me, indicating I should follow her up the stairs to our right.

'Good luck Jan,' called Jacques as I turned to catch up with my lawyer who waited impatiently at the bottom of the staircase.

I was funnelled into a cramped store room at the top of the landing. It was furnished wall to wall with shelves of books whose dusty covers implied they hadn't been moved for a very long time. Sarcastically, I mused this was possibly on account of the law having no use for reference books, because they simply made up the rules as they went along. No wonder the books were discarded on their shelves. Probably been there gathering dust since Napoleonic times! I propped myself up against the ageing bookcase and waited patiently in the claustrophobic contains of the abandoned storeroom, for Madame Caparros to arrive. No doubt, she'd want to touch base with a pre-hearing discussion.

How was she going to play it?

What were we going to focus on?

Had she understood all the paperwork I'd sent her?

Was she aware the references from a range of English professionals would prove extremely helpful in building my defence?

Time ticked by and there was no sign of her.

With only five minutes remaining before the hearing was due to start, she made a last-minute appearance asking me to follow her. Pausing briefly by the entrance door of the courtroom, she asked me to give her a brief summary of the key points. Surely that was her job, not mine? A force to contend with, I didn't dare challenge her. She stood raven-like in her black gown, her two lever arch files overflowing with evidence tucked firmly under each wing, hostage to the imminent grasp of her long sinewy clawed fingers. Her uneasy guile hinted at a capacity to swoop to pick at any morsel the opposition might drop at her feet.

'Have you read all the evidence?' I ventured, casting a look at the bundle of paperwork held captive in her grip. 'I don't think there is any more to add.'

Her head rounded towards me in a quick shrewd movement, like a bird of prey spotting its target.

'Madame, these files are meaningless to me. I've had neither time to read nor translate them all. Claude has just given his evidence and it is now your turn. Follow me.'

She left me no alternative but to do as I was told. Entering the room, Claude accompanied by someone I presumed to be his lawyer, sat opposite the doorway. Claude was wearing blue jeans and a white shirt without tie, top button undone. Clean-shaven as anticipated, and no doubt eager to play the role of victim as also predicted. Forcing myself to focus solely on the judge, I positioned myself in such a way so as to avoid Claude's direct line of sight. Despite my efforts, I was acutely aware of his eyes piercing into me. Not this time I vowed. I was introduced to the female judge and another woman who was apparently going to take notes. An informal room; no witness stand, no allocated seating for defence or prosecution. It belied the gravitas of the case. I can't remember if I swore some sort of oath. I was too preoccupied with throwing my absolute all into convincing the judge it was I who was telling the truth. Standing in front of her, she gave me a thinly diluted smile and with no provision for a translator, I began telling my side of the story and answering her questions as best as I could in my defence.

Claude's pretence of passivity was proving difficult for him to maintain. The more I spoke, the more vocal he became, interspersing and ridiculing my evidence at every opportunity. His latest technique involved uttering loud 'tutting' noises accompanied by a methodical side to side movement of his head to underline his utter disbelief. He was putting on a good show to indicate he was the persecuted, innocent victim in all this and totally beside himself at the extremes of my accusations. It felt as if the odds were stacked against me. I'd endeavoured to say everything I could within the confines of my limited vocabulary. My every day French didn't extend to a thorough comprehension of the legal jargon being used, so taking my seat, I prepared for defeat, head bowed.

There was nothing more I could do.

Claude, assuming he'd got the upper hand, made a string of derisive comments urging the judge to consider how my need for serious psychological help made me an unfit mother. It was upon hearing Claude's latest comments the legal raven in the form of Madame Caparros, swooped.

Plucking his very words from the air as they fell from his lips, she soared aloft with them, only to hover with a cry of, 'You deem that my client is in need of psychological help. Indeed, you may be right given what both she and her children have endured at your hands. And yet, were you not the person who pulled a gun on your ex-wife? You pulled a gun on her as a means of abducting your children! I have all the evidence here Monsieur Campait.'

She extracted a small set of A4 sheets held together by a purple paperclip, from one of her two files. Flapping them furiously in the direction of his face, in a spectacular show of dominance, she defied him to deny it. The odious smile on Claude's face vanished.

Her taloned words pierced his flesh, puncturing his ego, as his toxicity escaped into the air like mustard gas. Holding my breath, I watched with a bitter contentment as he slowly deflated. Wounded, finally rendered helpless, his lies, depravity, and cruelty bleeding out into the room. All eyes were upon him, bearing witness to his discomfort. As his head hung, so silence stepped in to answer loud and clear on his behalf.

Moments later, the judge ruled I be granted residential custody of Morgan.

We'd done it!

Finally, I'd beaten him!

Shaking the outstretched claw extending from the black wings of Madame Caparros' gown, I expressed my sincere thanks. I was in shock. Relieved yet disbelieving, I needed time to absorb the reality of it all.

'I'm convinced it was the last part of the hearing that changed the outcome of the case! I couldn't believe it when you produced those papers showing you had evidence of Claude threatening his ex-wife with a gun! Thank you so much for getting that additional information! How did you do it?' I asked eagerly.

I'd obviously underestimated this woman. She'd put the fear of God into me before we went into the hearing when she'd disclosed she'd not had time to read all the documents, never mind understand them! She'd shone through though, hadn't she?

A slow conspiratorial smile spread across my lawyer's face as her eyes glinted menacingly.

'Madame, I know this type of man. I have seen it on so many occasions in the past. He did not deserve to win. The gun and the ex-wife...' she tutted twice as her head nodded a no, 'I did not have any paper evidence at all!'

'But what about the papers you pulled out of the file?' I stammered, aghast.

'Just papers,' she replied dismissively, 'I cannot tell you what was written on them because I do not know and because it does not matter! All that matters is that it had the desired effect on Claude!' She laughed.

Case closed.

Her words summed up all I'd experienced. At any given point in time, reality could be an illusion, a guise, a front behind which the intricacies of deceit and manipulation reigned. Ludicrous to think a justice system had the gall to make rulings based on unfounded evidence.

It was bitter sweet; elated the result was in my favour but left with a sour taste in my mouth knowing there was no consequence for Claude or validation of the trauma we'd suffered.

Head spinning, I descended the long staircase to exit the reception area and stepping through its doors, out into the Autumnal sunshine. Caught completely off guard, someone stepped out from behind a pillar, violently grabbing my upper arm, forcing me to turn towards them. Before I even saw the face, I instinctively knew it was Claude by the ferocity of his grip. Tightning his hold, I could have cried out in pain but wouldn't give him the benefit. Although he was in full view of the public, his anger was so intense it no longer mattered to him.

Unable to break free, I was so relieved when a familiar voice said, 'My dear Jan. I was hoping to see you.'

My fears splintered, falling like shards of broken glass. It was my friend, Jacques exuding an authoritarian calmness as he surveyed the scene before him. Although retired from the force, he'd not lost his powers to de-escalate a situation and take control of it.

Speaking solely to me, making the point I was his only priority, and acting as if Claude were invisible, he said, 'I've been waiting to see you in the hope you can spare some time to have a drink with your old friend. Together we will raise a toast to this long awaited and much deserved, successful outcome for you and your family.'

I smiled with gratitude for his timely intervention. But above all, I beamed with a sense of blossoming elation, absorbing his words, anchoring their meaning, securing a truth beyond doubt.

A truth spoken by an honorable officer of the law who'd just confirmed Morgan's future lay with me. Claude was left with no alternative but to relinquish his grip.

Angrily dropping his arm to his side, his eyes narrowed as he spat his parting comment at me 'I will destroy you and I will never see Morgan again.'

I spun away from him, and linked arm with Jacques in true camaraderie style, as I turned my back on Claude for the last time, knowing I would never look back.

Chapter 68

It's true what they say. Objects come and go but memories are far more difficult to misplace or lose. Good or bad, they become passengers on your life's journey. Some are full of wonder, like a little bouquet of wild flowers; colourful, fragile and rare, to be nurtured forever. The joyous response to the news we were free, followed by a little bunch of boys celebrating at their chosen beach with a Scooby-Doo cake and a shrimping net. Unforgettable.

Equally etched on my mind, were the words of Claude's parting threat three months ago. Didn't he realise he'd never destroy me? No doubt he'd do his utmost to make the divorce and division of the assets as difficult as possible, but Morgan was by side, making me the richest woman in the world. And that was priceless.

Seated at the desk in my mum's attic bedroom, a pile of Christmas cards sat in their already addressed envelopes, waiting for me to insert my habitual annual bulletin. As yet, I was struggling to envisage how to begin to summarise the events of the year, let alone document them in palatable, easy to read format! My eyes fell on Tom's lucky stone protruding out from under the mass of triangular, yet to be licked envelopes. Picking it up and repositioning it on a scant patch of uncluttered space, an idea sprung to mind. I'd write a simple poem. It'd encapsulate all the feelings in a condensed form, without having to go into too much detail. After all, Christmas was a joyful occasion. It wasn't the appropriate time to be enclosing the horrendous truths of our year alongside yule tide greetings from me to each recipient.

In the same way I put an apron on to give me added incentive in the kitchen, I picked up my calligraphy pen, knowing it would optimise my creativity and began to write.

Dear All

Another year has passed and it's been incredibly eventful!

The boys and I have returned to live in Cornwall and we cherish being back home. Claude and I have separated and he continues to live in the house in France. Hopefully it won't be long until divorce proceedings are completed and I'll be in a position to sell my properties.

In the meantime, we have so much to be grateful for. I am thankful for the unusual friendships that have flourished both in places and between people I'd never have expected. As a little family of four (plus one dog!), we no longer take everything for granted. Instead, we appreciate even the smallest of things, which in themselves prove a great source of joy. Above all else, we are safe in the knowledge that we have each other. Unless I were to commit all that's led us to this place to the pages of a book, I hope for now, this will suffice

With love and best wishes, I'll leave you with the following thought:

*This is our year of celebration -
forto live with fear in freedom
is an exaltation in itself
but to live in fear, in captivity
is not living at all.*

Putting my pen down, I breathed a long sigh of relief, in the immense gratitude and appreciation of knowing I'd been given the priceless gift of writing the ending of our year, as it needed to be written. Every trial and tribulation had been worth every ounce of effort.

Our ordeal was over.

We were free.

I sat relishing the beauty of this moment, peace swaddling me in its blanket of comfort. Picking up a pencil, I began doodling daisies around the edges of my writing. Wonderfully modest little souls, with golden hearts, embracing a wealth of white petals, overflowing with good intentions. I'd seen them popping up in all their glory in the most hostile of environments, still managing to flower, rising, undeterred, between the gaps of unyielding flagstones.

Pure symbols of resilience. As a smile edged undeniably across my face, and for a fleeting moment, the flutter of a golden buttery scent touched the air with its warmth and was gone.

Epilogue

Returning to the safety of my beloved Cornwall, different types of challenges lay ahead. Firstly, we had to find somewhere to live. We weren't entitled to any type of benefit until we'd been resident in the country for two months. I was very grateful to have some money in a French account with which we purchased the basics. We lived in the camper van for six months until a two-bedroomed thatched cottage came up for rent in Mithian. I applied to rent it, knowing it would be beneficial for my sons to return to the security of a place they already knew and where they had friends. Given my situation, I was informed I'd need to pay six months of rent upfront. I sold the camper to pay for it. Although I know it was the right decision, I remember feeling very insecure because, without the camper, I'd no means of escape. Irrational thinking on my part, but I was so conditioned to living in a perpetual state of fear, the thought of being a sitting target, without the means of taking to the road to disappear, should the need arise, frightened me.

Perhaps Claude's threat of 'destroying me' was meted out by causing us as much hardship as he could muster. He took the reins in divorce proceedings, ignoring written communications and refusing to sign legal papers.

Although no longer physically present, he sought to remain in control from a geographical distance. The divorce finally came through on 15th February 2005. However, unlike the UK, France does not settlement of any assets at the time of divorce proceedings. This was to prove to be an insurmountable obstacle for many years. In the meantime, Claude claimed he was unemployed, without income and therefore unable to move out of the family residence. Given the properties were in France and we'd been married in the UK, led to a minefield of complications in terms of which law should be followed for the distribution of the assets. The case was passed on to experts for guidance. Three years of legal deliberation passed, and when it was decided I should be entitled to my properties, Claude's response was a silent one. In the end, even his own solicitor gave up trying to contact him. Without knowing where he was, legal hands were tied. I contacted Jacques and he kindly went to investigate, no doubt employing his policing tactics. He informed me Claude appeared to still be in residence although one of the post boxes had a different name written on it. Time fell away as quickly as the money I'd been spending on legal representation. Closure escaped me. I refused to give up but it was a burden continued to carry, to keep fighting, to remain strong, whilst knowing I'd never be free until I could sever all ties with France and everything I associated with it. It lay like an unhealed wound, continually festering under my skin. Sticking a plaster over the top of it, I attempted to conceal it in the short term, avoiding having to face the pain hidden underneath. It was not the answer. At regular intervals, the wound seeped through the dressing, a painful reminder of the rawness threatening to surface. In a bid to keep it hidden, I wrapped it steadily in an ever-increasing layer of bandages until I'd no option but to change the now unmanageable dressing. Whilst I concentrated on the tricky process of unravelling, my therapist cradled my fear, carefully administering the antidote via 'validation ointment'

Friends would ask 'how do you keep going, knowing how unfair it is?' The answer was simple. I would never give Claude the benefit of destroying me. I found my strength via my boys and in my discovery of the beauty of nature. Forming a deep and appreciative relationship with Mother Nature she bathed my wounds in inspiration and hope, whilst showing me how to appreciate the little things. Maybe things we'd miss if we didn't pay attention to detail; newly discovered pathways and unexpected symbols of hope surrounded me, once I learnt how to look. Reminders of all that is wonderful, reassured my mindset and gave me the courage to continue. I delighted in what I had and not in what I hadn't.

Years rolled on and when finances allowed I'd fork out in a bid to find a means of getting closure. I spent endless hours seeking evidence to prove Claude was gainfully employed. At one point I hired a private investigator who assured me he'd get the results I needed. Another thousand pounds left my bank account only to be presented with findings I'd already dredged off the internet myself!

In the early autumn of 2014 Morgan composed a letter to his dad in the hope he'd get a response. Now eleven years since Claude had vowed never to see Morgan again and he'd proved true to his word. No form of communication at all, not even a birthday card. Morgan deliberated long and hard, writing and rewriting his letter to his father, trying to present himself in a manner he hoped would initiate a reply from his dad. I helped him choose a likeable photo of himself which he included with his letter. It was a momentous occasion for

Morgan and so we walked to the post-box together to send it on its way. He waited for a response as the days turned into weeks which turned into months. Nothing appeared apart from a growing sense of abandonment on Morgan's part.

The beginning of 2015 ruled out all hope of Morgan reconnecting with his father when I received notification of Claude's death. He'd been living in a village near Perpignan for nine years, with an English teacher, whilst renting out our home and reaping the benefits. Armed with the news of his death, I tried to find a solicitor who could help me. While researching the internet, a friend of mine came across the name of a professional, based in Somerset, who was au fait with French law. Excitedly, I immediately winged him an email. It marked the beginning of a wonderful working relationship with David Barney to whom I will be forever grateful. In the pursuit of justice, he took my case on without charging any upfront fees. It was finally resolved seven years later, complicated further by Claude deliberately not writing a will, as well as the additional complications surrounding French inheritance laws.

Although free from abuse, the echoes as well as the consequences of it remain until this day. Claude impoverished us in so many ways: not only financially, but robbing us of our sense of self-worth, ability to trust, self-confidence and identity.

However, I cannot help but feel he had an accomplice, not an individual, but a whole legal system actively supporting and favouring the perpetrator. I hold the current law regarding The International Convention on Child Abduction to account. They are the 'enablers', the ones allowing this barbaric miscarriage of justice against mothers and their children, to continue.

I'm just one statistic in many and I'm one of the

lucky ones. Recently I had the unique opportunity to meet face-to-face with other *'Hagued'* Mothers from around the globe. It was an emotional, powerful and humbling experience. Sitting in a room full of women, we shared our stories, many of us feeling validated for the first time. It was a profoundly moving experience. Listening to these courageous women, my trials and tribulations paled in significance. With their permission, I'm dedicating the remainder of my epilogue to honour these courageously protective mothers and give them the opportunity to be heard.

Sarah Marie (USA)

"My name is Sarah Marie and I'm a Hagued, protective mother.
I've been forcibly kept from my children since December of 2019.
I have been charged with 'kidnapping' my own sons and facing 10 years in prison.
I will not live in fear.
I will not live in silence.
I will continue to fight for my boys."

Mothers such as Sarah lose custody battles due to their abuser knowing how to play the legal system, women whose alleged 'safe places' are raided by police and their children literally dragged away from them.

In 2019 Sarah fled from abuse with her two sons, escaping from the US to Canada in the hope of asylum. Soon after arrival, police stormed their Airbnb room in the middle of the night and arrested her at gunpoint. She told me:

"With a loaded gun to my head and three others pointed at me, authorities screamed in French and I was subdued on the floor, my children sleeping only a few feet away."

She had no time to hug her children or say goodbye. They were dragged away from her, only to be returned to their abusive father in the US. She was subsequently further traumatised by the penal system, before making the brave decision to revoke her Canadian citizenship in order to return to the US and fight for her children. Criminalised for her maternal instinct to protect her children, with whom she's been denied contact, she hasn't seen her sons since. Her fight for justice continues.

Mothers, such as Sarah are left suspended in the void of not knowing when or if they will see their children again. I simply cannot begin to imagine how this might feel as a mother, let alone as a child.

I learnt the plight of mothers making forced returns, accompanying their children back to the United States. Believing protective measures issued by The Hague ruling will keep them safe, they face a very different reality. It's not uncommon to find, unbeknown to them, their abuser has already initiated court proceedings and interim custody has been granted to the father, without any input from the mother. As a result, on arrival in the country, children are seized, and given back to the perpetrator, thereby enabling him to reassert control, and leaving the mother to fight for justice in an already biased legal arena.

Another protective mother explained how financial help from a friend proved pivotal in her custody battle. It enabled her to return to the country from which she'd fled, and rent a property over a significant number of years, whilst fighting for custody. She's adamant, without this financial support, she wouldn't have been successful. Money talks in legal matters, furthering the already established unequal weighting at the outset. Whereas the plaintiff's costs are automatically covered, the defendant's are not. Often already financially impoverished, the loving abductor is further disadvantaged with little choice but to return to the country from which she'd fled, dangerously isolated and alone, with no support network, cultural differences, language barriers, prevented from finding employment and potential homelessness.

Imagine an outlaw, constantly on the run with her children, living hand to mouth, moving from place to place in an effort to protect them. Currently hiding deep in the forest, only daring to come out when needing to buy essentials. Forced to live this transient lifestyle, knowing it's the only means of keeping yourself and your children safe? This is not TV entertainment. It's the lived reality of a mother who's already endured the unthinkable.

I was so fortunate to escape from Claude. In retrospect, being on the move in the camper van, never gave him the opportunity to grab our son. If I'd remained at the residence, as ruled by the High Court, until the time of the custody hearing, I'm certain Claude would have abducted Morgan, just as he'd done previously, when he secured custody of one of his other children, thereby making sure the child was physically present with his father at the hearing.

Imagine if the police had chosen to act on his orders, arrested me and handed Morgan over to his father. He'd have gained a legal advantage for the second time and I might never have seen my little boy again.

Some Hague Mothers are left to continue their battles spanning time and distance.

Anita (living in the UK)

"I have now not seen my children since 3rd August 2015 – seven years and counting. In the USA I am a felon – an international child abductor and non-payer of child support (an imprisonable debt) so dare not ever return. My children have lost life with their mother, lost their multi-faceted cultural heritage, family and language (I am half-Indian and we spoke some Hindi together).

I co-founded GlobalARRK in 2016, resigned in 2017.

I am proud to be a founding trustee of the new Hague Convention Mothers charity and hope that one day my children will see that I have never stopped fighting for them."

Ironically, I feel blessed to find myself in the enviable position of sitting amongst other survivors, united by our shared experiences. Some mothers never make it this far.

Cassandra Hasanovic was one such mother. She fled to Australia with her children, in fear for her life, convinced she was going to die at the hands of her abuser. However, under the Hague Convention, her pleas for help were ignored and the Australian Judge did not recognise domestic abuse as being intolerable. She was ordered out of Australia, and back to the UK. The protection orders granted in Australia were not enforceable in Britain. Cassandra won her custody battle but this further outraged the father of her children. Living in fear, on 29th July 2008, Cassandra's mother offered to drive her daughter and grandchildren to a domestic violence refuge. They never reached their destination. Cassandra's ex dragged her from the car and stabbed her to death in front of her mother and her children.

Our stories are many and varied, each as important

as the other. Hardships endured, selfless acts of courage, all centred on protecting our children. Unique in our individual experiences, but united by our unbreakable maternal instinct to keep our children safe, whatever it takes.

Roz, CEO, GlobalARRK

"Jan is one of thousands of families affected by this issue every year. After my own lived experience, I set up the charity GlobalARRK.

We are contacted by over 300 desperate families every year, all going through an international custody dispute.

Around 30% have been accused of child abduction under the Hague Convention (1980) after they tried to return home with their child.

Official reports say that over 75% of these cases involve a primary carer mother taking her child back to her home country after experiencing domestic abuse."

When is it right for someone to be condemned for loving and protecting your child?

Some of Us

🌼 Some of us are *Hagued* and live in terror every day that someone will burst through the door and take our babies away.

🌼 Some of us go on a family vacation and when we return we find ourselves facing Hague charges.

🌼 Some of us are *Hagued* and find ourselves trapped in a hostile or foreign country where we have no money and no resources.

- Some of us never even leave the country of our child's habitual residence but find ourselves *Hagued* anyway.

- Some of us are *Hagued* and win our Hague case only to be horrifically *Hagued* a second time.

- Some of us are *Hagued* and find ourselves locked away and facing criminal charges.

- Some of us are *Hagued*, never to see our children again.

- Some of us are *Hagued* and we don't make our 33rd birthday.

Throughout the world, *Hagued Mothers* fight with incredible fortitude. We fight for a right which should never be challenged in the first place, the right to protect our children. Firstly we fight to protect our children from their paternal abuser. Women seek refuge from domestic abuse on a daily basis. Protective mothers don't flee by crossing boundaries on a whim. It's not some twisted revenge tactic in our sick psyche. It's a last desperate act, leaping through the rare opportunity of a window of escape, taking the risk and running for all we're worth to a place of alleged safety. A place which in reality doesn't exist. A place whose judicial system criminalises us, acts complicit with our first abuser, and ignores both human rights and the rights of a child. A place in which we face another violation, this time via legal abuse.

I believe we live in a world where we're actively encouraged to label ourselves as 'survivors'. It promotes an ethos of not languishing in 'victim mode for too long. In fact, progress is calculated by the speed at which an individual is able to make the shift from victim to survivor. I'm not buying it. I'm not buying it for the simple reason that by defining myself as a 'survivor', I'm not only belittling my suffering but giving those in authority an excuse for not scrutinising their existing failures. I hold them to account.

Of course, it's so much easier for them if I'm a survivor as opposed to a victim. A survivor indicates there's some sort of positive shift that's taken place. It buries the trauma, negating it, lessening its impact and thereby frees the conscience of those with legal responsibility, leaving the need for change on the back burner where it will stay unchallenged. For this reason, I stand resolutely as a victim of domestic abuse, a victim of the gross miscarriage of justice and a victim of legal abuse until there's a review of the Hague Convention. A review which legally acknowledges, validates and effectively protects the victim.

For Every
Hague Mother

Where the Skylark Sings

The shrill of a skylark, high in the sky
aloft on the wind, I turn to her cry.
Far from the ground, feathered fleck in the air
soars high and alone – not one of a pair.

Energy focussed; she's calling to you
join in the song flight. She's one of the few.
Protecting her young, whatever the cost.
Freedom endangered must ne'er be lost

Fly high sweet skylark! With chorus combined,
we'll flock for justice, soul, body and mind.
Fly high for freedom! Our song long deserved
once borne on the wind, can ne'er be unheard.

Sweet symbol of hope, resilient and rare.
Bravely courageous, but sadly aware
how change can take time, so until it begins
meet me in the place where the skylark sings.

Jan Ford
11.10 2022

Why Skylark?

A skylark reminds me of freedom and embracing summer days, as a child, when my mother and I would meander through the valley on the way to our favourite beach. Hearing the call of a Skylark, high overhead, we'd loiter as we tried to spot the source of the sound, our eyes scanning for the tiny speck flying high in the sun filled blue.

Researching this bird, I discovered that it has a stronger attachment than most, to its young. Being fiercely protective, it finds ways of courageously moving both nest and little ones to a place of safety when danger is imminent. I guess you can imagine where I'm going with this!

Finally, when we first came back from France, Morgan started at pre-school and it was aptly named 'Skylarks'! The staff ensured that my son was protected at all times and alerted to the possibility that he was at risk of abduction by his father.

Hence, this was written to specifically honour every Hague Mother, sending love and blessings that you find fortitude for the battle and peace ever after.

References:

Useful organisations:

https://www.globalarrk.org/

https://www.reunite.org/

https://haguecollective.org/

https://www.hague-mothers.org.uk/

/hagueconventionmothers.org

https://www.herhaguestory.com/

Information about the Hague Convention on the Civil Aspects of International Child Abduction.

https://www.hcch.net/en/instruments/conventions/
full-text/?cid=24

My website

www.janford.uk